HOW TO BUILD
an
ENDURING
Marriage

KAREN BUDZINSKI

WESTBOW®
PRESS
A DIVISION OF THOMAS NELSON
& ZONDERVAN

Cover design by Terry Kole.

WestBow Press books may be ordered through booksellers or by contacting:

WestBow Press
A Division of Thomas Nelson & Zondervan
1663 Liberty Drive
Bloomington, IN 47403
www.westbowpress.com
1 (866) 928-1240

ISBN: 978-1-4908-4421-3 (sc)
ISBN: 978-1-4908-4420-6 (hc)
ISBN: 978-1-4908-4422-0 (e)
Library of Congress Control Number: 2014912448

Printed in the United States of America.

WestBow Press rev. date: 07/25/2014

Contents

Dedication

This book is dedicated to the crème de la crème
women who for over 32 years have attended
the classes, seminars, retreats, and luncheons
I have hosted to strengthen relationships.

Women who've wanted to learn and grow,
to take their relationships to the next level.

Women willing to step outside their norms,
to take responsibility, to keep on trying,
and to believe that they could be a part of
positive change, healing, and renewal
in their marriage and other relationships.

Women who had the humility to admit
things they did wrong, and the courage
to not take responsibility for others'
wrongs nor let those wrongs change them.

These amazing women have
encouraged me and stood beside me
in the fight to make sure
"happily ever after"
is not only for fairy tales.

Acknowledgments

I would like to thank the many women that have compelled and inspired me over the years to put my heart on paper—first and foremost my Mom, Patricia Girgenti, and most recently Lauren Kay, Kathy Andrews, and Karen Cynowa. My mom has always been an uncompromising example of a woman committed to unmitigated excellence in her life and relationships. Her life and love continues to inspire and challenge those around her. My sister, Laurie Piccolo, is the one with whom I walk through life, our arms linked together. Through every mountaintop and valley, she is there to encourage and strengthen me, with our number one goal in life the same: to hear "Well done, good and faithful servant" (Matthew 25:23 KJV) at the end.

I would also like to thank the self-professed "president of my fan club," my sister Diane Fisher. She encouraged and supported this project before it was ever birthed in my own heart. Her love lifted me, and when she left, she took a piece of my heart. I miss you so much, my sweet little firework. I know we will be together again. Your cheering still echoes in your absence. The story of your life, for those who will listen, accomplishes your vision of being a life coach.

I want to thank my husband and my best friend, Gary Budzinski. It has been a privilege to walk through life with you. You are a man of passion, integrity, and character. Your consistent dedication to the Lord shows in your life of excellence and devotion to your family. Thank you for living an uncompromising life.

I want to acknowledge my adult children and their spouses: Jesse and Amber Budzinski, Gabriel and Hannah Bahlhorn, Michael and Bethany Moon, Brandon and Christa Doto, and Daniel and Elizabeth Budzinski. You make the world a better place and shine so brightly. You have brought to life Psalm 127:4 and Isaiah 8:18. Thank you for continuing to allow me to be an important part of your lives.

I would like to thank my editor, Karen Porter, for the many dedicated hours you devoted to editing my manuscript. Your personal and timely attention to the edits and re-edits helped me immeasurably. You are a gracious and accomplished woman I have been privileged to work with.

Over the past four years, it has been inspiring and life changing for me to be a part of changing the world by teaching pastors and leaders in third world countries with Compassionate Touch (http://www. ctinternational.org). Not only are nations being changed, but each of their team members young and old will never be the same after attending a mission trip with them. I am honored to be associated with a mission organization that is making such an incredible impact.

I especially want to thank my Lord and Savior Jesus Christ. Your Word and Spirit have taught and empowered me how to live and give beyond my own limited understanding. Walking with You and learning to trust Your plans are always for "peace and not evil, to give [me] an expected end" (Jeremiah 29:11 KJV). Living by Your principles has allowed my days to be as You desired with the blessings of Deuteronomy 28.

"Now to Him Who, by (in consequence of) the [action of His] power that is at work within us, is able to [carry out His purpose and] do superabundantly, far over and above all that we [dare] ask or think [infinitely beyond our highest prayers, desires, thoughts, hopes, or dreams] – to Him be glory in the Church and in Christ Jesus throughout all generations forever and ever. Amen (so be it)" (Ephesians 3:20-21 AMP).

What to Expect From this Book

When you picked up this book, you made an investment and committed to excellence in your relationships. May you be challenged, humbled, and inspired to do and see things differently than you ever have before.

People who have the best relationships are those who realize that it takes extraordinary efforts. Olympic and professional athletes have coaches—not because they don't already know the ins-and-outs of their professions, but because they want to reach their fullest potential. These athletes continue to pursue excellence without slacking.

If you open your heart to some new ways of thinking and dealing with relationship issues, this book partners with you, like a coach, in your quest to reach your full potential in your relationships, offering help in the following areas:

- Learning what every man wishes his wife knew about his personal needs, desires, and points of view.
- Becoming more loveable to your husband, inspiring his love and desire towards you.
- Giving up control and allowing your husband the freedom to live his life with no fear that you are his judge and jury.
- Setting your husband free from unreasonable and unrealistic expectations.
- Achieving a better outcome by tweaking and changing yourself so that your husband's perception and perspective is considered.

- Avoiding common obstacles that hinder successful communication.
- Understanding the different roles in marriage and living within them without being obscured by or dominating the relationship.
- Identifying destructive habits that may be eating away at marital happiness.
- Preparing to get through potential problems without damage or injury to your relationship.
- Preventing financial matters from becoming a major hindrance in your marriage.
- Holding onto joy through the ups and downs of life together.
- Achieving true intimacy, love, and friendship with your husband.
- Refusing to take responsibility for abusive behavior by identifying and dealing with insurmountable and destructive issues.

Apply the information in this book. Knowledge is procuring the information, but true wisdom is applying what you learn.

As you read and share this book, stretch yourself: think and act outside of your comfort zone. I highly recommend the companion workbook to expand the impact of this book. With it you'll be able to personalize the principles. Keep notes on the results you see in your relationships as a result of lifting the bar for yourself and for your marriage.

Some of the principles and ideas may seem unfamiliar, but remember, our goal is to make our marriages incredible and out of the ordinary. Be willing to be brutally honest; look deep into your heart; and be open to adjust, tweak, and change. Be patient with yourself as you apply changes to better your relationships. You may slip and forget, but as soon as you realize it, pick yourself back up and keep applying what you have learned.

> "Those who built the wall and those who bore burdens loaded themselves so that everyone worked with one hand and held a weapon with the other hand" (Nehemiah 4:17 AMP).

Pick up your trowel (to build) in one hand and your sword (to fight opposition) in the other. We are going to start building and fighting for our relationships.

Preface

"And this I pray that your love may abound yet more
and more and extend to its fullest development in
knowledge and all keen insight [that your love may
display itself in greater depth of acquaintance and
mere comprehensive discernment], So that you may surely
learn to sense what is of real value [recognizing the
highest and the best and distinguishing the moral
differences], and that you may be untainted and pure and
unerring and blameless [so that with hearts sincere and
certain and unsullied, you may approach] the day of
Christ [not stumbling nor causing others to stumble]."
Philippians 1:9-10 AMP

Introduction:
The Importance of Relationships

If asked to list the most important things of life, most people would not list their material possessions over their relationships. When disaster strikes suddenly, people search frantically for family members because material possessions suddenly take the rightful place—behind the safety of loved ones.

The things we own, whether a little or a lot, do not define our value or who we are. Our relationships and our input into the success of the lives of others comprise true value. Each of us can testify to the investments others have made into us—those significant positive words or deeds that define how we live and the choices we make. Investments like these yield compounding returns.

> "For what is our hope or happiness or our victor's wreath of exultant triumph when we stand in the presence of our Lord Jesus at His coming? Is it not you?" (1 Thessalonians 2:19 AMP)

Why is it so easy to be distracted from the efforts necessary to build relationships? Because a web of never ending demands on our time catches us. Media and social expectations delude us so that we expect lavish lifestyles once known only by the rich and famous. We accumulate and maintain and update name brand and technical items that are outdated soon after we purchase them. Already stressed out by the rigors of increasing job demands, we buy into the need for extravagant travel and spa experiences to offset tangled nerves. Outlandish gifts assuage guilt in attempts to make up for lack of time spent with people. The result is a nation of people indebted to the hilt, without fulfilled and purposeful relationships, spending more money to anesthetize the pain of misdirected priorities.

Overloaded and overcommitted schedules take away daily choices. Time is money, and both are limited. Text messages, Facebook comments, Twitter notifications, and other social media take the place of communication with even the closest relationships. Even if we take the time to get together with someone, if they are still consumed with the constant influx and outflow of updates on media sites, we may as well have stayed at home and substituted virtual communication with them.

Relationships have no deadlines. Because we are so distracted, we fail to notice the slow yet steady breakdown of relationships. Relationships can be frustrating and need time and energy that simply isn't available. Rather than working through turbulence or trials, it is easier to focus on other things that we are more skilled at, hoping the problems in our relationships will just go away.

Besides, we may feel inept at problem solving, and because of the constant demands involved to keep relationships thriving, we treat relationships like once-valued technical toys or fashion items that are now out of date—simply replacing them with new ones. Unless we learn to give relationships the preeminence they deserve and work to keep them strong and flourishing, fractured and broken relationships will be littered along the paths of our lives. The demise of relationships filters down to the erosion of families. Society ultimately bears the effects of such erosion, since strong families are the anchor and stability of any strong society.

"And He said to them, Guard yourselves and keep free from all covetousness (the immoderate desire for wealth, the greedy longing to have more); for a man's life does not consist in and is not derived from possessing overflowing abundance or that which is over and above his needs." Luke 12:15 (AMP)

In order to invest time into relationships, we first need to learn the gift, the supreme gift, of being content with what we have. If we are thrust into the world of "never enough," we will be caught in the never-ending spiral of spending our lives for things that don't matter and need to be replaced. Instead, wouldn't you rather be able to prioritize and give relationships the preeminence they need in order to thrive?

"A godly life brings huge profits to people who are content with what they have. We didn't bring anything into the world, and we can't take anything out of it. As long as we have food and clothes, we should be satisfied. But people who want to get rich keep falling into temptation. They are trapped by many stupid and harmful desires which drown them in destruction and ruin. Certainly, the love of money is the root of all kinds of evil. Some people who have set their hearts on getting rich have wandered away from the Christian faith and have caused themselves a lot of grief. But you, man of God, must avoid these things." 1 Timothy 6:6-11 (GW)

Although relationships are as varied as the people involved, utilizing certain tools to build bonds remain constant. Whether relating to sons and daughters, grandchildren, nephews and nieces, uncles and aunts, parents, spouses, siblings, neighbors, bosses or employees, the tools and basic skills to maximize the potential in these relationships are the same.

We devote our energies to many time-gobbling activities that are transient and temporal, but when we invest in relationships our investment has the potential to be reflected for generations to come and for eternity. We cannot become distracted. We need to put our "deposits" into investing into relationships, ensuring that our investments cannot be taken away from us.

> "Stop storing up treasures for yourselves on earth, where moths and rust destroy and thieves break in and steal. Instead, store up treasures for yourselves in heaven, where moths and rust don't destroy and thieves don't break in and steal. Your heart will be where your treasure is. The eye is the lamp of the body. So if your eye is unclouded, your whole body will be full of light. But if your eye is evil, your whole body will be full of darkness. If the light in you is darkness, how dark it will be! No one can serve two masters. He will hate the first master and love the second, or he will be devoted to the first and despise the second. You cannot serve God and wealth." Matthew 6:19-24 (GW)

When we start out in any relationship, we usually put our "best foot" forward. We accommodate each other, and the relationship isn't inundated with responsibilities and demands. Of course, we like our relationships like we enjoy our airplane rides: without turbulence and with smooth landings. We soon realize that, with the ups and downs, ins and outs, and peaks and valleys life throws at us, a smooth ride isn't probable. The good thing about being in a marriage relationship is that, ideally, together a couple can cut the downs, outs, and valleys in half by carrying them together; and celebrate the ups, ins, and peaks doubly by appreciating each one together. While we get through these shared experiences together, we are building history with each other.

Relationship Histories

History in a relationship helps us look past a person's shortcomings of the moment to see the entirety of the whole package. History enables a couple celebrating their 50th wedding anniversary to be deeply in love, a child to look in awe at grandparents or parents, and parents to look in amazement and reflection as their children marry. History causes siblings to appreciate each other and be bound together by experiences shared from birth.

Our most important relationships have the potential to strengthen as time goes by. As you watch your child grow into an adult, you remember years of stages, special memories, struggles, defeats, and victories.

History had big benefits as I watched my Dad suffer with and ultimately pass away from Alzheimer's disease. I saw in him all the memories of him since I was little. I saw him as the big, strong shoulder to sit on, I saw him as the bigger-than-life Dad of my youth, as the fun-Dad organizing all sorts of activities and vacations as I grew older, as the Dad offering wisdom when I left my home to live alone, and as the Dad that fixed up every home I've ever lived in. Although my Dad was suffering with Alzheimer's disease at the end of his life, I had not forgotten everything he meant to me. The history of the relationship transcended the debilitating disease that took him.

I reflect at this same kind of history in my relationship with my husband. When I look at him, I see him as the fun husband I married, as the incredible father he became, not once, but five times in 5-1/2 years, as the new executive with his three-piece pinstriped suit and as the assured, wise, experienced senior executive he is now.

What are some of the key moments you have with your spouse that you cherish in your history together? What are some of the moments that make you smile? What are some of the ways you have both grown up together or faced challenges together? What are some of the things about him that you fell in love with, and what are some of the things about you that he loved?

Too often, we dismiss the history we have with our loved ones without a second thought. Does our "it can be replaced" mentality apply to people as well as things? People flit like butterflies from relationship to relationship. Wives leave husbands; husbands leave wives; parents run out on children; parents ask children to leave convinced either that they are better off without their families or their families are better off without them. More people come from broken families than from solid ones.

Even happily married couples may cultivate habits that may damage their relationships in the future if they don't tweak them. Like a tennis player with a few bad habits can still win the match, couples feel on top of their game. A tennis pro, however, spots the flaws that will ultimately cause harm and injury. This book will help you discover little things you may be doing in your relationships that may ultimately cause harm or injury as well, or further down the road a total breakdown.

With dreams and ideals for marriage broken, couples settle for mediocrity and sometimes misery. Many couples don't know where to begin to find help for their problems. Together we will look at some of the tools that can be used to repair fractured relationships.

If you want to go the distance and enjoy marathon relationships instead of short-term jogs, you first need to rise above the norm.

> "...When the enemy shall come in like a flood, the Spirit of the Lord shall lift up a standard against him." (Isaiah 59:19 KJV)

"...gather out the stones; lift up a standard for the people!"
(Isaiah 62:10 KJV)

Lifting the Standard

We can only be responsible for our own actions. We cannot control what others do, but we can control what we do to contribute to the success of our relationships. You can probably fake a quarter mile jog, but you cannot fake a marathon. A little jog involves little discipline, and a little effort. A marathon involves disciplined calculated investments of time and effort and is a huge demand physically, mentally, and emotionally. If you haven't dedicated yourself to the demands of training, you run a higher risk of injury and not finishing the race.

> "And God is able to make all grace (every favor and earthly blessing) come to you in abundance, so that you may always and under all circumstances and whatever the need, be self-sufficient (possessing enough to require no aid or support and furnished in abundance for every good work and charitable donation)." (2 Corinthians 9:8 AMP)

Athletes who want to stay on top of their professional game continue training. Serena Williams still trains with a pro to improve her tennis game. Tiger Woods works with a pro for continual improvement of his golf game. Successful executives hire a coach to provide guidance. If you want to improve your marriage, work on it with the spirit of a champion.

Your marriage cannot work unless you do.

Take a journey with me while we study and apply ourselves to live out our priorities in our relationships. The journey is designed to help us leave excuses behind as we apply ourselves to an extreme relationships workout. We will lift the ideals we have settled for in our relationships to new standards. Set aside pre-conceived ideas, commit to develop and apply new skills, and take a look at some of the priorities you may have unintentionally allowed to slacken.

Chapter 1

Who Am I?

We believe the other person should change to solve relationship problems. Although in some cases it seems to be true, unfortunately we cannot count on or demand another person to change. In addition, if we only expect the other person to change and believe he or she only is responsible for the shortfalls, we take accountability and responsibility off our own shoulders. We obscure positive steps that we could have initiated to change our relationships for the better.

Many relationship exercises focus on what you need or have a right to expect from each other. Focusing on self increases dissatisfaction and expectations. Instead, let's identify what will make us the best possible, and how we need to change. Whether your husband changes or not, you will find an unending source of joy and fulfillment in living out your best role and leaving the rest to the Lord. You will find out that whether or not your "needs" are met by a person, a career, or other people, there is a source of provision and joy available for you.

Good relationships aren't about controlling others, manipulating others, or remaking anyone into the person you want him or her to be. It is about looking in the mirror at the end of the day and knowing that, one day at a time, you lived your life that day making the most you could from it. Knowing that you made wise choices

1

and you weren't distracted by anything that wasn't in line with your maximized divine destiny. Realizing you are in control of your responses and able to maximize your potential—despite others' choices.

It has been said that you are three people: the person you think you are, the person others think you are, and the person you really are. Our goal is to make these three one and the same person. We will awaken our senses to discern where we are falling short of living the lives we dreamed of, and take concrete and tangible steps to do what we can to resurrect those dreams. Along the way, we will analyze some of the skewed ideas that have fastened themselves to our lives like leeches, taking away enthusiasm and vitality in our relationships.

My mom said that people living in the best times of their lives can sadly let those times slip by without appreciating them or realizing them. "Life is not a dress rehearsal," Rose Tremain said. You need to live the life you want to live today.

"Today you took a step. You either moved closer or further away from what you hope to be. Most people move further away. A handful overcome the negative inertia of this fallen world and moved forward. But nobody – nobody – stood still."[1]

That's the interesting thing that I don't believe a lot of people understand. Many people believe that if we do nothing we will remain the same. However, if you went out and cultivated a piece of land to plant a garden in your yard, but did nothing with it, *a lot* would happen. Any seeds floating by are capable of drifting into your plot of land and rooting themselves there. Weeds can also spread underground, establishing themselves with root and runner systems. If the ground isn't regularly worked with, it becomes much more difficult to remove the weeds. Even leaving a small bit of the root will result in the weeds perpetrating in your garden.

In the same way as an untended plot of land, doing *nothing* guarantees disaster in relationships too. You never "stay the same," but regress without realizing it until weeds have invaded and are rooted deeply into your relationship. Reworking a weed-infested marriage to become a fruitful harvest is hard work.

When my husband and I first got married in November 1981, we felt our relationship was exceptional, as many couples do on their wedding day. We were keenly aware that statistically most marriages end up in divorce, and we wanted to be sure ours wouldn't fail. I asked advice from older women who had solid marriages. I read books, compiled information, and taught a two-year course to women on how to be better wives. My husband and I taught marriage classes in Sunday school. We counseled singles who were planning for marriage, newlyweds about strengthening their marriages, couples experiencing problems, and couples who had separated. Through this process I became accountable to hold a high standard for my relationship.

I hope I can help you "lift the bar" for your expectations and perception of marriage and for your other relationships. I want to unveil the incredible opportunities available to you in the most important role in your life—being an incredible wife and partner. When the day is done, and when your life is over, the single most important relationship in your life (apart from your relationship with God) is the relationship you have with your husband. It should take priority over all other relationships. Being a wife is worthy of hard work, dedication, and learning to achieve optimal success and fulfillment.

Marriage is a relationship of the highest calling: one you entered into until only death can part you. You have committed to love, honor, and cherish another individual, no matter what the circumstances. This is serious business that demands your devotion, dedication, and fortitude constantly and consistently. Being your husband's wife should be the most important relationship you have on earth. When she first got married, Nancy Reagan said: "I had of course no idea what the future would hold for us. I only knew that I loved Ronald Reagan, and being his wife was then, as it is today, the most important thing in the world for me."[2] Are you able to say that? Is being your husband's wife the "most important thing in the world" for you? Does he feel that you hold your relationship with him as a top priority in your life?

A priority is a thing that is regarded as more important than another, the fact or condition of being regarded or treated as more important, the right to take precedence or proceed before others. Does your spouse know he is your priority? Do you live that importance out daily? What evidence could you show in a court of law to prove your husband is your priority in your day-to-day activities and considerations?

If your relationship gets better and better, it will not be by mistake. Consistent effort keeps your marriage strong and thriving.

Marriage can be the best thing on earth or the absolute worst. Although we are keenly aware of what our husbands could do to improve our marriages, we cannot control our husbands. Although you can't control whether your husband loves you more, you can control whether or not you are loveable and how you treat him.

I heard a speaker at a benefit say that the phrase "give 'til it hurts" should be "give 'til it feels good." When we learn to give beyond measure, we will improve our marriages. Be unselfish or you will be miserable.

One of our essential tools is to "give 'til it feels good"—as many things and in as many ways as possible—beyond measure and cheerfully.

And when we think we have nothing left to give, we are going to draw a deep breath and count on the Lord to help us keep giving beyond our own ability. When you truly give without expecting anything in return, an amazing benefit follows.

> "Do not think that love, in order to be genuine, has to be extraordinary. What we need is to love without getting tired. How does a lamp burn? Through the continuous input of small drops of oil. In Matthew, it is said, 'If the drops of oil run out, the light of the lamp will cease, and the bridegroom will say, I do not know you.' What are these drops of oil in our lamps? They are the **small things** of daily life: faithfulness, small words of kindness, a thought for others, our way of being silent, of looking, of speaking, and of acting. These are the true drops of love. Be faithful in small things because it is in them that your strength lies."[3]

We are going to give to our husbands in many small ways. We are going to allow him into our world. It takes a good deal of time and effort to explain struggles and insights we have and to draw the struggles and insights our spouse has to the surface. We are going to look for opportunities to brighten our husband's days with special little surprises here and there. We have to allow our husband "in" to share a confidence or heart matter, talk about concerns about the children or other relationships, or ask his opinion about something, and listen closely to show him how his opinion really matters. It takes time to be as close as we can be to our husbands, and to incorporate all he is (and isn't) into our homes and lives.

The movie *They Died With Their Boots On*, with Errol Flynn and Olivia de Havilland, is about General Custer (played by Errol Flynn) during the time preceding and during his "last stand." I love the words Custer says to his wife when he knows he'll never see her again: "Walking through life with you has been a very gracious thing..."[4]

What has walking through life with you been like for your husband? What would you like walking through life to be like with you? Fun? Energizing? Encouraging? Sadly, if you asked couples today, they might say, "Walking through life with my spouse has been a very trying thing." Or, "…a very stressful thing." Or, "…a perpetual roller coaster ride."

Is life better with or without you? What are you adding to the life of the person you love the most? Is life more fun because of you? Some spouses make it easier to live without them than it is to live with them. We need to learn to conscientiously and on purpose make it a benefit when we walk into a room. We want to try to make it so our loved ones can't stand not to have us around. We are going to add something to the atmosphere of the room at all times: and with purpose we are going to add something good. We are going to focus on making it so our spouse and children can't wait to walk through the door. It is going to be a relief when we're around, instead of a relief when we are not around.

What is Important to Men?

Relationship problems occur because we project our individual preferences and desires onto another person. When we want to do something nice for someone, we do something that we would appreciate rather than what they would appreciate. We aren't incredible wives because we keep a clean house, discipline the children, are involved with their children's education, or cook dinner every night.

Men wish wives knew what is important to men and what an ultimate wife is from a man's point of view.

First, let's look at a few excerpts written by men about what they consider a good wife to be:

"She must be beautiful, …not necessarily on the outside. She must be able to find the beauty in simple things… She must be able to find humor in the absurd. She must have a desire to care for me, and to let me care for her. She must know what forever means. She would be able to argue with me passionately and still respect my opinion. She must be kind. She must be honest and must be able to trust. She must want to look into my eyes at the end of our days and say 'We have done good things.'"[5]

★★★

"… I believe you must believe in and love God in order to love yourself and others. A 'good wife' is someone who respects 'all' people whether they are a Senator or a waiter in a restaurant. I also believe a 'good wife' is someone who understands the value of a family and therefore family at all costs must come first when decisions are made. A good wife is someone who maintains peace and order within the household, looks after the bills, education of the kids, the nutrition and social entertainment of the family. Also a 'good wife' is someone who is willing to speak out when/if there is something wrong (for example if the husband is doing something wrong). A good wife is also someone who accepts aging and so when she is 45 I don't expect her to need to purchase a new hot red convertible and pretend she is a teenager. A 'good wife' is also someone who doesn't put pressure on herself, husband or the kids if the situation does not call for it (for example tells me to take out $2,000 a month mortgage when I know we'd be better off with $1,000 monthly mortgage, or tells the kids they must get all straight A's in order to go to Disney World). A 'good wife' is someone who loves/likes to work things in-house before telling the Sis, the momma, the 'friend,' the grandma and whoever else. That's my idea of a 'good wife.'"[5]

★★★

"She needs to be pleasing to the eye. Attraction is what is going to start the relationship off. Then she needs to have qualities of your mother: that is what will make your relationship last."[6]

★★★

"Looking for gentleness and patience in communication. Looking for a friend who can love you when things aren't going perfectly. "[6]

★★★

"Looking for a woman that makes me forget about everything when I'm with her! "[6]

★★★

"In looking for a wife, confidence can make up for a lot. "[6]

★★★

One of my two nieces said of the other as a toddler: "She is my best friend. I don't like her." Married people who live together during the routine and ups and downs of life occasionally feel that way about each other. However, as you walk through life together appreciating and sacrificing for each other, you can become each other's best friend and like each other too. What exactly is a best friend to you? Are you those things to your best friend? Here are a few qualities I look for in a friend, and so I also try to be these things to my husband.

- Someone who understands and is willing to listen when I need to work through something
- Someone who will enjoy doing things I like to do alongside me
- Someone who is willing to help me when I am overwhelmed

- Someone who will listen to my behind the scenes information
- Someone I can trust with my secrets
- Someone fun to be around
- Someone who makes time to be with me
- Someone who is loyal
- Someone who will share his or her feelings with me and listen when I share mine
- Someone who values and considers my opinion, but still has the courage to voice and retain his own
- Someone who challenges me to be a better person

Make sure you know what you value in a friend and work on being those things to your husband. More importantly, find out what he values in a friend, and try to be those things as well.

When men find a good wife, they are devoted.

Antony left a wife and fought a war for Cleopatra, and then, after Cleopatra left with her fleet, Antony abandoned his fleet to be with Cleopatra, justifying the destruction of his forces by saying, "Give me a kiss; even this repays me." He then fought a war at sea for her. When Cleopatra portended suicide to bring Antony to her side, he didn't think life worth living without her. [7]

The Taj Mahal, built in 1631, is one of the Seven Wonders of the World, and the only true monument built to honor love. It actually changes colors at different hours of the day and during different seasons to depict the different moods of women. It was built by the fifth Mughal emperor, Shah Jahan, in memory of his third wife, Mumtaz Mahal. She married him at the age of 14, and she remained an inseparable companion of her husband till her death on June 17, 1631, at age 39. She died while accompanying her husband in a campaign to crush a rebellion, after giving birth to their 13th or 14th child (accounts vary). Her death so crushed the emperor that all his hair and beard were said to have grown snow white in a few months. For the love and affection she showed to her husband, Mumtaz Mahal received highest honor of the land—the royal seal. According to the legends, stories of her virtue spread all over the Mughal Empire.[8]

Mumtaz was quite a woman to bear thirteen or fourteen kids, truck around with her husband everywhere—even accompanying him to crush a rebellion, and still be such an awesome companion and partner her husband created a wonder of the world for her. She must have been loveable throughout her busy days. Her story takes away excuses when we have only a few children to worry about. Doesn't she inspire you? You can be wonderful to your husband too.

Another man recently spent his life savings and sold off all his family heirlooms to build his wife a replica of the Taj Mahal in her honor. He is in the process of building the 50 ft. by 50 ft. building in her honor but was stopped by lack of money.[9]

Napoleon Bonaparte's love toward Josephine shows how inspired a man can be by his wife. Napoleon left shortly after they were married to go to battle, and wrote Josephine:

"Since I left you, I have been constantly depressed. My happiness is to be near you. Incessantly I live over in my memory your caresses, your tears, your affectionate solicitude. The charms of the incomparable Josephine kindle continually a burning and a glowing flame in my heart. When, free from all solicitude, all harassing care, shall I be able to pass all my time with you, having only to love you, and to think only of the happiness of so saying, and of proving it to you?... I thought that I loved you months ago, but since my separation from you I feel that I love you a thousand fold more. Each day since I knew you, have I adored you yet more and more.

"Ah! I entreat you to permit me to see some of your faults. Be less beautiful, less gracious, less affectionate, less good, especially be not over-anxious, and never weep. Your tears rob me of reason, and inflame my blood. Believe me it is not in my power to have a single thought which is not of thee, or a wish I could not reveal to thee."[10]

Even though circumstances separated them, their love for each other never ended. When Josephine died, Napoleon shut himself away for days while in exile and went to her grave as soon as he could after he escaped. Because Josephine loved violets (she surrounded herself with them and their scent), Napoleon carried violets from her garden in a locket until he died.[11]

Listen to these notes written by men to their wives:

"The Star in the East was a miracle as was the Virgin Birth. I have no trouble believing in those miracles because a miracle happened to me and it's still happening. Into my life came one tiny dear and a light shone round about. The light still shines and will as long as I have you. Please be very careful when you cross the street. Don't climb on any ladders. Wear your rubbers when it rains. I love my light and don't want to be ever in the dark again. I love you – Merry Christmas – Your ranch hand."[2]

★★★

"I guess when I was young I thought marriage might be this way for a while: I never knew it could go on and on, getting better and better year after year."[2]

★★★

"This is really just an 'in between' day. It is a day on which I love you 365 days more than I did a year ago, and 365 less than I will a year from now. But I wonder how I lived at all for all the 365's before I met you. All my love, Your Husband."[2]

★★★

We may not have married a poetic man, or a man who even likes to write such letters to us, but all of us would like to be loved and appreciated by our husbands. Love is said to be a virtue. If we focus on consistently building good character in our lives, we will not only be able to love others more constantly, but we will become easier to love as well.

Chapter 2

A Woman of Character

Since we are going to focus on what we can actively do and pursue in order to love more and be more loveable, our first focus is going to be growing in character. One of my grandma's favorite quotes was, "Beauty is as beauty does." As we develop strong moral character, we learn to love others less superficially. As we demonstrate qualities that inspire others to see the value and strength inside of us, we are also loved more because of who we are then for what we look like. Our challenge begins with eight character traits that will inspire us to live with moral excellence in being an "ultimate" wife: virtuous, joyful, wise, encouraging, contented, loving, feminine, and healthy.

Goal: Virtuous Wife

A virtuous woman can be trusted. Can your husband trust you? Can he trust that you will do him good and not evil all the days of your life? That is the reference to the "virtuous woman" in Proverbs 31. It says there that the virtuous woman's husband "safely trusts in her, so that he needs nothing." He needs nothing. This woman can be counted on.

A virtuous woman is a hard worker; she is not lazy. She takes care of herself. She learns the skills and information she needs to know about: mending, cooking, baking, and homemaking, also computers, business deals, nutrition, and other things that are of value to her home. She gets up early and often stays up late. The virtuous woman, with her intrinsic worth, has really got it together. When she doesn't, she's working towards getting it together.

A virtuous woman is a woman her husband can be proud to be married to. When your husband talks about you to others, or others talk to him about you, what are they saying about you? Is your husband proud to tell his friends and associates about the things you are doing and the things you are involved in? About the caliber of woman you are?

Tips for Developing Virtue

1. Stop Talking Mid-Sentence.

Did you know you have the incredible power within you to stop talking mid-sentence? This power is one of the most powerful ways of exhibiting virtue. When you make a decision that only good things will come out of your mouth yet you hear yourself speaking otherwise, you stop talking. I have been giving the "stop mid-sentence" challenge to women for over 30 years, and when they accept the challenge, women feel powerful. Once you start using this power and see how much better you feel about the things you communicate (and stop communicating), you will not even want to complete any wasteful, destructive or polluting sentences. It's my challenge to you today: Stop talking when you hear yourself begin to say something that shouldn't be said.

2. Make Time for Service to Others

I'm sure your schedule is packed like mine, but if we want to be a virtuous woman, we will make time to help someone or a group of people who is less fortunate. Involve your children too. When

I committed to help Gilda's Club™, a cancer support community, my children were often with me as I delivered meals, helped people scrapbook, or cared for children while cancer patients underwent treatment or were in hospice. As we walked through the valley of death with two children under the age of seven and with several of my friends, my own children learned a new appreciation of health and a perspective of the gift of life. These experiences also gave our family a stronger sense of stewardship to use what has been entrusted to us to bless others instead of us seven and no more.

Whether it's volunteering at a hospital, at a cancer support group, or nursing home; whether it's being in charge of a Brownie troop or some other non-profit organization, a virtuous woman of character takes the time to give back to society. When you and I help others who may be less fortunate, the results show up in our lives.

- Children learn, by example, that it is important to take time for others, even while we're still trying to "get it together" ourselves.
- As the family's awareness of those who are less fortunate grows, they become less apt to complain about petty things.
- Your family will have an enhanced appreciation of the "gift of the present." I have always believed that the present is called the "present" because it is such a gift.
- You start a Scriptural principle in motion. "Give, and you will receive. A large quantity, pressed together, shaken down, and running over will be put into your pocket. The standards you use for others will be applied to you." (Luke 6:38 GW)

A virtuous woman exhibits virtues such as prudence, temperance, courage, justice, love, hope, faith, humility, kindness, abstinence, chastity, patience, liberality, diligence, faith, hope, charity, fortitude, justice, and self control. These virtues usually shine the brightest when tested. When you are tested, remind yourself it is time to see the virtue inside of you come to the surface to make your home a better place.

3. Do the Difficult Tasks First

When you make your list of things to do, choose the least pleasant task first. If I do not accomplish the least pleasant thing first, then I almost always drag my feet with other projects.

When I wake up knowing I need to scrub my floor that day, or to make a difficult telephone call, I used to invariably slow down the rest of my day just to avoid the inevitable. I would end up scrubbing the floor at 11:30 p.m. or putting the phone call off another day. Instead, if I chose to tackle the difficult chores at the first opportunity in the morning, I realized that thinking about these duties all day didn't bog down my thoughts and activities.

Rolling up my sleeves and getting the difficult tasks done first is not only a good discipline, but also the sense of achievement I feel provides a great kick-start to my day.

4. Grow Deep Roots and Bear Fruit

The root system of a tree spreads out about three times the distance of the canopy of the tree. It obtains and provides nutrients to the tree, as well as stabilizing and anchoring the tree into the ground allowing it to withstand strong winds and other forces.[12]

In the same way, if we have roots that go deep with the Lord and His Word, when we truly desire to be a "doer" of the Word and not just a "hearer," we will be blessed indeed; we will not deceive ourselves, and we will bear the fruit of God's Spirit in our lives. The more we obey the precepts, statutes, judgments, and commandments of the Word of the Lord, the more we will show His love and the fruit of His love to the world. My mom says, "The deeper the root the sweeter the fruit." The fruit of the Spirit of God, love, joy, peace, longsuffering, gentleness, goodness, faith, meekness, and temperance, or self-control (see Galatians 5:22) is a list of virtues that will manifest when you have a strong root system to anchor and stabilize you.

Psalm 1:1-2 (AMP) explains the root: "Blessed (happy, fortunate, prosperous, and enviable) is the man who walks and lives not in the counsel of the ungodly [following their advice, their plans and purposes], nor stands [submissive and inactive] in the path where sinners walk, nor sits down [to relax and rest] where the scornful [and the mockers] gather. But his delight and desire are in the law of the Lord, and on His law (the precepts, the instructions, the teachings of God) he habitually meditates (ponders and studies) by day and by night." Psalm 1:3 (AMP) explains the fruit: "And he shall be like a tree firmly planted [and tended] by the streams of water, ready to bring forth its fruit in its season; its leaf also shall not fade or wither; and everything he does shall prosper [and come to maturity]."

Goal: Joyful Wife

My sister has a sign hanging in front of the mirror in her bathroom. It reads: "You are looking at the person responsible for your happiness." A joyful wife takes responsibility for her own happiness. True happiness is not the kind of fleeting feeling a child has with a new toy or a giddy feeling that quickly fades. Genuine happiness is an overriding sense of joy about being the person you were created to be—doing what you were created to do, thinking what you were made to think, and speaking good words about good things. A joyful woman isn't a woman who retaliates or is a responder to others' problems or actions, but she is a woman who is response-able for her actions.

You will tend to look at your world from the glasses you choose to wear. I had a pair of pink colored glasses on my counter for quite some time to teach my children to look at their world "through rose-colored glasses" on purpose. What glasses color your world? Usually the glasses you are looking at the world through are colored with the character traits you exemplify. My mom's extreme love for people colors her world with love. When she looks at people or situations, love rules and everything is viewed through love. Another person may feel self-pity, and when they look at people or situations, they color others and events with the way they feel they were left out or victimized.

Because we see the world differently, several people can live in the same household, and later, when talking about it, each one saw it through the "glasses" they wore. For example, one of my siblings believes she grew up in a pretty perfect household; while another sibling only saw and dwelt on the negative aspects of growing up in the same household. We often laugh and wonder how it is possible that we grew up at the same time in the same home when each of us remembers it differently.

How you see the world changes your experience and affects your joy. This principle hit me particularly hard one Thanksgiving when I had a great day with my incredible family. All day my relatives, approximately 45 of us, enjoyed each other. We had a fantastic dinner, and a wonderful time being together, playing games, and watching football. When I got in the car, I said to my husband, "Did you hear what so and so said to me?" and I launched into something negative that was said at the beginning of the day about the way I looked. Suddenly I heard myself and I was totally disgusted. There were multitudes of wonderful things I could have focused on, yet I chose an isolated statement to triumph over the memories of the day. The problem wasn't with the day or with the person that said it; the problem was *me*. I didn't like myself at that moment, and I made a decision I would never again allow myself to concentrate on the one or two negative things about a day, but I would rather choose to focus on the good that happened.

If you have a grateful spirit, like the women I helped when I volunteered at Gilda's Club,™ you will find much to be grateful for every day. One woman, who had survived her battle with cancer, said she used to complain about the weather or little annoyances, but now she sees through the glasses of returning health, so she refuses to complain about small things again. She is happy to be alive.

When I decided to put different glasses on, I began to hold myself responsible and put myself in check when I started to look for or focus on negatives. My family has joined me in changing our glasses and thus the way we perceive our surroundings. When we leave an event or at the dinner table, we like to take turns telling our favorite part of the event or day.

Unfortunately, some homes only focus on negatives. Some women live with constant and harsh criticism, told and made to feel that they will never amount to anything. I have counseled people who have a difficult time believing that they can do anything correctly. You can have a transformation and change your thinking patterns. When you accept the forgiveness Christ died to give you to walk in fellowship with God, you are in Christ, and He makes all things new.[13] You are accepted[14] which means highly favored. And you have the Word of God and the Spirit of God to train you so that you are equipped for every good work.[15]

A joyful wife looks for the good in life. Knowing this about perspective inspired me to start asking each member of our family the best things that happened in their days. By focusing on the good things in each day, we trained our vision. We also made it a habit at our dinner table to take turns going around the table and saying one good thing about each person. Every person trained their eye to find the best qualities about each member of the family. On our family walks, to illustrate the concept that "you find what you are looking for," we would alternate looking for things "wrong" in the neighborhood with things "right." We would then talk about how much more enjoyable it was to look for the right things.

What are you looking for? You will see people, circumstances, and situations from the glasses you put on each morning. If you begin each day by reading the Bible, your focus will change too. You will see good things and your family will follow your lead.

When you learn to love righteousness and hate wickedness, you will have an anointing of true joy above your companions.[16] Also, in the presence of the Lord, you will find strength and gladness, or true joy.[17]

Did you ever walk along and not notice the little glittery pieces in certain parts of sidewalks? If you look carefully, and on purpose, you can spot little "diamonds" in the midst of the gray cement. But if you are rushing along, you will not see the little glittery pieces mixed in amongst the gray. Stop to see the leaves swirling in circles, the snow-covered evergreens, or the flock of geese overhead. Teach your children to look for the best things in each day. Make it a point to appreciate the good parts of each day and of each person in your life. Again, this is something that will not happen *by accident*: it needs to be a concentrated effort. Put those rose-colored glasses on. Retrain your vision.

Goal: Wise Wife

A wise woman has goals and works toward them. She considers the long-term ramifications of her actions as they relate to those goals. Don't lose perspective of how your actions today affect your long-term goals. I have a goal: I am determined to "live happily ever after" with my husband. At times, I've been convinced that I would be living that happy life by myself, and in my imagination at that. I live like I believe it, and because I don't give up my goal, even though there have been a few blips off the path, we are still heading there.

What is your goal for your marriage? If you aim at nothing, you will hit it every time. Write it down. For example, if you want a long and happy marriage, write, "I am going to celebrate my 50th wedding anniversary with the person I love the most." Post it and live your life to accomplish it.

Wisdom is sacrificing short-term pleasure or convenience for long-term goals. For example, when my husband comes home I want him to feel special and have a little down time. When I had younger children, it was difficult to rearrange my errands to be home so he could come home to his family and have a meal on the table. Bringing children with me on errands that I would rather have done alone, and giving up some of the things I wanted to do were very small inconveniences compared to the great benefit of my husband's comfort and sense of well being. Even after the children grew up and got married, I still run to the door to greet my husband to make him feel special, and he still can't wait to get home to his safe place where he is loved and appreciated.

Hard work and efforts pay off in the end, although often the sacrifices may seem painful. When running, I discipline myself to lean into the inclines as a challenge, and it increases the achievement of getting to the top. Sports and music lessons are great examples of sacrificing to achieve solid long-term goals. Those who have achieved recognition for greatness in music and sports didn't achieve it by accident; there are hours upon hours of unheralded sacrifices and disciplines that result in greatness. When I was 23 years old, I was to play Chopin's First Piano Concerto in E Minor from memory to close off a recital held at Ford Mansion. I spent well over a year learning over 60 pages of music, polishing it and committing it to memory. I spent endless hours doing various technique exercises so that my hands didn't cramp up during the most difficult pages. I sacrificed most of my social life that year in order to play the piece well.

In the same way, it will be discipline and extra effort that achieve extraordinary results in above-average relationships. Behind-the-scenes efforts and sacrifices will show up in the high caliber of relationships you enjoy. In the end, your relationships will show the dedication you applied to them.

A wise woman seeks counsel. I taught my children to seek help when they didn't understand something in school before they got so far behind they could never catch up. Bridges are built before storms make the waters rise. It is wise to seek counsel from someone who is succeeding at what you want to do (in other words don't seek counsel from someone who is not successful in building relationships). Go to a marriage seminar, read a good book, give some time and focus to making your marriage awesome before it goes unattended for too long. If you are having problems, seek out help right away.

A wise woman realizes that every little action and every little word contributes to the future success or demise of her marriage. It's as if each day you are given a packet of seeds to sow, and as you go through your day you throw your seeds into your field. You can be sure that those seeds will produce something in your future. The little seeds that seem so inconsequential are capable of producing an exponentially incredible harvest. Remember the seed for a tomato plant not only produces the tomato plant, but then each tomato produces hundreds more seeds. The capacity for each seed you sow should never be underestimated. The life you are living today is as a result of the seeds you have sown in your yesterdays.

Goal: Encouraging Wife

An encouraging woman is mature and knows the power of her words. If I ask you to think of a time when someone said something cruel that hurt your feelings, you could probably recount several instances going back to your elementary school days. Words are strong weapons; like a nuclear bomb, once set off there is no turning back. A wise woman realizes how powerful her words are and chooses them carefully. I once built a volcano as a science project to describe the power of words to my children. Destructive words are like lava; in a moment they erupt and flow destroying bonds and relationships that took years to build—and will take years to rebuild. If a critical, harsh, unhelpful thought crosses your mind, shut up. Don't poison your children or your husband by cruel thoughtless words. Be mature or get mature! It is unbelievable how quickly foolish women speak about the flaws of those they love. What kind of love belittles or demeans an individual, either in front of them or behind their backs? We need to remember the simple truth that the fictional rabbit from *Bambi*, Thumper, was taught by his mother, "If you don't have anything nice to say, don't say anything at all." Consider the feelings of your children and teens, too. Would you want them recounting your struggles and weaknesses to their friends? Speak well of your husband and your children; they will live up to what you believe about them. You expect your children and teens to control their words. How much more you should be able to control your words.

Do whatever it takes to grow up in the area of words. I discovered several three-word phrases that I practiced when I felt the volcano rising. With these little sayings running over and over in my mind, I was able to get through many situations without blowing it.

> Let it go.
> Lay it down.
> Give it up.
> Forget about it.

Knowing how to shut up isn't even enough. An encouraging woman also needs to know when to speak up. Is your husband clinging to the comments of others who compliment him because he doesn't sense your admiration of him? Do you leave too many good things unspoken?

My husband travels quite a bit. In order to help him keep up with what was going on in the house, so he didn't walk in without knowing what was going on in our lives, it was important for me to "speak up" when I often didn't even feel like talking. I gave him a little summary of each of our children so he would be aware of how to best jump back into our lives. I did not want my husband to be unaware and callous about our family dynamics because he had been gone. Because of this inside scoop, my husband was able to help our children through problems he may not even have known about because he was gone. When he came home from traveling, he then knew what to expect and why. Whether it was giving one daughter the opportunity to tell him about her first kiss, advising another daughter about how to handle a rigorous college schedule, or helping a son to determine the best college fit, I equipped him to seamlessly stay close to his children even with his demanding work schedule.

An encouraging woman knows how to communicate. Subtle hints don't work. If you feel something needs to be said, say it – don't expect others to know what's going through your mind or what you're dealing with inside.

An encouraging woman chooses her words carefully. The Bible says: Your words are a showcase, a china cabinet, – a display case of what is in your heart.[18] Are you building your home and those in it or ripping it apart?

Nancy Reagan said, "I [have] no blueprint for marriage, how to make it happy and long-lasting, but… mainly you have to be willing to give… I would add that saying how much you love each other – to each other and also in letters that can be read, and reread over the years – is a wonderful way to stay close. It is especially important in our busy lives to keep alive what really matters most: love, caring for each other, finding concrete ways to say it and show it, every day and in every way you can. It's what endures, after all, and what we retain and hold onto, especially in our hearts."[19]

An encouraging woman knows how to encourage herself and not lean on other people or circumstances. In 1 Samuel 30, when David returned to Ziklag, he found that the enemy had plundered his goods and taken all of his and his people's possessions. Instead of nursing the problem, he chose instead to encourage himself in the Lord, and then he went to battle, fought, and recovered everything. There was no one else to encourage David; he was in the wilderness and the people with him were discouraged and in despair and couldn't be counted on for encouragement. David did what we need to learn to do when we are discouraged, empty of resources, threatened, or just plain down. Although David was distressed, and everyone around him was grieved, he encouraged himself in the Lord. We need to learn to encourage ourselves in the Lord as David did (1 Samuel 30:6). The way we do that is by not focusing on the problems, and not focusing on the people who want to blame us. The word "encourage" means to fasten ourselves onto the Lord and trust in Him to lead and guide us to "recover all."

Goal: Contented Wife

A contented wife understands the "it is enough" principle. I taught my children from the time they were young to say, "It is enough." When it was time to leave an event where they wished they could stay longer, when they wanted more treats, when they wanted to stay up longer, just teaching them to say "it is enough" made my children realize they needed to be grateful for what they already had or did. Women often feel that if they had one more thing, then they could be content. If I could lose five more pounds, I would be happy. If I only had a few hundred more dollars... A bigger house... A better husband... A better job... Living in the "if only" breeds discontentment for living in the present.

We have seen more marriages ruined because of foolish women who wanted more and more and more. I heard that there are two ways to have more money—make more money or spend less. Learn to live simply. Learn to say, "It is enough." Enough to own, enough to maintain, enough to service, enough to focus on.

A contented woman frees her husband from being her "everything." Make a list of your needs, make sure they are needs, not greeds, and then, ask God to fill those needs. You may be surprised where the answers come from. Don't expect your husband to meet all your needs. Need social activities? Meet up with a few friends during the day and let your kids play at the park while you socialize. Need to work out or run errands? Have a babysitter come during the day so when your husband comes home you can have a wonderful family life. Your husband cannot be 100% responsible for your sense of well being. If he sees you happy and fulfilled, your husband will be freer to appreciate you and you will be more grateful for what he does for you, your house, and your family. Set your husband free from expectations.

If you don't release your husband from your expectations, he may become a "prisoner" of them. For example, you may expect your husband to give you a break when he comes home from work, and your husband could come home from work and meet that expectation. Since it was what you expected, however, you are not grateful: he only did what you expected him to do. On a different day, your husband could have an extraordinarily rough day at work and need a break himself. He could come through the door exhausted, with the intent of staring blankly at Monday night football. He could manage to clear the table, but then he sits down to watch television. Instead of being grateful he cleared the table, you are upset because you expected him to do so much more. Since he did less than what you expected, you are not only ungrateful for any of his efforts, but you are furious at how little he did when you expected so much. We need to set our husbands free from being the one totally responsible for fulfilling our needs. No one person can provide all you need. One of the best bonuses of freeing your husband from being the prisoner of your expectations is that your expectations will be put on God, Who is much better equipped to supply your list of needs than your husband is. God is "able to [carry out His purpose and] do superabundantly, far over and above all that we [dare] ask or think [infinitely beyond our highest prayers, desires, thoughts, hopes, or dreams]." (Ephesians 3:20 AMP)

A contented woman is grateful for what she has. I learned many years ago to expect nothing in order to become grateful for my husband's contributions to our family. Instead of being angry and agitated that he came home at 11 p.m. because his plane was delayed, I was happy to see him and grateful he came home at all. If you learn to expect nothing, you will become a more grateful person. A grateful person is a contented person. You will also become more empathetic and learn to see his point of view. This change of view is simplistic, and I know there are some situations where there are abuses that may need to be addressed, but, most of the time, this type of appreciation is one of the principles that made my marriage and even my other relationships better. Gratefulness is a beautiful attitude that you can decide to plant, cultivate, and grow. I was as grateful living in my little trailer when we first got married, fixing it up like a little dollhouse, as I am in my big beautiful home now. A grateful person is a person everyone wants to be around because she appreciates everything.

A contented woman is reasonable and realistic. Make sure your desires, whether for time, money, or expenditures, are in keeping with the reality of your budget and are reasonable. In the same way, don't expect a quiet introverted guy to be the life of the party; don't expect a sports fanatic to miss sports games; don't expect a guy who has a physically demanding job to come home raring to go. Not reasonable and not realistic.

Goal: Loving Wife

A loving wife thinks the best of her husband. She honors and respects her husband for who he is; and doesn't constantly focus on who he isn't. This honor doesn't mean that you don't realize your husbands limitations; rather that you purposefully don't allow his shortcomings to blind you from seeing his positive and strong qualities as well. Have you loved your husband enough? Do you appreciate the things he does for you, or are you always harping on the things he doesn't do? Nancy Reagan wrote: "In the climate of today, I think it would be good for all of us to focus on the positive, the true, the things that really last, on character, humor, commitment, and love, and on the happy memories of a wonderful man and his life."[19] "Summing it all up, friends, I'd say you'll do best by filling your minds and meditating on things true, noble, reputable, authentic, compelling, gracious— the best, not the worst; the beautiful, not the ugly; things to praise, not things to curse." (Philippians 4:8 THE MESSAGE)

When someone loves you, they usually think the best of you. You want to be around them! When someone is critical of you or you know they just don't like you, you try to avoid them at all costs. It's the same way in your marriage. When we delight in our husbands and think the best of them, they will want to be around us more. If we are critical, they will avoid us.

A loving wife is genuinely interested in what her husband is interested in. Nancy Reagan said, "I was, I suppose, a woman of the old school: If you wanted to make your life with a man, you took on whatever his interests were and they became your interests too."[19] Old school or not, the principle rings true.

Dana Reeve was a great example. She married a famous movie star, and was a movie star herself. She was a constant companion of Christopher Reeve (who played the role of Superman). After her husband became a quadriplegic following a tragic horseback riding incident, Dana told Christopher: "I still love you no matter what. You are still you," and she became his chief supporter during his 9-1/2 year ordeal and throughout his dedication to find and fund a cure for spinal cord injuries. After Christopher's death, she became the chairwoman of the Christopher Reeve Paralysis Foundation, which funds research on paralysis. She never returned to her own acting career, because what was important to her husband became important to her too.

Dana wore Christopher's wedding band on a chain around her neck. She explained how she missed his companionship: "I would really like him here. It's very disorienting to be one person instead of the team we always were."[20] She continued, "I made a vow to Chris when we married that I would love him, and I would be with him in sickness and in health. And I did OK with that. But there's another vow that I need to amend today. I promised to love, honor, and cherish him until death did us part. Well, I can't do that, because I will love, honor, and cherish him forever".[21]

A loving wife makes a place for her husband to come alive. Have you delighted in being a part of your husband's goals and dreams? Have you supported his ideas? I love the song by Stephen Curtis Chapman, and the words have become a mission for me to my husband:

> Cause what I really want to say
> Is what the sun would say to the sky
> For giving it a place to come alive
>
> It's like a tale too great to be told
> It's something that my heart can only show
> I'm gonna take my whole life
> Just to let you know
> What I really want to say[22]

Goal: Feminine Wife

When I first got married, my husband and I began the task of combining our two households into one. It wasn't long before our home smelled like vanilla candles and cute curtains adorned the windows. Tastefully placed plaques, framed photos, and guest towels were obvious signs of a woman living in the home.

A woman's creativity makes a home an expression of hospitality, warmth, and femininity. Being feminine doesn't mean being frilly or putting floral furniture in every room; however, your home should reflect the style, grace, and effort of a woman who cares about it.

God built men and women with differences and the way we dress, the way we act, and how we present ourselves reflect those differences. Try hemming a pair of pants, sewing on a button, arranging flowers in a vase on your table, or organizing a messy drawer. Develop the feminine part of you and the creative task of making your house a home.

Try it and see. Your feminine side will appeal to your man.

Goal: Healthy Wife

As we work on being the best we can be, it is imperative not to neglect our health. Energy and strength are investments in our marriages and other relationships. When you eat healthy foods, you feel better. You have a twinkle in your eye, and a pep in your step. When some people walk into the room, you can feel their positivity and energy come in with them like a breath of fresh air.

If you aren't sleeping well or eating healthy foods, vitality will not be a part of who you are. If I eat junk foods or food on the run, or substitute coffee for sleep, I run out of energy. If I let myself gain weight, I get more lethargic and lose the energy to accomplish my goals. Realizing these hindrances to my goals and overall health encourages and inspires me to keep putting solid efforts at maintaining good health.

You have to give energy to get energy. My grandfather was over 70 years old and yet he walked almost every day. Until the day he died, energy was part of his personality, and with it he encouraged and uplifted others. He told me to walk on the treadmill, even if it were only for 10 minutes at the end of the day. He recited the dangers of drinking pop, eating processed foods, and eating too late at night. My grandfather had a servant's heart and was constantly busy doing things for others. It seemed as if his time multiplied. I believe that, in part, he was able to do so much for others because he took good care of himself and had the vitality and energy to give.

Good health also involves what you fill your mind and spirit with. Right after I got married, and before I had children, I found myself singing a popular country song on my way into work. All of a sudden I jolted as I heard the words coming out of my mouth, and I realized that those words were never going to contribute to the kind of life and marriage I wanted. I began to take a strict inventory of the songs I listened to and sang, and I was surprised at how many of them were off color from the way I wanted to live.

Be careful of the things you see and hear because those things become part of who you are. If I fill my head and heart with good music, podcasts of my favorite preachers, and the Word of God, and wholesome movies and entertainment, the natural outcome is that good things come out of me too.

Be the best you can be. Take steps to address a few health areas where you have slackened your efforts. Heed the words of Winston Churchill, "Never, never, never give up!"[23]

Goal: The Ultimate Woman

So what are you aiming for? If your greatest dreams and goals are separated from your marriage, re-focus. Work hard to be awesome: virtuous, joyful, wise, encouraging, contented, loving, feminine, and glowing and healthy.

Where are you now? Have you neglected yourself to the point where you don't have the energy or vitality to be the wife you wanted to be when you first got married? Have you let your ideals go and succumbed to the lazy slacker sitcom attitudes (accompanied with a lot of sarcasm, yelling, and eye rolling) prevalent in the breakdown of our society? Have you lacked the discipline or character necessary to be the person and wife you aspire to be?

Get lost in the work of understanding your husband better, being the best person you can be, and in the process making your husband look and feel good and be the best he can be.

The end result will be what is said about the woman of virtue in Proverbs 31:28 and 31:31 (NKJV): "Her children rise up and call her blessed; her husband also, and he praises her …Give her of the fruit of her hands, and let her own works praise her in the gates."

To My Precious Child from Your Heavenly Father:

Attached is a new sheet of paper. It has never been written on. I have a special assignment for you today:

Please write anything you want on this paper. This paper is how you want to live today.

Notice the paper is blank. That means leaving any unforgiveness, bad attitudes toward others, bitterness or anger out of it. Give all others a fresh start in your heart, and write with an appreciation for others, knowing that I do the same for you today.

You can write something you learned from other papers in your past that you don't want to forget today, but you cannot re-write your past.

You can write something you hope for in your future that you want to remember today, but right now, you cannot write your future: you can only write your "today".

Write with reckless abandon—I want you to throw yourself into this day and live 100% in it—don't hold back.

I want you to write without fear. Know that I am with you today to walk with you. Look at the Bible and the accounts of all those who have gone before you. Trust Me.

I want you to write with Me in mind. You know the plans I have for you. You know what I have told you is good for you and what is not. Just as you don't have to call your parents to make every little decision because you know what they would say, don't think you have to ask Me for every little decision. You know which relationships I will bless and which I will not; you know what things I will bless and which I won't.

I want you to soak up the gifts I've given you today: the people, the places, the events. I want you to be the most amazing culmination of you there can be today. Be a wise steward over the things I've put into your life today, and make a difference in the lives of others, at the places you go and at the events you attend today. Once today is gone, some of the people, places, and events may never be there again. But know that I will never change.

Write your own paper. No copying. No cheating. No asking someone else to write for you. No blaming someone else for what is written on your paper. Only you can write your today and take responsibility for your today.

Write with courage. It takes courage to face new challenges, climb new mountains, face new difficulties. Do all you can and leave the results to Me.

This day is only a day quickly passed and gone. Give all.

And when tomorrow comes, I will give you a new paper to do the assignment again.

Love, Your Heavenly Father

Chapter 3

Control Freak

When I began teaching relationships classes in 1981, I did so with materials that were outdated and much of the information was inappropriate for the twenty-first century. Because some of the material was so archaic, the material really discouraged women from accepting some of the information even though it was worth paying attention to. However, general principles that keep marriages and relationships strong never change:

- Sex. If you give your husband your body, feed his ego, and feed him he will cherish you forever. Women are the ones that make sex complicated.
- Men need to be accepted for who they are. Most of the time we don't think about changing them until after the wedding.
- Men need to be respected.
- Men want to know they are a top priority in their women's lives.
- Men have strong ego needs; they do not appreciate having their pride deflated.
- Men love joyful and happy wives.
- Men don't want you to fix their problems, but they appreciate your confidence in them and your encouragement.
- Men like their women to be feminine and not try to act like men.

- Men want their wives to be their lovers, and do not appreciate being "mothered" by their wives.
- Men don't like women who act like they are smarter or braver than them.
- Men appreciate kindness and generosity in their women.
- Men look to their wives to make their houses peaceful homes.
- Men appreciate when their wives look the best they can.
- Men like when their wives are grateful for gifts they receive, regardless of whether the gifts are expensive or inexpensive.
- Men like to feel they are the "kings of their castles."
- Men appreciate it when their wives can stretch a dollar.
- Men appreciate women that they can trust. Men aren't usually petty, and they don't want wives that gossip about them nor about others.
- Men like women that aren't insistent that everything being done their own way. Men want to be respected for the way they do chores and activities even when it is different than the way their wives are used to.
- Men appreciate being asked for favors, opinions, money and time in a respectful way rather than being pressured or commanded.

A quick internet search on what men wish women knew for success in marriage will reinforce that these timeless principles are still predominant for successful relationships. Blogs and forums restate strong timeless principles for marriage that I have read and taught over the past few decades.[24]

We want to live up to our potential as the best wife we can be and go back to the pattern for marriage established 2,000 years ago in the Bible—the pattern that worked.

The book *Sacred Influence: What a Man Needs from His Wife to Be the Husband She Wants* recounts how David McCullough found a letter by John Adams written to his wife, Abigail, in the heat of the Revolutionary War. He said, "We can't guarantee success in this war, but we can do something better. We can deserve it." [25]

Later McCullough read another letter by George Washington, which used the same line, referring to words in a play called *Cato*. It can help us transform our marriages. Explaining, McCullough said, "That line in Adams' letter is saying that how the war turns out is in the hands of God. We can't control that, but we can control how we behave. We can deserve success." [25]

You can't control another person. You can't guarantee how everything will turn out when another person's actions are part of the outcome. But you *can* behave in such a way that transformation is encouraged and likely.

McCullough's book also tells about Napoleon Bonaparte's letter to his wife telling her, "I insist you have more strength. I am told you are always crying. For shame. That is very bad…. Be worthy of me and develop a stronger character. Make a proper show in Paris…. If you are always weeping I shall think you have no courage or character. I do not like cowards. An empress should have heart." [25]

I like the saying "Be worthy of me." This should be the goal of every husband and wife—to be worthy of each other.

Scripture gives several directives for what it means to "live worthy."

In Matthew 10:38, we are told that any person who doesn't take up his cross daily to follow Jesus is not worthy of Him. In other words, using the most sacrificial example of all time, being worthy involves great sacrifice.

Romans 16:2 (NLT) shows us that Paul told the Romans to receive Phoebe in a way worthy of the saints. In Ephesians 4:1 (AMP) they are told to live a life "worthy of the divine calling to which you have been called." Simply put, wives should receive their husbands in a way worthy of a husband, and we are to live a life worthy of the calling to be a wife, a helper, a lifelong partner. [25]

The focus is not taking responsibility for how another person acts, or trying to manipulate another person into acting a certain way. Instead, we seek to control our actions, responses, and reactions.

How can you tell if you are entering control freak territory? How can you see the warning signs and take action against them? Some of these selfish tendencies are easily spotted in others' lives and seldom recognized in our own unless we step back and take an accurate assessment of them or have someone, who loves us honestly and specifically and nouthetically,[26] critique us in these areas. If any of the following signs are surfacing in your life, take note.

1. You make plans and commitments for your husband before you check with him.

   Making plans on your own probably indicates you are used to having things go the way you plan or the way you want them to more often than not. Instead, grant your husband the courtesy of deciding whether or not he wants to participate in the plans before you finalize them. Tell him and others that you need a go-ahead from him before confirming plans. He will be delighted to have a say in how things are planned.

   My husband is so busy that I am in charge of our calendar, as limited as it is with his extensive travel. He actually *sends* people to me to make plans. However, before I finalize any plans, I make sure he is available and whether it is something he wants to do. I also try to anticipate his feelings by asking questions like, "Are you sure you want to commit to this engagement when you are just getting home and will want to get together with your children (grandchildren)?"

2. You monitor your husband.

You listen for incorrect English, scrutinize his table manners, or get annoyed because he crunches cereal (or ice), slurps his soup, or picks his teeth. Instead, work on your tolerance level. Love "...is not easily provoked" (1 Corinthians 13:5 KJV). The problem isn't really how your husband chews; the problem is with your acceptance and patience.

3. You speak to your husband in the wrong tone.

Maybe it's something you've heard too often on television or in the movies. You may need to reassess what you would like your role to be in your marriage. Calm down and communicate to him with the same respect and honor you would like to be spoken to. Listen to your tone and tweak your style if you have adopted some bad habits. Drop the condescending verbiage, and learn better communication strategies so that he'll want to listen to you rather than tune you out.

4. You need to be in control of every situation.

When you need something done and insist it be done exactly how you want it regularly, without considering the schedule or needs of your husband, or if you find that you are so limited in your choices of restaurants or movies that it cuts out any other opinion, you need to step back and examine why you expect your husband (and probably others) to adjust to your wants instead of accommodating his ideas. When someone else takes control and you more strongly assert yourself to take over, you may not only have insecurity issues, but the control freak may be taking over you. To reverse this tendency, practice going with the flow and letting others make choices when they are with you.

5. You tell him what to wear and how to handle his personal grooming.

   There is nothing wrong with helping your husband pick out an outfit if he likes you to, but if you constantly nitpick his appearance, you are encroaching over to the "control freak" arena. If you find yourself telling him how to get his hair cut, whether or not he can grow a beard, setting up waxing appointments for him, or constantly belittling his appearance, you are definitely in "control freak" territory.

6. Your strong opinions are negatively affecting other relationships.

   Although strong people are often respected, when the feelings and opinions of others' aren't considered, it gets old after awhile. If your mother, your sister, your family or your close friends make statements here and there, be open to giving someone else a chance to make a decision. Back off to allow others' input. Force yourself to play a game you really don't like for the sake of playing a game with the group. Watch a movie that wouldn't necessarily be your first choice because someone else wants to watch it. Go to a different restaurant than your favorite one; expand your choices to include more of other's desires. Chances are that if others are noticing your inflexibility, you are exhibiting some of the same control freak tendencies at home too, so take notice.

Philippians 2:21 (THE MESSAGE) says, "Most people around here are looking out for themselves, with little concern for the things of Jesus." We all have a sin nature inclined toward selfishness. In addition, our society has bent and molded and shaped us to "get all you can, look out for #1, and go for the gusto." Jesus calls us to humble ourselves, to deny ourselves, to consider others better than ourselves, and to love without expecting anything in return. Marriages are stronger when we actively look for ways to consider our mate's needs above ours, and to sacrificially love, with supporting and convincing actions—without expecting anything in return.

What you feed will grow, and what you starve will die. Feed only the actions and attitudes you want to grow; stop feeding the actions and attitudes that need to go. When you feed an action, you make provision for it, you fuel it, you add to it. When you starve an action, you take away provision for it, stop adding fuel to the fire, and stop adding information to it.

What are some of the things a woman wants to change in her husband?

1. Habits that annoy us —bad table manners, eating junk food, bad moods, complaining, quick to anger, leaving things and clothes around the house, interrupting, crude language, or smoking.
2. How he spends his time or money—too much time watching or playing sports or computer games, napping or sleeping, hanging with the guys, at work or work related activities, or even at church and church activities. Neglects to phone when delayed. Constantly checks his email. Spends too much money on hobbies, extravagant clothes, or expensive sporting events, or falls for risky investing schemes.
3. Neglected duties—fails to keep up with routine home and car maintenance.

4. Social behavior—loud or overzealous in public, not courteous, interrupts, contradicts, brags, and exaggerates. Picks questionable friends, or isolates himself and doesn't want to do much socially.
5. Desires and vision—lacks confidence, indecisive, or afraid to take advantage of opportunities, resulting in missed opportunities. Either has no desire to get ahead or is consumed with success. Unrealistic dreams or desires that require incredible risk.
6. Leadership—fails to be the family leader or to correct and train or take an interest in the children.
7. Moral and religious standards—uninterested in attending church, no interest in personal spiritual growth or the spiritual well being of the children. Lax about violence and sexual content in the TV and movies.
8. Finances—mismanagement, unwise spending, stingy, extravagant, or expensive hobbies.

If your husband has some of these faults, what do you do when you are painfully aware of them? Are you able to accept your husband and look to his strong side and the things he is good at, or are you determined to control and correct your husband's weaknesses? Some women actually feel that helping their husbands change is something they are doing because they love them so much.

However, when you find yourself trying to change your husband, ask yourself why you will not accept him the way he is. If you truly accepted your husband for the way he is, with his goods and bads, ups and downs, you would not try to change little things that annoy you about him.

While at a marriage retreat, my husband and I were instructed to write down the things that bothered us about each other on a piece of paper. When we exchanged our papers, I was shocked to find that my husband had come up with only a few things. I was embarrassed that my paper was full of things. Realizing full well that I can be much more annoying than my husband helped me understand that my list was a reflection of a critical and faultfinding spirit.

We are not talking about abusive or threatening situations, but we are addressing annoyances and differences that are inevitable when two diverse personalities come together. We will address abusive situations that cannot be tolerated, ignored, or winked-at in a later chapter.

I have often looked back on when I began teaching marriage classes a month after I got married. In one class, with a group of strong women, we listed some of our husbands' behaviors that bothered us. A few of them voiced some fairly common complaints, most of which are included in the list above. We made a commitment to turn a blind eye towards our husbands' faults and concentrate on the things we loved and appreciated about them instead. Approximately twenty years later, I happened to see several women who had attended the original class—women still in my life. When I asked about their husbands, it was funny to hear that one husband was on the couch watching television after a hard days' work, another was on a hunting trip, another golfing, and my husband was traveling for work—the very things we had listed that bothered us the most twenty years prior. Some behaviors do not change, but our attitudes can. Knowing that each of the women adjusted her attitudes illustrated to me that acceptance contributes to the success, freedom and enjoyment of my marriage.

Why do we even want to change our husbands? We may see blind spots that he doesn't see but are overtly obvious to others, and we just want to help them. Sometimes their faults embarrass us and we want to change them to better our own public image. Other times, we think that if our husband changed, our life could be easier or better. Many times, discriminating women are keenly aware that their husband should change for his own good. Maybe you are facing a situation that has spiraled out of control and if your husband doesn't change, he is headed for disaster. Maybe your husband is involved with things that demand intervention in order to save your marriage relationship.

In any event, whether it is a situation that you need to address or not, Proverbs 21:9 (THE MESSAGE) tells us it is, "Better to live alone in a tumbledown shack than to share a mansion with a nagging spouse." Interestingly enough, human nature is inclined to avoid pain more than seek pleasure. If it is more painful for your husband to come home and try to deal with you or to live with a woman he doesn't feel he can ever make happy, it becomes easier for him to just walk away. I have met newlywed husbands who worked incessantly just to avoid going home to their demanding wives. It is so sad that husbands would rather be at work than at home, which is supposed to be their safe place.

In truly accepting our husbands for who they are, we have to be sure to do the following:

1. Be reasonable and realistic, knowing he has strengths as well as weaknesses.
2. Examine yourself for pride, self-righteousness, and inflated feelings of superiority, and see these harmful character deficits as the sins they are.
3. Purposefully and willfully release your husband from your grip and give him permission to be himself.
4. Give up the roles of being your husband's image consultant, trainer, or 24/7 critique manager.
5. Don't compare your husband to any other person.
6. Refuse to see anything except good in your husband.

7. Learn when to <u>speak up</u> about what you admire in him, and when to <u>shut up</u> when faced with things you don't admire.

Regardless of the reasons or justification for wanting to change our husbands, when we analyze the reasons *not* to try to change them, it is easier to see why we need to let these things go. Once we come to the understanding that we need to let go of changing our husbands, we can then look at *how* to identify and change even the nicest control freak habits we may have fallen into.

Chapter 4

Giving Up Control

Why *shouldn't* you try to control your husband?

1. Not my responsibility.
    Goal: Knowing your place, staying there, and enjoying it.

First and foremost, it is not my role to change my husband. When we got married, there was nothing in any ceremony, license, or understanding that set me up as judge, jury, or image consultant for my husband. Most probably, a good reason you won your husband's heart is because you didn't judge him; rather, he felt you admired and respected him.

One thing that really helps me to know how to handle a lot of situations and realize what I should be doing in particular situations is knowing my role. What is your role in your husband's life?

Is your role to change him? Do you let him know he gets on your nerves or point out his faults? Do you recite things your father always did to accentuate what he doesn't do? Do you leave articles lying around, or worse yet, read them to him thinking he'll catch on? Do you drop hints or coax him to improve? Do you try to make him feel guilty or play the martyr role in front of others?

If we are careful to operate within our role or responsibility, not only are we set free from being "in charge" of who our husband is, but we set our husbands free to learn, change, and grow independently of doing so in answer or obedience to us or because of our authority and demands.

When you are operating in the role of judge, jury, or image consultant, it is impossible to live the role as wife, lover, friend, and soul mate at the same time. When you have taken on one role, you obscure the other. You have to make a choice and pick one role and go with it. Men thrive on your admiration, and a critic's role by definition is not to admire but rather to express an unfavorable opinion of something. You can't be looking for good and bad at the same time. Start looking for actions, character, or strengths to compliment in your husband, and you will find them.

It is better to influence a man than to demand things from him. A man's temperament, personality, and position as the leader of the home make it difficult for him to take orders from a woman. Our role as the second in command wields great impact. Ralph Waldo Emerson said, "Who shall set a limit to the influence of a human being?"[27]

When we set our husbands free from answering to us, we set them free to be the person they are, and we can work on who we are. Freedom inspires our husbands. Marriage is not an excuse to stop working on your behavior and character because you are so busy working on your husband's.

When other people tried to conform me into their ideas of what *they* thought, I resisted, or at best, if I changed my actions, it was a burden to me. However, when the *Lord* put something on my heart that needed to change, it became a *freedom* to me. For example, when I had my third baby I wasn't able to practice piano enough to justify lessons every week. When my husband told me I'd have to quit, I resisted, resenting the fact I had to "give up" one more thing. Shortly afterwards, when the Lord put it on my heart to quit and confirmed it through several people, I was able to give up piano lessons, trusting that the Lord had another chapter in store for me.

It became apparent that even if I could manipulate my husband to change his behaviors, it was a burden to him and he often resented it. By making my demands I stood in the way of what God could impact my husband to do. If I get out of the way and leave the results to the Lord, many times I can be a part of influencing my husband to change in a more positive way. Also, in so doing, he becomes less resistant to change because it wasn't in answer to my demands. Because I chose to love and respect my husband regardless of whether he changed some of his actions or attitudes, he knows I still love and admire him in other areas, leaving the responsibility between him and God.

Your husband   You blocking him   God
                 from hearing from
                 God

After you move out of the way, your husband has no excuse to hide behind and has to answer for his behavior himself. That's the freedom of letting God speak and staying in your role as friend, lover, and soul mate. Because we women tend to have more insights, encouragement, support, and emotions, and see much deeper than most men, we think we can intervene. However, before a woman is close to living up to her potential, she often becomes more worried about changing her husband than she is about changing herself.

I love the way THE MESSAGE Bible states this problem:

> Matthew 7:1-5 (THE MESSAGE)– "Don't pick on people, jump on their failures, criticize their faults — unless, of course, you want the same treatment. That critical spirit has a way of boomeranging. It's easy to see a smudge on your neighbor's face and be oblivious to the ugly sneer on your own. Do you have the nerve to say, 'Let me wash your face for you,' when your own face is distorted by contempt? It's this whole traveling road-show mentality all over again, playing a holier-than-thou part instead of just living your part. Wipe that ugly sneer off your own face, and you might be fit to offer a washcloth to your neighbor."

Just think of where you will be if all that energy you spend on manipulating and changing your husband is redirected toward being the best you can be as a wife. You will not only learn unconditional love, but you will grow in every character definition of the fruit of the Spirit of love, joy, peace, longsuffering, gentleness, goodness, faith, meekness, and temperance.

It should be a huge relief for you to relinquish the job of changing your husband. "You're supposed to be the leading lady of your own life..."[28] was an epiphany to Iris in the movie *The Holiday*. You are the leading lady and what are you doing to live the life you wanted to live? Your part. Not your husband's role, but your role: your lines and what you say, where you go, and what you do.

In your role as wife, lover, and friend, learn to recognize when you are operating outside of that role. Refuse it. Starve that behavior. Make choices to move away from actions representing roles you shouldn't be taking on.

2. It extinguishes his love for you.
   Goal: To keep putting firewood on the love fires and avoid extinguishing love.

Just as a fire needs to be fed, so does your relationship. If you think you are staying the same, you are probably heading backwards. Numerous factors contribute to extinguishing love. Unfortunately, men tend to take more mistreatment than women without saying anything. They may retreat into a shell, stop trying to impress their wives, and lose the delight to discuss situations with her feeling she is too critical and doesn't see the best in him. He may turn his attention to other things that will distract him from thinking about your relationship, such as hanging out with his friends more, watching an overabundance of television, playing video games, or working as often as he can. Sadly, many men will suffer through a lot without saying anything and then one day they are finished. They get up and they walk away. Then the wife comes to me shocked and surprised that "one day" her husband just "had enough." He was done. The problem usually has been building and building and building without resolution.

Let's face it: your husband would never be romantically interested in his mother. The moment you take on a mother role with your husband, you are throwing water all over the fires of romantic love and you can be sure those feelings will be doused in a hurry if he looks at you more as a mother image than his lover, friend, and wife.

At the website affaircare.com, there is a list with several things that extinguish love. As you read through this list, mark off or check the ones you feel you need to stop throwing on the romantic fires in your relationship:

- ❖ Emotional Neglect
  - Scorekeepers
  - Fault finders
  - My way or the highway (controlling)
  - Bottomless pit (enough is never enough)

- ❖ Spiritual Neglect
  - Will not forgive
  - Lack of personal transparency
  - Smoke and mirrors (deception)
  - Disrespectful judgments

- ❖ Physical Neglect
  - No tender touch
  - Withholding sexual fulfillment
  - Abandoning physical attractiveness

❖ Financial Neglect
  ▪ Ongoing unemployment that isn't part of a mutual understanding
  ▪ Unwilling/Unable to live by a budget
  ▪ Hidden debt
  ▪ Hidden spending or overspending
  ▪ IRS or legal financial trouble (judgments, liens, etc.)

❖ Family Neglect
  ▪ Refusing to leave and cleave
  ▪ Not making time for personal adult time (including recreation)
  ▪ Not making time for each child individually (child rearing)
  ▪ Inequitable distribution of household chores
  ▪ Getting too comfortable; giving up

❖ Social Neglect
  ▪ Irritating habits (discourteous)
  ▪ Independent behavior
  ▪ Not sharing activities or free time together
  ▪ The silent treatment or not listening actively

❖ Security Neglect
  ▪ Angry explosions
  ▪ Attack dog (verbal/emotional abuse)
  ▪ Passive warmonger (passive–aggressive)
  ▪ Physical abuse
  ▪ Not being a safe haven.[29]

As you look at some of the things listed for kindling love, see where you are adding kindling wood to your relationship:

❖ Emotional commitment
- Love: Do you make sure your spouse feels a loving emotional connection and commitment from you?
- Value: Does your spouse believe he is valued by you?
- Respect: Does your spouse believe you respect him?
- Trust: Does your spouse trust you and see you as trustworthy? Do you trust him and see him as trustworthy?
- Acceptance: Does your spouse know you accept him for the person he is?
- Appreciation: Do you express appreciation for your spouse and the things he does?
- Affection: Do you express affection for your spouse in words and actions?
- Admiration: Do you admire your spouse and say so out loud?
- Understanding: Does your spouse know you understand him?
- Forgiveness: When your spouse does something wrong, do you forgive him and let it go forever—never to be brought up in an argument?

❖ Spiritual Values
- Do you support your spouse's spiritual values?
- Do you and your spouse have a shared spiritual life?
- Do you respect your spouse's beliefs?
- Do you have spiritual transparency about your spiritual beliefs?

❖ Physical Commitment
- Touch: Do you regularly touch your spouse?
- Kissed: Do you kiss regularly?
- Hugged: Do you hug regularly?
- Tenderness: Do you regularly cuddle and hold hands?

- Intimacy: Are you sexually active with your spouse?
- Attraction: Are you physically attracted to your spouse (his hair, body, grooming, clothing)?

❖ Financial Commitment
  - Is your spouse able to provide for family and children?
  - Does your spouse actively participate in providing for family and children?
  - Are you able to pay monthly bills without going into debt?
  - Can you live a lifestyle that's mutually acceptable to both you and your spouse?
  - Does your spouse contribute to family income?
  - Does your spouse contribute to paying off family debt?
  - Are you able to plan for future financial stability?
  - Are you able to plan for future needs such as kids' college?
  - Can your spouse live by a budget?

❖ Family Commitment
  - Does your spouse make time for adult time alone with you?
  - Does your spouse make time for the children individually?
  - Do you ask your spouse for help with household chores in a reasonable way?
  - Do you enlist your spouse with raising your children?
  - Does your spouse say 'yes' more than 'no' whenever possible?
  - Do you offer your spouse a "day off" now and then?

❖ Social Commitment
  - Do you include your spouse in your social activities?

- Do you support and encourage your spouse in social situations?
- Do you share fun and enjoyable activities together?
- Do you share joy and laughter?
- When others are around, is it obvious you are a couple in love?
- Do you like to spend your free time with your husband?
- Do you offer your husband free time at home?
- Are you a companion to your spouse?
- Do you listen well to your spouse and express both interest and caring?

❖ Security Commitment
- Do you support your spouse in times of crises?
- Do you turn to your spouse in time of crises?
- Do you stand by your spouse?
- Are you loyal and committed to your spouse and your marriage?
- Do you present a united front with your spouse (against relatives or the children)?
- Is your relationship secure and not "in the balance" over a fight?
- Are you there for your spouse when you feel he needs you?
- Are you a "soft place to fall," a safe haven, for your spouse? [30]

It should be your goal to be sure you are not constantly dousing love and instead kindling it. Your actions every day are bringing you closer to total extinguishment or total acceptance and love. The results involve your choices moment by moment. You choose which way you will act and respond. Again, you are responsible for your actions and not your husband's. When you purpose to work on yourself to love someone the way you committed to, good things are bound to follow.

3.   It makes you seem self righteous and proud.
     Goal: To be humble and give your husband the freedom to grow.

When you are constantly trying to change your husband you appear self-righteous and proud, and self-righteousness and pride are worse problems than many of the things that bother you about your husband.

Unfortunately many women view their husbands as a "home improvement" project. They believe that the way they show their husband love is by telling him how he could improve. Most men aren't as worried about constantly improving as much as they are interested in being accepted for who they are. A man will change on his own when his goals or vision changes. Every one excels in the areas where they feel confident. If a woman is constantly letting her husband know she is disappointed in him, suggesting ways he could improve, or reciting his weaknesses, he will retreat and believe that there is really nothing he can do to make her happy. He will stop trying if his efforts are not recognized or brushed over. He will not be inspired to better himself in areas he has been told repeatedly that he isn't effective nor efficient at. Men excel when they are appreciated and valued. First and foremost, a man should feel accepted and appreciated is by his wife.

Remember to give your husband the same freedom that God gave him: his free will. Accept him for who he is, realizing that as a human being he is part virtue and part vice. Choose to look to the good things he is rather than the things he lacks. Admire your husband, and put him first in your life. When you give him this personal freedom, his mind will function without barriers and he will be receptive to new ideas, even yours, and encouraged to be the best he can be.

Shakespeare said, "A true friend is one that knows you as you are, understands where you have been, accepts what you have become, and still gently allows you to grow."[31] Accept your husband where he is and allow him the chance to grow.

Pride constantly tempts us to focus on changing our spouses while neglecting our own weaknesses. Concentrate on your own growth so you can avoid the sin of pride. It is not wrong to hope for positive changes in your husband, but you will definitely have a better and more enjoyable marriage if you stop seeking to change your husband and instead work on your own character.

God can use your marriage to teach you how to love. If you don't run from the challenges that marriage presents, your marriage will make you a more unselfish, stronger, and wiser woman. Proverbs 9:10 (AMP) tells us, "Hatred stirs up contentions, but love covers all transgressions." This means that when you are hateful (objectionable, abhorrent, obnoxious, unpalatable, unpleasant, disagreeable, distasteful[32]), strife and discord will invariably follow. Conversely, when you choose to love (be devoted to, admire, be benevolent towards[32]), it covers, or from the Hebrew word *kacah,* fills up what is lacking in others' lives.

This Scripture verse has another vantage point as well. When we choose to love instead of hate, we will wipe out sin in our own lives. Not only with the way we choose to feel towards our husbands, but also with every relationship we have. When you truly love someone you will not sin by judging, criticizing, being jealous or envious, looking down at them, or holding them captive to perfectionism or even to a standard you have for your own life but they don't have for theirs. Love will prevent a multitude of sins from entering your heart. Choose love: without ceasing, fervent, extended and stretched out love. As the Bible puts it in 1 Peter 4:8 (THE MESSAGE): "Most of all, love each other as if your life depended on it. Love makes up for practically anything."

What about those things your husband does that really bother you? Only when your husband receives a steady diet of praise and true appreciation can he be motivated to overcome his weaknesses and become a better man. Appreciation can inspire a man, child, or any individual grow to a higher potential. I knew this from the way my mom raised me and I lived it out while raising my children. I refused to have any other kind of love than the kind in 1 Corinthians 13:7 (KJV) that "bears all things, believes all things, hopes all things, endures all things." I chose to believe the best about my children, despite any minor lapses they were going through. I told them, "I know you will make the right choice," many times and prayed that they did. Even if they *didn't*, they were able to see the results of the wrong choices and see for themselves the reasons our family chose to live differently than other people did. That way, as my children grew into adulthood they knew that they had parents who believed the best about them. Knowing we believed in them lifted them to another level.

One of the things I appreciate about my husband is that he never tries to change me. There has *never* been a time in our lives together where I have felt unloved. I am a more "emotional girl," and I have had to *work* at making sure that *he* never feels less than totally loved and accepted. Because emotions tend to sink to the lowest place, this involves taking responsibility, accountability, and having maturity over the words I blurt out, the feelings I recite and rehearse in my heart, and the things I mull over in my mind. In other words, my *soul* needs to live out its regenerated life, which is much more powerful if my *spirit* controls my mind, will and emotions than if I am tossed about by the events of each day.

Karen Budzinski

There is a song I particularly like, called *Who Will Love Me For Me*
by JJ Heller:

> He cries in the corner where nobody sees
> He's the kid with the story no one would believe
> He prays every night, "Dear God won't you please
> Could you send someone here who will love me?"
>
> Who will love me for me
> Not for what I have done or what I will become
> Who will love me for me
> 'Cause nobody has shown me what love
> What love really means
>
> Her office is shrinking a little each day
> She's the woman whose husband has run away
> She'll go to the gym after working today
> Maybe if she was thinner
> Then he would've stayed
> And she says...
>
> Who will love me for me?
> Not for what I have done or what I will become
> Who will love me for me?
> 'Cause nobody has shown me what love, what love really means
>
> He's waiting to die as he sits all alone
> He's a man in a cell who regrets what he's done
> He utters a cry from the depths of his soul
> "Oh Lord, forgive me, I want to go home"
>
> Then he heard a voice somewhere deep inside
> And it said
> I know you've murdered and I know you've lied

I have watched you suffer all of your life
And now that you'll listen, I'll tell you that I..."

I will love you for you
Not for what you have done or what you will become
I will love you for you
I will give you the love
The love that you never knew[33]

To love your husband, for who he is, in spite of his shortcomings, is an attribute that pleases God. If you can learn to love, really love, it is the strongest force there is. God *is* love (1 John 4:8 KJV), and when you walk with the Lord, if you get out of the way, *He* will love *through you.* You need never run out of love.

Most human dysfunctions stem from a lack of love. When someone really loves you, it inspires you to want to be better for that person. I want to love my husband more unconditionally because of the way he loves me, not because of the way he picks at me. Romans 5:8 tells us that "while we were yet sinners, Christ died for us" (KJV). Can we show our spouses that while they are yet imperfect we can die to our selfishness and our agendas to just love them? Joyce Meyers wrote a book titled the *Love Revolution*, which reminds us that for our love to be revolutionary, we need to practice love every day, until the culture of selfishness gives way to a new culture of concern for others. Just reading through the Table of Contents for her book, you can readily see problems inherent in our society where we need to be challenged to a "love revolution."[34]

Do you really believe you are a better person than your husband is? You need to humbly see your own weaknesses so you can accept his. When you demand that someone change for your sake, you are trying to bend the world around your comfort, your needs, and your happiness. That's pride, arrogance, and self-centeredness—and God can never bless that.

Recently, a dear friend of mine said, "You are so kind all the time." I replied, "In my life, I have needed a lot of grace from others; it has made it easier for me to give grace having received so much of it." I believe the same rings true with our relationships: when we are willing to give grace, it will be much easier for the recipient of that grace to give grace back.

Freedom of choice is one of the most fundamental laws of life. Mankind does not develop or experience happiness without it. God was fully aware of this principle when He created man and placed him on the earth. He allowed the forces of evil to be present to tempt him and to try him. He knew from the beginning of time that many men would fall into sin and reap the bitter harvest that comes from disobeying the statutes, laws, and commandments God gave us to instruct us in the ways of life. But He also knew that without freedom, mankind could not grow and develop. Man has to be given a choice and make that choice himself. If God could risk man's future happiness in order to extend to him his precious freedom, a woman should allow her husband this same privilege. Let him do what he wants to do, and be what he wants to be without you assuming a role that even God Himself doesn't.

Men need freedom of choice when it comes to spiritual matters as well. Until the end of time there will be wars fought over religious rights and choices. It is a right that God allows us to choose whom or what we will serve. A wise woman will allow her husband the freedom to choose in this very important area of life. A woman I met in England years ago had been praying for her husband. He wanted nothing to do with church or God. On Sundays she asked him if he would like to go to church with her. Every week he declined. She continued to love him and respect his leadership role in the home and allowed him to choose. After almost 30 years, one morning she got up to go to church and he was getting ready to go with her. He turned his life over to Christ that day and continued to go with her every week after that. When a man's opinion is respected, he is freer to consider his wife's or other viewpoints than if he feels cornered.

Steven Stosny wrote an article titled *Freedom to Love*. He asked, "When did 'I love you' degenerate into 'Meet my needs!'" He states: "To be free to do something, you must be free not to do it. We are free to love only to the extent that we aren't forced into it by guilt, shame, fear of abandonment, or, worst of all, the interpretation of vulnerable feelings as emotional needs. No matter how seductive 'I need you,' may sound in popular songs, the partner who needs you cannot freely love you.

"If someone needs you, he or she is more likely to abuse you than to give freely of love and support. Most painful conflicts in committed relationships begin with one partner making an emotional request— motivated by a perceived 'need'—that the other, motivated by a different 'need,' regards as a demand. Any disagreement can feel like abuse when the perceived 'need' of one party to be 'validated' crashes headlong into the 'need' of the other not to be manipulated.

"'If you loved me, you'd do what I want (or see the world the way I do),' one argues.

"'If you loved me, you wouldn't try to control me,' the other counters.

"The problem is not in the language the couples use or even the content of their arguments, which is why communication and problem-solving techniques rarely help over time. As long as they perceive themselves to have emotional needs that their partners must gratify, their desire to love is reduced to 'Getting my needs met,' which the partner often perceives as, 'You have to give up who you are to meet my needs.'

"Ultimately, the freedom to love is a core value issue. Which is more important to you, getting your perceived needs met or loving freely? Which gives you the better chance of being loved freely in return?"[35]

Stosny's observations explore the differences between "toddler" love, driven by perceived needs, and "adult" love, driven by desire and values.

In the movie *What About Bob,* Bob walks around grasping saying, "I need! I need! I need!" It is a good catch phrase: if I hear myself sounding "needy" I break into the Bill Murray voice: "I need! I need! I need!,"[36] and it jolts me back to the reality of how ridiculous I sound.

Once you stop expecting your husband to be perfect, and once you give your needs to the Lord, you can learn to love your husband for who he is, and set him free to grow.

Do small things with great love

37

4. It doesn't work.
   Goal: To give it up.

The most compelling reason why you shouldn't try to change your husband is that it doesn't work. It causes your husband to retreat into a shell, creates discord, cools romance, and often causes your husband to want to stay away from you.

When my toilet overflowed and I couldn't plunge it, I knew I couldn't use it: it didn't work. I left the plunger in the toilet because I didn't want anyone thinking it was operative. Why bother? It didn't work. In the same way, the fact that trying to change your husband doesn't work but does the opposite means you should give that up too. When you put the squeeze on your husband, you squeeze the life right out of him.

When you find fault with yourself and others, it becomes a habit, and you tend to do it more and more. Soon you will find that people avoid you, because no one wants to be around someone who is finding fault all the time. You can become a magnifying mirror—magnifying to any one who dares to come close what they are missing or lacking or what they do that is just not your taste. How long can you stay in front of that magnifying mirror that makes your pores look like they are to the 100th power? Not many people are drawn to that kind of negative magnification for long. Always seeing the negative is not a winsome personality that is going to make others want to be around you.

Stop criticizing yourself, your husband, and others. Look for good things and rehearse them when you find them. Build up rather than tear down people and relationships. If you have developed a habit for being critical, break it. Start today.

"It is better to dwell in a corner of the housetop [on the flat oriental roof, exposed to all kinds of weather] than in a house shared with a nagging, quarrelsome, and faultfinding woman." Proverbs 21:9 (AMP)

"It is better to dwell in the corner of the housetop than to share a house with a disagreeing, quarrelsome, and scolding woman." Proverbs 25:24 (AMP)

A man expects his wife to be the one secure haven where he can relax, be himself, and feel secure. When you are constantly dissatisfied with him, he feels insecure and unappreciated, just as you would feel if he was constantly picking on you. The reverse effect then takes place: any incentive to strive to be better is thwarted and extinguished. Resentment, arguments, defenses, retreat, and discord abounds. Your efforts to change him cause the exact opposite as he tries to defend and hold on to who he is. It is just not worth it and it doesn't work. The damage to your relationship and problems in your home are not worth gambling away. When it becomes more important for you to love him than to change him, the love and harmony in your home will reflect the wisdom of that choice. Ultimately, it is more inspiring for your husband to be the best he can be for someone who loves and appreciates him for who he is than to try to do something nice for some one who is always looking to pick you apart.

While driving through Italy, Gary and I had a lot of time to be together. Gary seemed amused at my conversation, but was definitely more in tune to driving than talking I longed to talk as we spent time together.

I said, "Gary talk to me."

"About what?" he asked.

"About anything. What do you like, what don't you like, what are your dreams, what plans do you have for anything, who do you like, what problems at work are you experiencing, what is your favorite vacation, best memory, worst memory, most funny thing that happened to you… anything! I just want to hear you."

After thinking for a few seconds he said, "That is a lot of stuff to talk about…"

Then there was silence. After a short while of looking around and driving some more, I decided to be content and carry on my conversation.

I was happy to talk about what I observed, to note unusual sights, and notice all sorts of details. Gary was happy to drive and look around a little—in silence. I decided I would rather let Gary be content in who he is without trying to pull conversation from him. We are different personalities and enjoy the same things in different ways.

I did manage to "test" his knowledge of foreign words with my Italian language phone tutor. He had me in stitches with his consistently inconsistent pronunciations of even the most basic Italian words. A further indication that he really wasn't too interested in little details!

The best way to love someone is to allow him to feel safe with you. To know that whether he is in the mood to talk or not, that you love him and accept him just the way he is.

Sometimes it is the opposite situation: Gary will need to vent or I will need to vent over something. Once while running through the airport with our five children and suitcases, with barely enough time to grab lunch before the next flight, Gary frantically was looking for our meal voucher coupons. When I began to ask him the routine questions about where they could be, he bellowed out in an embarrassing tone, "I just need the vouchers!" To be safe with someone is to know that they will look beneath your tone and words and see your heart and believe the best in you. You can pour your heart out, and, if needed, restate things that need to be restated because they came out wrong the first time, or because they were misinterpreted.

The worst thing to do in a disagreement, when trying to reach a conclusion, or in a misunderstanding, is to defend yourself. When a team is on the defense in sports, they are determined not to let the opposition break through. When you are on the defense in a conversation, the person talking to you will never feel any opportunity to break through either. If you're on "de-fense" there is a dividing fence between you.

When your spouse knows that discussing his feelings with you will end up in a debate, he will soon learn that your motive is not to understand but to undermine. He will give up. Love is demonstrated by bearing, believing, hoping and enduring when faced with opposition.[38]

I love this poem about Friendship:

> Oh, the comfort –
> The inexpressible comfort of feeling safe with a person,
> Having neither to weigh thoughts,
> Nor measure words – but pouring them
> All right out – just as they are –
> Chaff and grain together –
> Certain that a faithful hand will
> Take and sift them –
> Keep what is worth keeping –
> And with the breath of kindness
> Blow the rest away.[39]

If your spouse does not feel safe with you, but feels that you have him "jumping through hoops" to become what you want him to be, you need to make some changes. Keep your tone gentle. Ask him, "This is what I understood you to say..." or, "Is that what you meant to say?" Make your spouse feel safe and enjoy the "inexpressible comfort" defined in the poem above.

If you want your husband to love you, be loveable. He needs to feel safe around you and secure in who he is (and who he isn't as well.). Maybe right now you don't really feel there is anything to admire or appreciate about your husband. If not, look for his potential, which is a very real part of a person. Think of things he has done in his past, how he handles his work, how he relates to others, the strong points others appreciate about him. See him as others who admire him see him. Listen to what he talks about. Let him know some of the things you appreciate about him, no matter how trivial they seem.

Look at some of his faults and determine if they are a negative expression of something positive. For example, if maybe your husband is obsessive or demanding, it may be a negative exhibition of his being a hard worker and a pursuer of excellence. A strength can often display itself as a weakness. Look beneath the surface to see the driving force behind the outward behavior and try to inspire the positive demonstration of that strength. This principle applies to raising children too: our children's strength is often shown in their weaknesses, or in a misuse of that strength. A wise mother will train her children on how to address those weaknesses and turn them into strengths.

For example, I had a strong willed child who had temper tantrums all the time. The problem was not her strong will (which was later important in her life to swim against the tide of popular opinion to make right choices), the problem was in the demonstration and abuse of her strong will through temper tantrums. Tweaked and turned around, her strong will became her greatest asset.

I apply the principle to my life too, especially when learning new skills. When I work on concert piano pieces, I begin with the part of the composition that is the weakest and practice it so much that it becomes the strongest part of the piece. If you apply the same principle to weaknesses in your character, you will grow as a person.

Request to a Wife

Dear wife, I need adoring looks,
The kind I read about in books.
I want esteem, I want affection.
Please, darling, beam in my direction.
Don't, dearest, frown and squint your eyes.
Don't cut me down to proper size.
Oh, do not fear and do not doubt me.
I want to hear the good about me.

So, if you'd be in married clover,
Make over me.
Don't make me over.

Richard Armour[40]

Tara Parker-Pope wrote, "It has become clear that many marital disagreements simply can't be solved. In one study, researchers interviewed the same couples four years apart. To their surprise, 70% were still talking and fighting about the same problems in exactly the same way as they were four years earlier. The result has been a push for 'acceptance' therapy, encouraging partners to accept the enduring foibles of their spouses rather than trying to change them."[41]

Putting some of these habits into practice will help you as well: you will end up liking yourself even if no one else changes.

Chapter 5

When Something Has to Give

In an ideal world, we would truly hear what each other is saying in a relationship and take tangible steps to solve situations that are frustrating or problematic. Unfortunately, too often one person in the relationship is willing to do anything possible to achieve a better relationship, but the other person remains unyielding or unresponsive. This roadblock creates, frustration, isolation, and eventually the waning of the love that binds the relationship together.

Sometimes it is imperative to address and change abuses in your relationship. When your husband is blind to his own faults and they are negatively affecting you, as his lover and friend you may be able to show him. If he is abusive, you cannot allow that to continue and think it is all right. If you are not allowed basic freedoms and are living under threats and accusations, you need to address the situation.

There are some important things to remember before you bring up a sensitive situation.

1. Handle With Care. When you try to give constructive criticism, handle the situation with discernment and delicately. Your husband may resist change and immediately become defensive if you begin to challenge any habits or

choices. Be prepared to be provoked, verbally attacked in the same or a different area, resisted, and possibly even ignored. Many times when I have been approached or made aware of something I was doing that needed to change, I had to hear it from several people in several different ways before I changed my mind. Once you present your case about the need for change, allow time for him to ruminate, reflect, and come to a conclusion himself.

2. <u>Blind Spots.</u> We all have blind spots. I drove a Suburban for many years and discovered the blind spots in that car are large. So I learned to use the mirrors. A wise woman sets up a warning system in her marriage. A system to alert her to her blind spots before a crash actually happens. I regularly ask my husband if there is anything he would prefer I change regarding my habits or actions. He does the same with me. By keeping the climate open to suggestions for change, we are both ready to hear and tweak whatever is necessary to reach the full potential for our union together.

This approach should be a normal occurrence in relationships. During a yearly review, an employee meets with his or her boss to find out what he or she has done correctly to produce positive results. He or she also hears what needs to be fine tuned because the results are less than positive. This review often precedes a bonus or raise, which takes away some of the negative emotions that come from being on the hot seat.

We instituted the same policy when raising our children so that they would be able to handle constructive criticism as they grew older. We asked our children to describe other family members reviewing his or her demonstrated strengths and areas that needed improvement.

Confrontation isn't easy. But if you believe a certain behavior will cause a problem in your husband's future, you will take the time and the risk to confront him. If he takes time to confront you, realize that it is probably difficult for him too. If he cared less he wouldn't even bother to put your relationship on the line to try to help you. Knowing someone is taking the time and risk to confront you should make you want to hear what they have to say.

When someone confronts you, carefully listen to what he or she is saying and hear the heart behind the words. Consider if what they say has any merit. Even if you don't feel you acted in a certain way or did what they believed you did, examine yourself. If there is no merit, or if it is not possible for you to address the criticism, move forward. If it has merit, tell the person you will try to change and ask him or her to pray with you or hold you accountable to the change.

Perspective is important. In sports games, the perspective of the umpire or referee actually becomes part of the game. So whether the ball is "in" or "out," the ump or ref makes the call based on his or her perspective.

Imagine if three people stand equal distance apart and hold a huge globe and each person explains what they see. Although everyone is holding the same globe, each perspective is different. Be sure that you consider your spouse's perspective as important. He may offer valuable insight from a different angle.

3. <u>Purify Your Motives</u>. I need keen insight on what I hope to accomplish when I open my mouth in any confrontational situation. It is easy to make mistakes in how or why I communicate something. "All of us make a lot of mistakes. If someone doesn't make any mistakes when he speaks, he would be perfect. He would be able to control everything he does." James 3:2 (GW)

Psalm 39 has given me some helpful guidelines:

❖ Keep my mouth with a *bridle* while the "wicked" (which comes from a Hebrew word meaning *morally wrong, actively bad,* or one that *did wrong*) is in my presence. (verse 1)

❖ *Hold your peace* even from speaking *good.* You may need to make sure you *have* some peace to hold onto first! Peace is the *absence of negative emotions.* Make sure your emotions are not negative if you are going to be talking about sensitive matters! (verse 2)

❖ Pray and ask the Lord to give you insight to your weaknesses first, ending up knowing that your hope is in the Lord. (verses 4-7)

❖ Ask forgiveness for any wrong motives or sin. (verse 8)

❖ When you open your mouth, let the Lord be the one speaking *through* you. (verse 9, emphasis mine.)

If you tend to blurt out the wrong attitudes or words when faced with a difficult situation, try memorizing Psalm 39.

I also like the example of Queen Esther in the book of Esther in the Bible. She spent twelve months or so in cleansing and purification treatments before she approached the king the first time. This wasn't just a splash of perfume and a quick makeup application: this was a twelve month cleanse and purification (which meant to scour and polish) with essential oils so the cleansing, purification, and sweet fragrances exuded from her very presence. If we take time to be sure we are pure and have a "sweet smelling fragrance" from the inside out, I believe we could approach our husbands with better results.

The difference in Esther was dramatic. King Xerxes' former Queen, Vashti, was noted because she was "lovely to look at" (Esther 1:11). But the King saw a different beauty in Esther: "...the king loved Esther more than all the women, and she obtained grace and favor in his sight more than all the maidens…" Esther 1:17 (KJV). Vashti was lovely to look at, a word that means with the sight of one's eyes. However, in the description of the King's reaction to Esther, the Bible records a word for sight that means, "interested in the very presence of someone." In Esther's case, her presence alone gave her favor, not only because of the way she looked, but also from what emanated from within.

4. <u>Timing is Everything.</u> Esther also knew about timing. She didn't run into the King's presence and ask for big changes. She made him a nice dinner (twice!) and knew when it was appropriate to ask (not demand). She put out the reason she was asking and the King quickly determined what she needed and responded to it. Oh the value of timing.

When you play tennis, if you are able to hit the ball while it is in front of you, there is a "sweet spot," where not only do you have more power and control, but you can use core strength instead of just hitting with your arm. If you hit the ball early, although you may surprise your opponent, your swing will not have the same impact. If you hit the ball too late, you will overwork your arm and it will be more difficult to hit your intended target area. Timing is everything. In the same way, we desire our communication to hit the "sweet spot:" not too early, surprising your spouse and diminishing the impact, and not too late, overworking it and struggling to hit your intentions in the communication. Be discerning enough not only to accommodate your preferred timing in communications, but ensuring that it is a good time for the one you are communicating with as well.

5. <u>Increase Your Chances of Being Listened To.</u> A friend told me how her husband would never *hear* her frustrations when she communicated to him. He didn't seem to understand how upset she was, so he did nothing to change the behavior

that caused her such irritation. I suggested she learn to do what I learned while visiting Italy: learn to speak as much as possible in the language of the one you are trying to communicate with. She was using enough actions and words, but she wasn't communicating in a way that made it easy for him to understand.

Your words and actions help him become receptive to your communication:

a) The discussion shouldn't be lengthy. "Under pressure or stress the male brain's spatial function is activated and he will stop talking; the female brain's function of speech is activated and she may talk nonstop."[42] Realize that males often will shut down emotionally and verbally to avoid confrontation. There is actually a term for it: *stonewalling*. The definition is what it sounds like, and is more particular to males: "to delay or block (a request, process, or person) by refusing to answer questions or by giving evasive replies."[43]

b) "Approach your spouse with precise complaints rather than attacking your partner's personality or character."[44] Dr. John Gottman, one of the nation's foremost experts on predicting divorce, has shown that arguments and fights that many believe are signs of problems can actually be some of the healthiest ways couples can make adjustments that will keep them together.[44] Men need to be able to fix things: when you attack them generally it presents a situation that is impossible to fix and becomes frustrating; however, addressing a single issue makes a solution possible.

c) Enjoin him to work with you. I love finding out the etymology of words to get a clearer picture of what a word really means. The word *enjoin* means *toward joining* or *toward attaching*. When working through issues, your objective should be to lasso your husband (or any one for that matter) to be in the circle with you working towards the best possible win-win outcome. Enjoining may take a bit of creativity on your part. If your husband begins to feel you are pushing him away or that he is not part of the solution, you may as well stop talking because solutions will be almost impossible. Examine your processes, and ensure they are *enjoining* both (or all) parties to a resolution of the problem at hand.

d) Be winsome in your approach. Why would your husband even want to consider your needs or your point of view when those needs come across as demands, threats, or accusations? How do you communicate with your husband when you need to? I suggest taking a winsome approach. In other words: "win some" to your viewpoint. The word is derived from words meaning "agreeable, pleasant, pleasure, delight."[45]

Often when I begin to communicate about something important to me, and it seems my husband is tuning out, I become increasingly emphatic and passionate about convincing him to see things my way. As he feels backed into the corner, he tends to either push his way out of the corner or shuts down and enters the passive "stonewalled" stage, either of which only fuels my passion and exuberance to convince him. If my adrenaline starts pumping, I need to slow down quickly because the intensity will become scary. If you ever feel even remotely that your intensity is too high for valid communication, try looking in the mirror; it will verify whether you are frightening to look at or winsome. Your choices are to either give it up until you can be winsome or to waste time that you can never gain back. Before you get to the point where your communication will end with resentment, bad feelings and a nonproductive argument, give it up. Once you feel yourself going on a tangent that makes you scary looking and ugly, consider a different road into your husband's heart.

e) Lighten the intensity. In her book, *Fascinating Womanhood*, Helen Andelin devoted an entire section to handling anger with the trust, love, and innocence of a child.[46] There are several reasons why this child-like (*not* childish) type of communication can be so effective:
   - It keeps situations cute instead of ugly.
   - It is void of intense emotions like hatred, resentment, and bitterness.
   - It can bring laughter into the word cesspool.
   - It uses feminine appeal and makes your husband feel more attracted to you.

Examples of Solutions Based Communication

I asked my husband not to leave his gun out of the gun case. For some reason, he kept leaving it out. Rather than bringing it up constantly, I hid it and when he asked me where it was, I simply told him, "We really can't leave the gun out so I hid it," and then I told him where. After a few times, my husband realized it was easier for him to put it away where he could find it again without finding me. If it is occasionally left out, I tell him, "I'm frightened of the gun being left out with so many people around. Can you make more of an effort to put it away?" Approaching your husband in a feminine way such as "would you consider…" or "it would mean so much to me if you would…" or "would you mind very much if…" will get you an ear and consideration faster than demands and accusations. But if you are not living a life that shows you are on his team, and you are a selfish, nagging, critical woman, or if he feels insecure around you or in his home, he may not have a favorable response to your suggestions no matter how you put them.

Instead of acting ugly and being scary, I choose to be cute with my overworked intense husband. I have found that I achieve better results that way. Instead of demanding attention from him, I may come up and tap him on the shoulder until he realizes it (which sometimes can take quite a few taps). Then I'll say, "No one is paying attention to me." He will start laughing and ask what I want him to do. If I badgered him into paying attention to me, we wouldn't have so much fun with it, and it could be a chore.

If he has been inconsiderate or uncaring about something I'm going through, I will look at him sweetly and ask, "Remember when you used to really care about my feelings?" Rather than accusing, threatening or badgering, I make him think about what he did or didn't do and give him a chance to change his mind.

I would rather invite my husband into my life than to demand it. I purposefully work on making it fun and desirable to be with me, and I put effort into making sure that my husband will enjoy himself more with me than without me.

Rather than demanding that he help with the groceries, for example, I will go up to him and squeeze his arm muscle and say, "Hey, are those muscles just to look good or do you think they can help me get these groceries into the house?" Usually that kind of an invitation inspires my husband to help me more than any demands or guilt trips would.

I've enjoyed considering alternate ways to express my frustrations other than nagging. I want to be my husband's lover, not his mother. In order to do so, I find a substitute way to work out my frustrations other than taking them out on the one I love the most. If I can't express things in a cute, non-threatening way, I will hit the treadmill or work furiously on cleaning or sewing or something that will not result in destroying the relationship we have worked so hard to build.

It is far better to express my feelings in a nice way than to ignore them. I was told early in my marriage that it was wrong to have disagreements in front of our children. I disagreed. I believed it was important to demonstrate to our children that we don't always agree, but there are ways to work through differences to get to a point of agreement. Sometimes it may mean that I don't get my way. My way may actually be considering my husband's needs as more important than mine. So actually his way becomes "my way."

At the end of the day, I can look in the mirror and know I am working on being the best "me" I can be, and that I am trying to become pleasant to live with on purpose.

Important Considerations

1. When he is abusive.

"Marriage and family are important to God, but just as important to him are the individuals within those marriages and families. God does not value men more than women, or the institution of marriage more than the people who are in it."[47] When a husband purposefully and continually behaves with cruelty and insults, you must protect yourself.

Sometimes women allow their husbands to mistreat them, believing that they are helping keep the relationship together. But allowing your husband to mistreat you is allowing him to stumble and sin. No one should wound or verbally or physically abuse you. Codependency, by definition, means making the relationship more important than your value as a person. Do not shrink back or retreat into a shell. Instead, respect yourself and do not tolerate despicable treatment from any one. Remove yourself from danger and seek professional help before you put yourself in harms way again. We will look more at communicating through special problems later. But know that you are not doing any person a favor by allowing him to sin and abuse you and making excuses for it. If your husband is morally wrong, lying, disrespectful, cruel, or in any other way sinful, you can't just deny it and overlook it. If you do, that is a weakness in your own character, and instead of pulling him up you are lowering your standards to his. Something inside him knows you to be better than to take it. Think of some times when you had a lapse but a stronger person alongside you held their ground and it became an encouragement for you to become a better person. Only in the face of compromise and unjust behavior can this moral strength become obvious. "Factions have to exist in order to make it clear who the genuine believers among you are." (1 Corinthians 11:19, GW)

If you have lived in such a way that your husband can trust you and knows you are for him and not against him, and if you are doing all you can to build a good relationship with your husband, he should sense that you have the ultimate good of the relationship in mind. If he doesn't, there may be serious issues underlying routine abuse. The substance of this book does not address how to handle serious abuse issues that demand professional help. Do not take the blame for abusive reactions, his controlling you, or his errant behavior or compulsions. Don't wait to seek help until you are over your head or wounded either physically or emotionally.

If your husband is abusive to your children, you must protect your children. Know the difference in a man who is simply firm in disciplining his children and one that is abusive. Firm discipline is a masculine tendency that should be respected. I made it my job to read all the child-raising books and take great care to "build self esteem" and institute "cause and effect" and other supportive psychological training with my children. With all my charts and systems in place, my husband would come through the door exploding because toys were left out in front. I felt he didn't even take time to understand why we left everything out; and that his explosion was undoing some of the training I had done for weeks. I still knew enough principles that kept my hand over my mouth at those times: first and foremost, children tend to respect a firm father and love him because of his firm training. Secondly, it was more important for our children to feel my support of their father's authority, especially when I didn't necessarily agree with the process, and to know we were united in purpose. If I had stepped in and made my husband feel ineffective or unsure of his methods, he would have gladly receded and left the training to me. Instead, when my children became teenagers, that *deep voice* carried the weight it needed to in order for my children to have a strong authority to answer to for their actions.

When he goes too far or acts in a way that is damaging or injurious to your children, you have a responsibility to protect your children from any danger. You aren't *punishing* your husband or condemning him for his actions, but you need to protect your children. If you are firm, but kind, your actions may inspire him to seek help and lead him to see the need for positive changes.

2. Addictive and damaging behaviors.

Addictive behaviors such as gambling, alcoholism, pornography, or other compulsive vices are difficult to accept due to all the problems that accompany them. You need to gain an understanding for the addiction. Addictive behaviors start as bad choices but quickly plummet to becoming addictive physically, spiritually, emotionally, and socially. Addictive behavior releases a substance in the brain, dopamine, which not only releases an overriding feeling of pleasure or satisfaction, but is also linked and embedded into the memory. This substance causes a craving to repeat the activity until it is compulsive and eventually leads to a physical demand on the body to recreate the feelings of pleasure or crash to depths of despair. Addictions are difficult to overcome. The only way you can even remotely understand this kind of behavior is to do without all food or drink for three days. Or give up coffee, sweets, or another habit. You will soon get the picture, to a slight degree, of what you expect when asking someone to give up something they are addicted to. Again, the substance of this book does not address how to handle serious addictive and compulsive behavior issues that demand professional help. You are not to blame for his addictions. You can, however, examine your reactions and be sure that you are not making the problem worse by your responses. Realize that these are serious problems and your husband needs help; do not procrastinate getting professional help. As you work through professional help for your husband, you keep working on your own failings and watch for bad attitudes, harbored unforgiveness, impatience, or a critical spirit. If you will focus on areas you still need to grow in, you will be more forgiving for your husband's failings as he seeks freedom and accountability.

When you are married, you have a right to expect your husband to be faithful and to consider you. If your husband is having an affair, be sure that you did not do anything to drive him into the arms of another woman. If you did, change your behavior. If he doesn't end the affair, you need to firmly let him know you will ask him to leave if he continues in the affair. You cannot live with a man who is unfaithful; it is wrong morally and you cannot allow him to live in sin without repentance. Even if you need to separate, try to win him away from the other woman if possible. He is on a road that promises to destroy not only your marriage, but his own spiritual destiny as well.

3. When his faults cause him problems or failure, and he is unaware of the problem.

If your husband makes the same mistakes over and over, you may be the only person that cares enough to take the time to try to help him. For example, my husband enjoys doing a lot of things with and for other people. Because his time is so limited due to his demanding work and travel schedule, he tends to over commit.

One day as we were leaving church with our five little ones, I heard Gary's brother say, "See you in a few hours. Glad you can help me move!" Walking a little further, a friend of Gary's said, "See you at golf in a few hours." We hadn't even gotten to the parking lot when my brother-in-law said, "See you around 3." When I asked, "How are you going to do all these things in one afternoon?" my husband was silent. When we got home, however, I heard him call his friend and say, "Karen said I can't golf today." I laughed so hard, shaking my head at him. I gave him an "A" for wanting to do so much, but he had committed to participating in too many activities at the same time. He now tries to be more careful of his commitments so that he can manage and appropriate his time more suitably for the priorities he wants to live out, His zeal to do things with others still makes him fall prey to over commitment sometimes, so I still help him pull back a little.

When facing a problem with your husband's behavior, choose to believe the best about him first. If past disappointments make you suspicious, at least be reluctant to believe his character could allow such a lapse in judgment or taste. Tell him you can't imagine a man of his caliber would act in such fashion. Indicate that if such bad judgment happened, there had to be an explanation. Continue to have faith in him and let him know that you continue to do so despite a temporary lapse.

In dealing with lapses of character or judgment, you have to remind him that you love and accept him just as he is. You may need to assure him that the suggestions you are making are for him to be more successful and effective and so that he will not be so misunderstood amongst others. Be sure that before you correct him you are certain his behavior is actually causing problems and not simply irritating you.

4. When there are things you can't live with (or without).

For example, I love to exercise by running, power walking, or working out. When my schedule or his did not permit me the time to take an hour to exercise, I learned to be reasonable and realistic. I knew some days would more easily accommodate my exercise than others. I was willing to stay up late and get up early, so we sacrificed financially in order to purchase a treadmill.

Other things may include making time to see your parents, family, or best friend; a hobby that is "part of you," such as sewing, playing an instrument, or sports; a special interest that you thrive on, such as history; a yearning to travel; or a desire to have pets or children.

Be careful that the "things you can't live with (or without)" category doesn't become too expansive. Try to make the "things you can't live with (or without)" category a few things that impact you more directly.

I saw a video once about a woman with four children. Her husband had died and she was speaking at his funeral. She said something like, "Every one knew my husband to be the brilliant wonderful man he was, but there *was* another side to him. He snored loudly. He left his things out. And the wind from behind never ceased while he was sleeping! Why am I telling you that? Because I want my children to know that I would do anything to have any of his bad habits around again because that would mean he would still be with me."

"Normal day, let me be aware of the treasure you are. Let me learn from you, love you, bless you before you depart. Let me not pass you by in quest of some rare and perfect tomorrow. Let me hold you while I may, for it may not always be so. One day I shall dig my nails into the earth, or bury my face in the pillow, or stretch myself taut, or raise my hands to the sky and want, more than all the world, your return."[48]

Purposefully Defining Your "Normal" Day

Where are you now? What role do you have in your husband's life? How does he describe you to his friends and co-workers? Where do you want to be? What have you done, said, or shown that gives him something good to say? We are going to look at some positive ways to improve bad habits, and for those who don't have any bad habits, we are going to help you not create any!

Is your husband first in your life? Does he feel like he is top priority to you? What are some of the activities or hobbies that demand our attention and threaten to push our husband lower on the list than he should be? My husband and I decided to integrate into our marriage that if one of us asks the other to do something, that thing becomes top on the list of priorities for the other person. For example, one day a few friends were over. Because of the change of weather, it was extremely hot in the house and we couldn't open the windows because the screens weren't in. My husband was returning from a weeklong business trip. My husband walked through the door, briefcase in hand and full suit on, exhausted from traveling all day. Before he even took his suit off, though, he put the screens in, because he knew it was important to me. The part of the evening that reflects the most about my husband, though, is that my friends knew before he even came home that he would put the screens in immediately.

I do the same for my husband. If he asks me to do something, I do it as immediately as I can. Little courtesies like this that we put in place show each other that we are number one on each other's priority list.

When I volunteered at Gilda's Club, there was a beautiful woman there who had Parkinson's disease and cancer. Although she walked with a walker and was all bent over and shook incessantly, and although she was weak and tired, we all knew that whatever it took, she would get to the bathroom and put her lipstick on for her husband before he picked her up. That little effort showed him that she still wanted to look her best for him.

What do you do when your husband is about to come home from work? When he walks through the door, do you stop doing what you are doing and go to greet him? When we were little, we were taught by my mom to do a few chores before my dad got home: we picked up the clutter and put everything in order, and we stood by the door waiting for him to come inside. My mom spent a few minutes in front of the mirror to look good, and I even remember her changing her clothes sometimes.

When my husband came home from work, I taught my children to do the same thing. I had good examples, and wanted to just keep it going. My grandfather had this wonderful ability—whenever he saw you he acted like it was a very special event. I couldn't *wait* to see him because I always knew how visibly delighted he was to see me. I wanted to show my husband the same delight when he came in the door.

Some wives feel that when their husband walks through the door, it is *their* turn to walk out and get things done or to hand him a baby or a vacuum. I feel it is very important when coming home to his "safe place" that he has a few minutes to unwind from the traffic, the work pressures, or just from being away home. I always gave my husband this courtesy and made his coming home a special time where he could feel he was coming home to his "castle." Clear away the clutter, light a candle or have something cooking in the oven, and have your chores done. Make it so he can't *wait* to come through those doors.

The world can be a cruel place, and places of work can leave a man feeling undervalued and unappreciated. I know that in the corporate dog-eat-dog war my husband has to engage in every day, he appreciates more and more the sanctuary I have made our home to be for him. I tried to create an atmosphere of celebration, laughter, and love. This sanctuary will never happen by accident; it has to be *on purpose* and with strategies and action plans to plant the seeds that result in such a harvest.

I never rehearsed problems nor did I let our children run at him with their problems when my husband first came home. Give your husband a chance to unwind, and let him know he is the king and he has arrived at his castle. Remember, if you make him feel like a king, your position next to him will be as his queen.

Wives complain that their husbands come home to sit in front of the television set, but I believe sometimes a man just has to "tune out" from the pressures of the day, and many men are able to relax by watching sports or something on the television. At night, my mind goes a mile a minute and I can't get to sleep unless I put something on television to distract me from thinking. Your husband may be the same way. If you make your home a place of peace and order where your husband can renew himself in body and spirit, you will find he will be more excited to get home than to be away.

Even though you may work outside the home and feel that you are entitled to dump on him when he gets home, resist this attitude. Treat him the way you would like to be treated. Let your home be his "safe place." If you need your home to be more of a "safe place" for you too, don't pressure your husband for it. Make arrangements to have your sitter stay an extra half hour or make provisions that don't rob either you or your husband from much needed down time.

If you have chores or running to do, try to do those things *before* he gets home so you are not cutting into valuable and precious family or rejuvenation time. Hire a babysitter during the day or take the children with you. I often took the children with me on errands, shopping, and even to my dentist appointments. I had five children in five and a half years; it was quite a challenge. However, the result was much better behaved children because I had to train them to be well behaved since they were with me running errands so much.

I raised my family to know that at home they would always be treated well and loved and protected. Our home was every person's "safe place" where they could rest, be appreciated and loved, and be equipped for the battles of life. It was a place to hang their hat, and lay their armor down, where their needs would always be considered. This starts with the head of the home. Many moms tend to put their children's needs ahead of their father's needs. This is so unwise. Teach your children that they are *not* the center of the universe; this teaching will pay big dividends when they become teenagers and have already learned to respect and acknowledge authority figures in their lives.

Does your husband know you consider his needs above your own? How do you demonstrate this? You don't have to do *every*thing, but you need to do *some*thing! Are you who you really think you are? The people that know you the best are the people you live with. If they are not impressed with your character, you have some work to do. Even if people who don't live with you *are* impressed, they don't see you when things are tough and not necessarily going your way, so their opinions are ones without all the facts. Learn to live from the "inside out" so that you are more concerned with what those who love you most think of you than what other people who know you least do.

Realizing that my husband doesn't have to be everything to me allows him to be something and helps him to know that I choose to love him even though I don't expect him to be perfect. Accept the fact that you can't be all things to all people either. You will find a newfound freedom that helps you be secure in who you are, but also in who you aren't. You will become less concerned about what others think about your husband (or children) and more concerned about what your husband and children think of you.

What defines you? Are you working hard at your relationships or are you bored and discontent? I believe that all boredom and discontentment comes from the distance between the potential you should be living up to and the actual way you are living. If you roll up your sleeves and work at it, you will close that gap between the two and live up to your potential, pushing boredom and discontentment and all associated negative behaviors out of your life.

One of the promises we looked at in Proverbs 31:31 (KJV) is, "Give her of the fruit of her hands; and let her own works praise her in the gates." The key word is "works." Let's get to work these next few weeks and do our part to make our marriages and relationships better. Rather than controlling your husband, work on improving your own attitudes, behaviors and responses.

I know that choosing to accept your husband at face value is not easy. It is so difficult that many women give up trying. Any advancement to a better, happier life is difficult. As Christians we have to love our enemies, do good to those who hate you, and try to have perfect hearts. We don't set aside these goals because they are difficult. We press toward the mark for the prize of that high calling (Philippians 3:14). And the results are tremendous if you learn to accept your husband at face value. For years he may have suffered the plaguing thought that you are dissatisfied with him. Your assurance that you accept him as he is will remove doubts from his mind and come as a relief. His appreciation for you and his response can be life changing.

I love the equation of change posted in the book *Sacred Influence*. It states that your marriage isn't just a number on a scale of 1 to 10; rather it's a mathematical equation: $x + y = z$. Your husband may be the *x*: a number you absolutely can't change. But if you change the *y* (that's you), you influence the overall result of your marriage: *x* + *2y* = *q*. That's both the beauty (change is always possible, even if only unilaterally) and the frustration (the nature of that change is limited and not guaranteed) of human relationships. It's why we focus on how it is possible for a woman to *influence* a man, not on how a woman can *change* a man.[49]

Even if your husband never changes, you can make your marriage better by changing yourself or changing your responses to him. You need to be the best you can be, living out being an amazing godly woman and living with strength and wisdom. You need to live the Spirit-filled life God called you to live. While you are setting your attention to that, the Lord will infuse you with new love and gratitude for those in your life, beginning with your husband. When you start to work on your own weaknesses, you will have a new understanding for his.

What is your purpose in life? It is to be the best you can be for the glory of God. Then make your impact on the world around you. If you are overly concerned with just changing your husband, you are sure to miss out on the larger purpose that God has placed you on the earth for. God gives your husband a free will, and part of your role in life is not to take that away. Your mission starts at home, but ultimately will impact the world. Stand up to the challenges your marriage relationship gives you and allow the Lord to change you and speak to you in the valleys, and then take those relationship victories and begin applying them to other relationships and demonstrating how to truly love to the world.

"I have no way of knowing whether or not you married the wrong person, but I do know that many people have a lot of wrong ideas about marriage and what it takes to make that marriage happy and successful. I'll be the first to admit that it's possible that you did marry the wrong person. However, if you treat the wrong person like the right person, you could well end up having married the right person after all. On the other hand, if you marry the right person, and treat that person wrong, you certainly will have ended up marrying the wrong person. I also know that it is far more important to be the right kind of person than it is to marry the right person. In short, whether you married the right or wrong person is primarily up to you." – Zig Ziglar[50]

Chapter 6

Reasonable and Realistic

Romantic comedies are ruining your love life! That's the latest from researchers at Heriot-Watt University in Edinburgh, Scotland, who say that love on the big screen sets up unrealistic expectations. Here's the information, courtesy of the BBC: In the study, one group of volunteers watched a romantic comedy, while another watched a drama. Afterwards, they all answered questions about their attitudes toward love and dating.

The results? Those who watched the romantic film were more likely to believe in fate and destiny and they had a stronger belief in "love at first sight." In the follow-up study, these beliefs didn't prove to be helpful. Fans of movies like *Runaway Bride* and *Notting Hill* were less able to communicate with their partners. Why? Because many believed that couples who are really in love should "just know" what each other wants. Even if you're certain that you know the difference between onscreen and real life, you're still susceptible.

Researcher Kimberly Johnson warns that this "movie effect" is subtle. She says that romantic films capture the excitement we feel in a new relationship and since we identify with the characters, it's easier to buy into unrealistic ideas, such as the idea that lasting love can happen in a few days. Romantic movie watchers also have unrealistic expectations from their partners and their relationships in general.

They [expect things]... that should be part of a relationship on occasion, everyday life isn't like that. That can cause dissatisfaction. Now, this doesn't mean you have to give up your movie dates. Just skip the romantic comedy and catch a thriller instead.[51]

How reasonable and realistic are *you*? Where do you get your notions of a perfect relationship? Your expectations of how your husband should act? Your ideas of what your family should look like? Are you able to really appreciate your man for who he is, not for some ideal you think he should be?

To appreciate a man means to set a just value on him, to esteem him for his full worth, and to be grateful for him and what he does for you. Having a keen sense of appreciation can be developed; it is not necessarily an inherent trait all human beings are born with. Usually, in fact, women tend to look at the worst things in a person rather than the best.

When we had younger children, we were on such a strict budget that we had to save for a long time before we could purchase items for our home or family. After we had saved quite some time, we were finally able to purchase beautiful violet wallpaper for the girls' room, with matching bedspreads. I was thrilled. When I came home, my hard working husband had wallpapered the entire room, but I immediately noticed that the focal wallpaper border was hung upside down. My husband was not about to rip the wallpaper down and start over, so I had two choices: to live with it joyfully or to live with it miserably. Although my normal tendency was to focus on the thing that needed to be fixed, I retrained my eye when I went in the room to focus on the other parts of the wall that were done correctly or the bedspreads, telling my husband that it was okay, and would serve to remind us that only God is perfect!

Philippians 4:8 (AMP) – "For the rest, brethren, whatever is true, whatever is worthy of reverence and is honorable and seemly, whatever is just, whatever is pure, whatever is lovely and lovable, whatever is kind and winsome and gracious, if there is any virtue and excellence, if there is anything worthy of praise, think on and weigh and take account of these things [fix your minds on them]."

The greatest most powerful force on earth is love. Love is the essence of God Himself: for God is love. When we learn to love, really love, as God does, unconditionally and without stipulations, we are most like our Father God. Being loved can be someone else's foolishness or blind puppy love; but when we love God's way, it is a fruit of His Spirit in us. When all is said and done, there are three things that remain, 1 Corinthians 13:13 (GW) tells us: "...faith, hope and love. But the best one of these is love." Love can be *learned*. Titus 2:4 (GW) instructs the "older women to wisely train the young women..." "to <u>love their husbands</u>." (Emphasis added.) Open your hearts to truly learn how to better love your husbands.

1. <u>See With the Eyes of Love</u>.

Learn to see your husband through eyes of love. John 7:24 (GW) reminds us to "Stop judging by outward appearance! Instead, judge correctly." 1 Samuel 16:7 (GW) puts it this way: "...God does not see as humans see. Humans look at outward appearances, but the Lord looks into the heart."

Seeing with eyes of love takes a little practice and a lot of maturity. It takes a conscientious effort to not see someone else's faults. To see your husband with eyes of love is to really see him and appreciate him in a way that no one else does. It is seeing his potential as part of his person, seeing his intentions, seeing his struggles, yet choosing to focus on his victories in spite of his faults.

The eyes of love see with the entire love chapter, 1 Corinthians 13, in mind: "Love endures long and is patient and kind; love never is envious nor boils over with jealousy, is not boastful or vainglorious, does not display itself haughtily. It is not conceited (arrogant and inflated with pride); it is not rude (unmannerly) and does not act unbecomingly. Love (God's love in us) does not insist on its own rights or its own way, for it is not self-seeking; it is not touchy or fretful or resentful; it takes no account of the evil done to it [it pays no attention to a suffered wrong]. It does not rejoice at injustice and unrighteousness, but rejoices when right and truth prevail. Love bears up under anything and everything that comes, is ever ready to believe the best of every person, its hopes are fadeless under all circumstances, and it endures everything [without weakening]." 1 Corinthians 13:4-8 (AMP)

One day while visiting with my mom in her back yard, she exclaimed, *"Just look* at this yard and how beautiful it is! I never get tired of coming out here and looking at all the special things I love about this yard." I realized that she had just voiced a similar sentiment about her little front porch. I said, "Mom, you see everything as better than it is."

She is like that with people too. People love being around my mom because all they feel is the love and admiration she has for them. She chooses to leave the rest to God and just love the gift(s) each person brings into her life. As an extra bonus for the way she loves, my mom lives in victory. Many people her age are swallowed up in misery, bitterness, unforgiveness, envy, jealousy, and a lot of other sins. But by covering others' sins and choosing to love, my Mom doesn't allow herself excuses to sin against others. She chooses to love. She gives others room to grow, to change their mind, to become better people, and all the while they know she is on their team cheering them forward. "The fire of love stops at nothing—it sweeps everything before it." (Song of Solomon 8:6, THE MESSAGE)

In your relationships, learn to see with the eyes of love. Purposefully see people (and places) as "better than they are," viewing the history you have with them, their role in your life, their potential, and the little talents and strengths and gifts they may not even be taking time to utilize yet. Let others know you are on their team, and make it difficult for them to disappoint you. Let them know you expect good things from them; you will be amazed to see that many people are badly craving someone to draw out the good that is in them.

2. <u>Concentrate On What Really Matters</u>.

In magazines and books, women are characterized and portrayed as wanting and loving only superficial things about men—how they look, their position in society, and how much money they make. Looks, position, and money aren't the best criteria to define a successful marriage partner. What defines "success" in your marriage? Do you have a vision in your mind of what your husband should be like? Do you expect him to be like your dad, your brother, or your friend's husband? If you really want to appreciate a man for who he really is, you need to determine what defines a successful man to you. You have to be realistic and reasonable and be sure the things that you appreciate are achievable and possible. You need to develop a sense of values—values that really matter. If you only appreciate things that are fleeting and temporal, your joy and contentment in your relationship will be the same.

Appreciate and treasure character traits in your husband, such as honesty, dependability, kindness, love, or loyalty. When you appreciate and express your appreciation for virtue, your husband and others will know that the things that matter most to you are things that make them a better person. Ultimately, appreciation will result in a stronger relationship too, because it will not be superficial.

The way we look at activities, pursuits, and others usually starts with the way we look at self. When you center your life on temporary fleeting activities and pursuits, your priorities will have to change to revolve around activities and pursuits that may not even be a priority to you. You will find that you really aren't able to consider others' feelings or needs because yours are taking up too much time. You will become hypercritical of others for their outward appearance, and you will rarely notice or focus on the characteristics in the lives of others that transcend the temporal test of beauty to be character qualities that matter for eternity. For example, I used to tell my girls, "You show me a super-buff, dressed to the T, suntanned, perfect-looking guy, and I'll guarantee that's one guy that doesn't have time for many things besides himself, the gym, and the tanning booth."

I was guilty of this at one time in my life too. I was training for the marathon, and running was a passion for me. I even missed an important baby shower because I was running. I let everything revolve around my running schedule and made no accommodations for any one or any activity that didn't involve my training. I learned that even when something is a useful, it has to be kept in its proper perspective. 1 Timothy 4:10 (THE MESSAGE) reminds us, "Workouts in the gymnasium are useful, but a disciplined life in God is far more so, making you fit both today and forever."

When you live out priorities that really matter in your own life, however, you will naturally appreciate others for things that really matter as well. When you find yourself concentrating on all the wrong activities, start looking first at how you prioritize your own life. Don't allow yourself to live out of balance; concentrate on how much time you spend on your external beauty and how much time you spend developing and demonstrating character and your inner beauty by spending time in the Word of God, in church, ministry, helping those less fortunate, and other such disciplines.

When you develop inner beauty, character, virtue, and wisdom, you can stop grasping at the unattainable "fountain of youth" and focus on beauty that is incorruptible and unfading (1 Peter 3:3). You can smile at the future (Proverbs 31:25), because you know that "... beauty evaporates, but a woman who has the fear of the Lord should be praised." (Proverbs 31:30, GW)

When my children were dating, I told them that they could not expect a person to possess every good trait in their late teens and early twenties. The important thing to look for, I told them, is someone who is dedicated to excellence in all areas of their lives. With such a person, although he or she may not have achieved a full roster of qualities yet, with a dedication to excellence in their lives you could be sure they will always be growing and challenging themselves to be better. "The ways of right-living people glow with light; the longer they live, the brighter they shine." Proverbs 4:18 (THE MESSAGE)

3. <u>Be Grateful for What He Does For You.</u>

Notice and appreciate the many little acts of kindness your husband does for you. Being ungrateful cannot exist with contentment. You will never be content with your husband if you are not grateful for him. Gratefulness needs to be cultivated; in other words, you need to promote its growth. Are you grateful for him picking up groceries, putting gas into your car, emptying the trash, carrying heavy loads, or other things he does for you? Are you looking for so much more that you can't even see or appreciate the things he does? Do you appreciate the time he spends with his children? I cannot tell you how many times I have heard young moms undermine their husband's efforts because they feel he should do certain duties around the house. Even if these chores are his duty, how nice it is to be appreciated, and how much it does for a relationship. Are you grateful that he works hard every day? Maybe you work as well, so you find it difficult to appreciate his work because of the fact that you work too. Wouldn't you like him to appreciate the fact you are working? You can't make him appreciate you, but at least you can treat him the way you would like to be treated.

If your husband is required to exert extra energy on one area in his life, other areas may be temporarily lacking. You need to verbalize your acceptance of this reality. Many times when I am sewing or making a craft, I tell my family, "I can't be creative and neat at the same time." I expect them to understand. While I am working on these classes, I let every one know that other areas in my life may be put on the back burner for a while. It is unrealistic and unreasonable to expect that I can take on a huge project and keep everything else going at the same pace at the same time.

One thing we have to learn is when you put one hat on, another hat may have to be put aside temporarily. I find many women who expect their husbands to be working on many different aspects of their lives, expecting each area to meet perfection. If your husband is going through a tough time in his career, he may not be able to help around the house as much or be as involved with the children for a period of time. Work through tough times together and let your husband know you don't expect him to take on a huge project that demands his time and energy and efforts and not let something else slacken. Once you learn how to be reasonable and realistic, you can clearly spot when you aren't being so and adjust your expectations.

When my husband had to make a career change unexpectedly, I came home to find him sitting on the edge of the bed very disturbed. It was just after we had sent our oldest son to go to college out of state, and we also had our other four children at a private Christian school that was costing us thousands of dollars. Although inwardly I was freaking out, I told him I was proud of him for being a man of integrity, and that I had confidence we would make it through. I told him now that the children were older I would go back to work short term so that he could take the time to interview and secure a position that would be right for him. I let him know I would make whatever sacrifices were necessary until he found a new position. I went to work at a law office in Novi. Jumping back to work after being out of the work force over twenty years found me at a computer working on Excel and Access programs instead of typing on a Selectric™ typewriter. I worked hard, going between school activities for our children and work, starting part time but then assuming so much responsibility that I became the office manager and had to hire an assistant to keep up with the work load. Once my husband was settled in his new job, which took a little over a year, I was able to quit. While he was looking for another job it would have been unrealistic or unreasonable for me to expect him to do anything else but look for a job. It became his full time position, and even though he was at home, if I thought he was home to make my life easier, it wouldn't have given him the time he needed to find his next job. It was time to focus on being the one helping him up at the time he was down. Too many wives, when their husbands are down, are so focused on the impact on their own lives that they are not able to be the one helping pick their husbands up, or they don't look for creative ways to do so. This totally wipes out one of the main reasons why the Bible tells us, "Two are better than one; because they have a good reward for their labour; For if they fall, the one will lift up his fellow. But woe to him who is alone when he falls and has not another to lift him up." Ecclesiastes 4:9-10 (KJV)

Maybe your husband doesn't do much around the house. Maybe he comes home exhausted and it's all he can do to fall on the couch until it's time for bed. Maybe he is going through physical or job trials that render him unable to do much. In that case...

4. <u>Appreciate What Kind of Man Your Husband Is.</u>

Unfortunately, our fast-paced society places a great emphasis on productivity. So much so, that we have become *human doings* rather than *human beings*. When my grandmother had a series of strokes and couldn't accomplish much, she felt her entire purpose in life had been taken away from her. She felt her life was without value because she couldn't *do* things for everyone. We were delighted to just have her around us, but she never felt that she was valuable until she could accomplish small chores from her wheelchair again.

If you have gotten so far away from really appreciating your husband that you can't even imagine anything to be grateful for, look back at the history you have together to remember the things that attracted you to him in the first place. Were there times he was thoughtful or considerate in your history together? Remember what bonded you together and try to recite a few of those things to him.

Have you appreciated the pursuits that your husband has dedicated himself to become good at? Maybe your husband went to trade school, or maybe he took an online course or soldiered through an internship. My dad had a sixth grade education, but he had so much wisdom and common sense that every person who knew him became the recipient of many of his golden nugget philosophies and proverbs about life. At his funeral, the funeral directors said they had never seen so many people pass through a funeral home; over 1,600 people came for the one-day viewing. Many people considered my dad their "second father" or acknowledged what they learned from him that their own fathers had never taught them. In the midst of having his own six children and seventeen grandchildren and being active in their lives, my dad was pouring wisdom wherever he went. He taught me that you don't have to have a formal education to impact others.

Appreciate your husband's efforts: his education, common sense, willingness or ability to fix things, or his skill at finding the right person to fix things if he can't. What special talents does he have? Is he a good communicator, or is he patient to work through problems?

Is he a good negotiator, salesman, or time manager? When a wife is looking for ways to appreciate the gifts inside her husband, she can magnify those gifts.

These character traits are like finding diamonds; you don't find them just casually walking along not paying attention. You may have to go into dark caves (bad or tough situations), pay attention, and you may find a little nugget here and there. But what value it is when you find something! You excitedly want to share the good news. This is the way it should be when you find something good in your husband. Don't expect to find a mine full of diamonds; be realistic and reasonable, and know that in the midst of some crazy days with some unbelievable demands, your husband still has character glimmering here and there which is worthy of mention and valuable to find.

Are there any physical features you admire about him? Any time he demonstrates strength and fortitude? Does he play or participate in sports? Maybe the only thing you can concentrate on for now is that he has great eyes or hair. Find something and start somewhere appreciating your man. Maybe the problem has been compounded and turned into a cycle; he hasn't done anything you feel is worth commenting on or appreciating, which has killed his motivation to even try to do anything noteworthy. You have gotten out of the habit of expressing any appreciation as much as he has gotten out of the habit of doing anything worth appreciating. Some one has to break the cycle, why not you?

Remember, we are talking about being "reasonable" and "realistic" as far as his physical features go. Do you *really* want a man who looks like a body builder or you can't compliment him? If he is built to the hilt, I can promise you he will need to be at the gym *every day* to work on that. So be careful what you criticize him for; his lack of muscle may be something to *compliment* him on because you know how difficult it is that he can't work out at this stage in his life because he is focused on other priorities. The thing I *loved* about my husband when we started dating was that he was *one* guy that I dated who *wasn't* overly concerned about his image, his looks or what he wore or drove. It was a *relief* for me to go out with someone who wasn't self absorbed.

I have a friend that has a lot of problems with his knees and shoulders, and a few health issues on top of it. Because of his health problems, it is difficult for him to get to the gym. But he loves when people comment on his calves. He has great calves and he is really strong. Look for and find strengths to compliment your husband on. Remember, we are being reasonable and realistic. We're not looking for perfection, just like we can't keep up with looking for perfection in our own bodies, but we are told in Ephesians 5:29 (GW), "No one ever hated his own body. Instead he feeds it and takes care of it as Christ takes care of the Church." It's the only guy's body you are one with, so start appreciating it!

We need to become more reasonable and realistic not only in appreciating our husband's body, but in the way we feel toward our own body. 1 Corinthians 7:4 (AMP) says, "For the wife does not have [exclusive] authority and control over her own body, but the husband [has his rights]; likewise also the husband does not have [exclusive] authority and control over his body, but the wife [has her rights]." We are so used to looking at Photoshopped commercials, movies, and magazine photos that we feel inferior and have a poor self-image. You may not be driving the number one car in the world, but you still should love and appreciate it. Your husband has his rights over your body, and it doesn't have to be perfect for him to love it.

1 Peter 3:3-4 (GW) says, "Wives must not let their beauty be something external. Beauty doesn't come from hairstyles, gold jewelry, or clothes. Rather, beauty is something internal that can't

be destroyed. Beauty expresses itself in a gentle and quiet attitude which God considers precious." It isn't that what you look like doesn't matter at all: in fact you should take care of yourself so that you look the best you can. The warning to wives in this verse is reminding us that our focus should not improperly be on something corruptible that will not last.

In Charles Swindoll's book, *Strike the Original Match,* he says: "Cecil Osborne refers to a person who possesses this over-emphasis on the externals as a "narcissistic woman." She is one who... ...has an inordinate self-love. She is unduly preoccupied with her face, her body, and often with her own interests, which she perceives as an extension of herself... A man married to a narcissistic woman is in for trouble. If the world does not continue to praise her and if he does not cater to her infantile whims, she may develop any number of physical or emotional symptoms... A narcissistic woman constantly seeks to be the center of attention. She seeks flattery and is engaged in constant battle for popularity. She is sometimes a 'psychic scalp collector,' flirting with men in order to prove to herself that she has not lost her attractiveness...

"For the woman who genuinely wants to be a godly wife, my advice is to give greater attention to your inner person - those 'imperishable qualities' - than to your physical attractiveness."[52]

Appreciate your husband's achievements. Has he won any trophies and medals? Has your husband received a positive review at work? Has he received a note or commendation? Men don't love to keep those trophies and medals around for nothing; they love to be recognized for what they have worked hard to achieve.

If you are not interested in these achievements, then where is your interest? If you are not interested in how your spouse's day went, then whom do you think should be interested? If you don't get excited about what makes your spouse happy, then who do you think should? If you don't cheer your spouse up after a hard day, then who do you want to cheer him up? If you don't know the little things that mean a lot to your spouse, then who do you want to keep track of those things? If you are not interested in the little details of your spouse's day, then who do you want to be interested in him?

If you aren't the shoulder for your spouse to cry on, then whom do you want to lend a sympathetic ear to him? If you don't appreciate him, then who do you think should? Make sure that you are the stars in your spouse's eyes, the pep in his step, the lift to his spirit, and the wind beneath his wings.

My husband treasures little weird artifacts that people from work give to him. They may be symbolic, such as a vial with a spice in it, or obnoxiously ugly, like an unusual flag with something like "no frogs" written on it. But no matter what it looks like, if he attaches it to an achievement or an event he was proud of, he wants to keep it. Some men get a hole in two or a hole in one and have the ball mounted on a trophy with the date on it. Some men love their bowling trophies, or the awards they received from running races or winning championship games. Give your man a place to display these mementos he is so proud about.

I must admit, that is very difficult for me because my husband has so many keepsakes like that. When he worked at one company, it was eagles. Everything was either a statute or knickknack of an eagle or had eagles on it: awards, cups, hats, letter openers, signs, and glasses. As these items started invaded our living space and crowding us out, I set up an office area in our house for Gary with plenty of display cases for him to put whatever he wanted in them. His office became his trophies and collectibles showcase.

When he went fishing with his sons, each caught a fish at different times. He had both fish stuffed to commemorate the occasions. We put those plaques in our recreation room, and I am glad we have a place up north now so I can send those plaques into the pole barn!

A wise woman knows that these keepsakes represent value to her man because it makes him feel important, showcases an achievement, or commemorates something momentous he did in his life. We need to be careful to not diminish the value of these souvenirs. Remember, a lot of these past achievements represent success to him. It is wise for us to use these things as a reminder that it's very appropriate to announce and be proud of some of our husband's achievements.

Applaud your husband's achievements past and present. Make him know you believe in him. Make your husband feel like a winner with you. It is interesting during football season how many times men will want to leave when the team they are cheering for is way behind. I have heard many comebacks on the radio from the parking lot, because even if we have great seats for a game or we are with friends, my husband will walk out of the game early if he feels there won't be a comeback. Make your husband feel like he is on top of his game with you. Look for ways to cheer him on and stop blowing the whistle making him feel there is no hope for a comeback.

The more you admire your husband, the more he feels like a real man and has the courage and initiative to step out in his role even more. The more he feels like an appreciated and admired man of integrity when he is around you, the more he will want to be around you. When someone sees all the good in you, you aspire to show them even more of that side of you. It is as the Roy Croft poem states:

> I love you,
> Not only for what you are,
> But for what I am

When I am with you.
I love you,
Not only for what
You have made of yourself,
But for what You are making of me.
I love you
For the part of me
That you bring out;
I love you
For putting your hand
Into my heaped-up heart
And passing over
All the foolish, weak things
That you can't help
Dimly seeing there,
And for drawing out
Into the light
All the beautiful belongings
That no one else had looked
Quite far enough to find.

I love you because you
Are helping me to make
Of the lumber of my life
Not a tavern
But a temple;
Out of the works
Of my every day

Not a reproach
But a song.

I love you
Because you have done

More than any creed
Could have done
To make me good
And more than any fate
Could have done
To make me happy
You have done it
Without a touch,
Without a word,
Without a sign.
You have done it
By being yourself.
Perhaps that is what
Being a friend means,
After all.[53]

When you appreciate who someone is without requirements, you become a safe place for that person to share deeply, usually what he doesn't share with any one else. Having decided early in our marriage that what was important to my husband would be important to me, I have learned to establish a place for my husband where he can safely share his goals, dreams, and plans with me. Even when his ideas are not exactly mine, or not necessarily a goal I would have focused on, I try to help find a way for him to achieve his goals. I often have to sacrifice or postpone achieving my goals in order to help my husband reach his. Philippians 2:3 (GW) says, "Don't be concerned only about your own interests, but also be concerned about the interests of others." It is a good discipline not to always make everything about me and my dream and goals. If I really put things in perspective, it should be a goal and dream of mine to help my husband achieve his goals and dreams in the first place. So actually when his goals and dreams are realized, mine are as well if one of my goals is to put him first. Know what things are on your husband's list of things to do, or his "bucket list," and help him accomplish some of them as your goal.

5. <u>Appreciate the Norm.</u>

Many women believe that when they marry their "Prince Charming" he will fulfill all their dreams and be all they lack, and they can live "happily ever after." This is an illusion. Soon we realize we married a regular person with ups and downs, and we become disillusioned. You become disappointed that your spouse is not as good or valuable or true as you had thought. Disillusionment is disheartening and causes you to lose determination or confidence, shaking or destroying your resolution. If you find you are losing heart and determination, if your resolution or confidence is waning, be sure to keep building up your faith and trust in your husband and in others so you don't lose heart. Be more realistic and choose to love and appreciate your husband for who he is in order to have your "happily ever after."

Too often, we are reluctant to compliment our husband or express appreciation for him, thinking if we do he will not address other areas in his life that we wish he'd work on or change. So any little compliment given to him by another woman entices him. Many husbands find themselves in the arms of another woman because she simply took the time to hear him and respond to his need for admiration. To visually illustrate this concept, consider a sponge. When the sponge is soaked in water, excess water isn't needed or soaked up by the sponge. However, when the sponge is parched, it will soak up every little drop of water given to it. When your spouse leaves the house, is he a parched sponge or a soaked one? One that has been starved of basic attention, compliments, and appreciation, or one soaked with attention, compliments, and appreciation? Make sure you "soak" your spouse with attention and compliments so he isn't a parched sponge ready to soak up any compliment that comes his way.

No husband comes in a perfect package. No husband can do it all. No wife is perfect either. Your job, as a wife, is to fight to stay sensitive to your husband's strengths. Resist the temptation to compare his weaknesses to another husband's strengths while forgetting your husband's strengths and that other husband's weaknesses. Would you like your husband to compare your weaknesses to another woman's strengths? Treat your husband the way you expect him to treat you.

6.   <u>A Strength Could Be Hidden as a Weakness</u>.

2 Corinthians 12:9 (THE MESSAGE) says, "…and then he told me, My grace is enough; it's all you need. My strength comes into its own in your weakness. Once I heard that, I was glad to let it happen. I quit focusing on the handicap and began appreciating the gift. It was a case of Christ's strength moving in on my weakness." When we are weak in character, the grace of Christ can become our strength. The same is true with your husband. Unfortunately, it is easier to see someone's strength from the misuse of that strength before the grace of Christ tweaks and changes it. For example, if you are decisive, you can be seen as argumentative or stubborn. If you are gentle or kind, it may be seen as weakness. If you are confident, without Christ's grace you may seem obnoxious. If you are tenacious, without the grace of Christ you may be unyielding or uncaring. Look for strengths beneath what you see as a weakness. Look beneath the surface and you may find strengths that the grace of Christ can turn into your husband's greatest assets.

7.   <u>A Weakness Can Display an Issue Running in the Background</u>.

Often while working on my computer, a program will seem to almost stop responding. I will type a word and the computer will take several minutes to catch up with the word I typed. Often the spinning wheel will kick in and make me wait even longer. Upon investigation, usually I find that there are too many programs running in the background. I have to close out those programs because they are taking up energy.

You may not realize the unresolved issues, hurts, past events, problems, and demands running "in the background" of your husband's life. You may try to deal with the frustration of what you see on a surface level: too long a pause or no response at all, the inability for him to respond correctly or with a good attitude, or abrupt communication. What you don't often see is *why* he is responding in a way that isn't normal or what you expected. Look beneath the surface to discover what is "running in the background," and causing the unacceptable communication.

If a husband is defensive and disagreeable, arguing over little things so much that the family walks on eggshells around him, he may drive his loved ones and family away. The question isn't necessarily, "Why is he so mean?" The question could be, "What may be running in the background?" Look beneath the surface. He may feel unappreciated. He may have suggested ideas at work that weren't given value or accreditation. That promotion or a raise he wanted may have been given to someone who doesn't have the best interests of the company in mind. He may feel thwarted in his efforts. To top it off, his wife and family don't understand or recognize his hard work.

When my husband seems distracted, forgetful, negligent, or thoughtless, I look beneath the surface. I discover that his email inbox is full and the pressure of his job weighs on him. We may be talking, but his mind is miles away trying to figure out problems and solutions for his job. He doesn't feel his job is more important, but it is demanding and pressing—so much so that he can't put the load out of his mind.

Your husband may not be the handyman you expected him to be when you got married. Maybe your dad was great at fixing things around the house, and your husband won't even try to fix anything. He may not be interested in painting or renovating the house. Maybe he doesn't feel like even investing money into making the house look good or in maintenance. The lawn may be a disaster. Underneath the surface he may be exerting a lot of energy away from home toward being successful. If he repairs others' houses or is a carpenter or tradesman, by the time he gets home he may need a break from his routine. One of the ironies of life is that a plumber's house often has plumbing problems, an electrician's house often has electrical problems, and a painter's house often needs painting. Who can blame these men? When a man gets home, he wants to get away from the day's pressures and he trusts that his family will understand.

The more reasonable and realistic you are, the more you will be able to appreciate your husband and truly understand his needs and desires.

One of my daughters came in the door one day. She was visibly disturbed, irritable, and on edge about a minor misunderstanding we had. Normally, something trivial wouldn't create such a problem for her, but on this day, she was touchy and irritable. Realizing this behavior was atypical for her, I touched her arm and asked, "What is wrong?" She burst into tears and told me how another issue bothered her so much. This unrelated problem complicated little daily difficulties.

A man may never burst into tears or tell you what is bothering him under the surface. Often a psychological coping mechanism called *displacement* is in place. Displacement moves a frustration or hostility away from the actual problem's source to a safer person or situation. Realizing this psychological process alerts you when your husband is difficult to live with because of hidden stresses running in the background.

When someone hurts me or is inconsiderate, I realize I can't change that other person. But I can take responsibility for myself and determine that I won't behave the same way. I try to avoid the kick-the-dog-syndrome.

8. Expecting the Bumps in the Road.

I personally like my relationships the same way I like my airplane rides—without any turbulence. Realistically, wind currents in the air guarantee a few bumps along the way and potholes guarantee a few bumps while driving along the road. The good news is that planes rarely crash because of turbulence; the bad news is that relationships do crash because of it. What if, at the first sign of turbulence in the plane, everyone jumped out? Or beside every pothole, people abandoned their car? Sadly, the first sign of turbulence in a marriage sometimes leads to divisions.

Marriage is a destination. There will be unrealistic expectations, turmoil, and failure. But the destination is a loving, warm, understanding relationship so it is worth a few bumps and turbulence.

Acknowledge your husband's lapses without hanging those lapses over his head. Allow your husband to relax in his own home. Make sure the demands in his life do not come from you. Make a special place for his special treasures. Buy furniture he likes. Make sure your husband knows how valuable he is to you. Learn his goals and aspirations. Understand why he works so hard.

Enjoy and love your life on purpose. You are stuck living with the bad stuff; you may as well appreciate the good stuff. For a long time, I focused on all the deficits in my life and things I had to do without, not realizing that my focus obscured many benefits and conveniences I actually did have. I complained about all the hours my husband worked, failing to recognize all the benefits I had because of his work. I wore myself out with my bad attitude. I was consumed with what I didn't have. I played a martyr and victim.

It was disgusting—even to me! At that point, I decided to put a stop to my bad attitude. Part of the process was letting the many naysayers around me know that I would no longer entertain negative comments about my husband's work schedule. The next part of the process was to think right thoughts.

I did what the Bible told me to do—I didn't say "Lord help me not think wrong thoughts." I pictured my mind as a frying pan heated with the oil of the Holy Spirit where defeating, wrong thoughts would just sizzle away. Like a fisherman casting a line, I cast wrong thoughts out as far as I could, and put right thoughts there instead—by choice. You and I are responsible for what we think, so choose to think thoughts that build rather than destroy. On her Facebook page on April 23, 2012, Joyce Meyer said, "When we fill our thoughts with right things, the wrong ones have no room to enter."

I would rather be reasonable and realistic so that I can sincerely appreciate my husband. I would rather feel secure in who I am, knowing that I can't be all things. These choices are daily. And the choices provide a good balance for my husband, my family, and me. I love my friends and family without demanding perfection. I refuse to expect perfection.

Because I don't expect people in my life to be perfect, I don't crumble when someone disappoints me. Marathon runners know that mile 18 of the 26.2 miles is considered a wall because that point is the hardest physical and mental challenge. Many runners can't get past the wall. When I ran a marathon, I trained to expect the wall. I was prepared, hydrated, paced myself, paid attention to little rubs that could cause blisters. Because I anticipated the wall, I got through it and to the other side.

In the same way, you know marital problems will come. We can learn adequate problem solving and communication skills before the problems come. By preparing beforehand, you will be equipped to get through the tough times as effectively and with as little damage as possible.

James 3:2 (AMP) says, "For we all often stumble *and* fall *and* offend in many things." No one is exempt. Your husband will positively let you down at one point or another. In many ways. Being reasonable and realistic is to know this and choose to love in spite of it and regardless of it, and not be shocked, dismayed, overwhelmed, overwrought, and undone when (not if) it happens!

Chapter 7

Admiration and Appreciation

When my family complains about little flaws they have, I like to point at a tree or some beautiful thing of nature nearby. I say something like, "Look at that tree. The bark and the leaves and the roots are not perfect, but the tree is still beautiful. You don't have to be perfect to be beautiful!"

One of the most glaring lapses in a woman's character is ungratefulness. Being ungrateful not only contributes to frustration in your marriage, but it can douse water all over your spouse's efforts to please you. When someone is ungrateful, it takes all the joy out of doing something special for that person. Choose to be grateful and look for opportunities to express gratitude for even the smallest displays of affection and consideration.

When a husband or anyone doesn't feel appreciated, it is easier for them to withdraw than it is to convince that person of his or her worth. Maybe your husband doesn't feel valuable or appreciated by you. Perhaps he hasn't done much to try to persuade you otherwise, which has made the situation even worse. "Words kill, words give life; they're either poison or fruit—you choose." Proverbs 18:21 (THE MESSAGE) Choose to convey your love, commitment and appreciation to him. One simple choice and accompanying actions can arrest a downward spiral and turn things around.

Johann Wolfgang von Goethe wrote, "If you treat a man as he is, he will stay as he is, but if you treat him as if he were what he ought to be and could be, he will become the bigger and better man."[54] If your husband learns to trust you and your sincere appreciation and gratitude, he may begin to live up to your opinion of him. Have you ever walked into a room where you knew someone was mad at you or just didn't like you? You almost take on the characteristics of what they believe about you. It becomes a type of self-fulfilling prophecy as you encounter that person. That is the same way your husband feels when he suspects you don't appreciate him. What you believe about him reinforces that behavior for bad or for good.

You can't manipulate or motivate your husband to work on his character; however, when you truly believe in him and choose to see the best in him, he is more apt to want to live up to the good you see in him. Admiration is the number one need for men, yet it isn't something he can get for himself. Admiration must be given to him by those who love and appreciate him. Men appreciate being admired by others, but especially want to be appreciated by their wives. A woman who refuses to focus on his weaknesses, but instead chooses to find things to admire, is a woman he will cherish. Appreciation not only wins the heart of your husband, he will aspire to be a better man for it too.

The more you compliment your husband, the more your love for each other will grow. Try it. A woman may argue, "I can't admire my husband unless I feel like it." She may never feel like it! Emotion follows action. The feelings grow after the compliments and sincere appreciation.

Since I worked in the corporate world, I know first hand how difficult the workplace can be. Usually the day begins in rush hour traffic, or in my husband's case, he faces rush hour traffic, plus airport traffic. People are increasingly difficult to work for and with, and company quotas that are often impossible to meet. Most workplaces overload good workers and expect them to do the work of several people. Making money is hard work.

When my children were growing up, I taught them to be frugal and shop around when they needed to purchase something. I required each one to budget and save. I helped them understand that the money we spent represented my husband's life. Although I worked part time, my husband brought in most of the money. I wanted my children to know that dollars were equal to hours of life given up to earn a paycheck. My children learned that when we spent money, it was available because of great sacrifices. My husband was happy to know that we realized and recognized the sacrifices that were made to provide for our family. He knew we refused to take for granted the incredible over-the-top efforts he expended at work.

Another thing I realized while working is the tremendous pressure to meet quotas and target numbers. As in most workplaces, my husband's company implements a once-a-year review. When that time of year arrives, my husband mentions the review several times. I can tell he is apprehensive. I mark my calendar so that I will be sure to ask how it went and especially if he was given credit and felt appreciated. When my husband came home with a raise or a promotion, I made a big deal out of it. I not only verbalized my congratulations, but often I'd make a special night to celebrate. When my children were younger, I told them, "Your dad got a bonus! That means he was working so hard and making such a big difference at work that he got more than his normal pay! Aren't you so proud of him?" If a man's wife doesn't make a big deal over these types of things, who will? Stop, acknowledge, praise, and celebrate.

Men need admiration. I used to laugh because my son used to want me to sit and watch him play his computer game. He was great at it and wanted me to acknowledge it. This need is pre-wired into men;

most men may not even realize that it is part of their makeup. When parents observe manly qualities about their boys and express their admiration, it builds confidence and helps growth into manhood, encouraging all the potential within.

It was usually not my girls who wanted me to sit and watch them, but my boys often did. How delighted they would be if I sat and watched them build Legos™ or K'Nex™; or play Rock Band™, Dance Dance Revolution™, or a computer game. When I did, it built a bond between us. The boys basked in my admiration for them. "Watch me." "Watch me." In their sports games, they looked over to catch my eye before going up to the plate or out on the field, or if they did something noteworthy in the game they looked up to be sure their Dad and I saw it. Feeling so admired by his parents, and with such a bond, your son is fortified against youth problems that lie ahead and threaten his sense of identity. Because many parents do not understand this acute need, admiration is sadly lacking or even sometimes purposefully withheld. Although some men seem to do well without a lot of praise, there are more men that end up seeking praise from their jobs, social networking, or other places when they don't get it at home.

Once a man graduates from school, begins his career, and launches out with his first home or apartment, it is exciting for him to be able to make decisions. Once my sons approached their twenties, they wanted to exercise their right to choose and do what they thought was best. They were anxious to start accomplishing their big plans and great ideas. Each one needed me to take the time to listen to their plans and dreams. Each one wanted someone to see the possibilities. Someone who wouldn't cut him down, ridicule him, nor criticize him. A man craves admiration and the woman who freely gives it to him is cherished.

To encourage maturity in your husband's ego (instinctive maleness) means helping him to maintain a positive self-image by recognizing and appreciating his God-given drives. If a wife sincerely compliments his strength, his patience with the children, his spiritual judgment, his wise decisions, his handsome appearance, and his drive and aspirations, these comments help him to have a good feeling about himself and consequently a better feeling toward others. You will have to learn to accentuate his positive traits and eliminate emphasis on the negative. Teasing him about things that already bother him, and calling him names even in jest, are damaging to his confidence. Making derogatory or sarcastic comments about the way he reads or the way he prays makes him withdraw or over-react, especially when the teasing is done in front of others.[55] Although he may not say anything about it right away, anger, resentment, hostility, or other negative displays of character may come to the surface later.

When your husband has basic feelings of self worth, he will be able to turn outward with love and concern for others and be seen by others as caring and loving. In addition, his response will be more caring and loving toward you. If he does *not* feel good about himself, he tends to turn inward, is more concerned about himself and his problems, and is seen as selfish and disinterested. He may quickly and negatively respond to minor irritations. Often, this is the result of an unhealthy ego in a man.

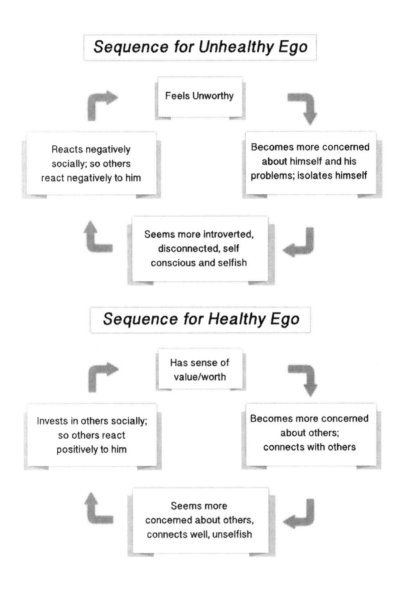

If your husband has negative tendencies resulting from an unhealthy ego, it will take much time and prayer and creativity to help these feelings turn around. When he feels good about himself, he is more concerned about others; he will look out for other people and appreciate them. When he receives positive reactions, he will consequently feel better about himself.

If your husband is seemingly the opposite of the healthy ego illustration above and his behavior is egotistical and he brags to everyone about his wonderful accomplishments and natural abilities, he may have an underfed ego and you may be the only one who can help him. For example, one woman's husband was known as egomaniac. Every conversation he mentioned how many great things he had done and the great ideas he had; he was not just good at things, but he was the best. His wife cut him down when they were alone or with others. Later, she realized that he could be starved for admiration, she understood that the reason he kept feeding his ego was because she was not feeding it. He was after approval. She corrected the situation by commenting on what a good guy he was and some of the things he had accomplished. He no longer needed to brag to impress people to gain love and approval, so he changed almost miraculously from the braggart he had become into a likeable man.

Another woman became increasingly aware of and sensitive to her husband's faultfinding and criticism of her in public. He often made her the brunt of his jokes. Then she realized that she rarely praised him or expressed faith in him when they were alone, in front of their children or friends, or even before God. Slowly and wisely she began to express what she had thought, but not said. It was not long before he began to refrain from making cutting remarks about her, and on occasion commented to others about her good points.[55]

When you realize your husband's ego is not in a healthy state, how can you help? There are several basic considerations you can integrate into your life. These tips will strengthen any relationship.

1. Be Sincere.

Your husband will know whether you mean a compliment or not. Start with a compliment that is sincere. Do you appreciate his sense of humor? Do you appreciate his diligence? Sincerity is of utmost importance when it relates to a man's sensitive ego needs. If you don't sincerely appreciate him in your heart, examine every part of your relationship to discover some good things. Even something simple can show your husband your sincere appreciation of him. You can say something like, "We've had our ups and downs but I'm glad you chose to marry me!" I've told my husband that if I have to get older, at least I have the privilege of getting older with him. At other times, I have told him that if someone has to drive me crazy, I wouldn't chose any other person but him.

In Matthew 12:34 (GW), we read, "You poisonous snakes. How can you evil people say anything good? Your mouth says what comes from inside you." What do you rehearse in your heart when you think about your husband? Is your focus on what he is not, or are you purposefully thankful for the traits and qualities that make him who he is? He will know your true feelings either from the words you say or the way you glance at him or your body language, or the way you communicate. One woman told me that she "did all the right things" for her husband, but she hated him. I told her that he knew that she hated him. She vehemently denied it until I told her that body language, tones, and looks (which you cannot cover up) clearly demonstrated what she really thought of him. I asked her not to change her *words,* but to change her *heart.* She accepted the challenge and she and her husband happily are models of a happy marriage to several grandchildren.

Psalm 139.23-24 (AMP) says, "Search me [thoroughly], O God, and know my heart! Try me and know my thoughts! And see if there is any wicked or hurtful way in me, and lead me in the way everlasting." Jeremiah 17.9 (AMP) tells us, "The heart is deceitful above all things, and it is exceedingly perverse and corrupt and severely, mortally sick! Who can know it [perceive, understand, be acquainted with his own heart and mind]?"

Jeremiah 17:10 (AMP) reads, "I the Lord search the mind, I try the heart, even to give to every man according to his ways, according to the fruit of his doings." Look deep. Do you truly and unselfishly love your husband and do you communicate that love to him? Ask the Lord to reveal any areas that cause you to fall short in your love for your husband, any ulterior motives to change him or to make your life be easier, or any wrong attitudes that will ultimately hurt your marriage.

Once your heart is right, make sure you have cultivated sincere appreciation before you express it. If you are not sincere, your husband will know it and believe you are trying to manipulate him for your own benefit.

Often, women don't notice when their husband has done something worthy of their attention. Men may comment about something they've accomplished, but if women aren't quick to pick up on it, they may not mention it again.

2. Speak Specifically.

Don't speak in generalities. What do you admire about your husband? Is it a particular character trait that you can recount when you saw it demonstrated? Was there an incident that made you proud of your husband? Observe him and listen to him so you will be able to see specific things to admire in him. Just seeing isn't enough, however, if you don't let him know what you see. It takes a little practice to say things vocally. When you can tell him *when* he demonstrated the qualities you admire in him, he will know you mean it.

Your marriage will improve when you can vocally and specifically let your husband know:

- you are glad you married him,
- you realize you may not have understood him in the past,
- you can ask for forgiveness when you are wrong, and
- you want to show him you love him just the way he is.

3. <u>Begin Gradually.</u>

If you have gotten out of the habit of complimenting your husband or verbalizing his strong points, begin *gradually*. Compliments may seem awkward for you to do if you have not done them before. One woman felt too embarrassed to compliment her husband for being firm about his convictions. Despite feeling awkward, she began to voice her admiration of him, because she wanted to be sure he knew how she felt. One day, he proudly told a friend some of the statements she had said to him. It didn't take long for her to realize how much she needed to say these praises out loud. Her husband began to ask her out on dates and plan other special events. Once he knew how much she cared, he was free to care more for her rather than being on the defense all the time. If you feel uncomfortable, step out and do it anyway. Your discomfort is further confirmation that you need to keep practicing until it is *not* uncomfortable. I have learned to be *comfortable* feeling *uncomfortable* in situations where I need to step outside my comfort zone.

4. Be Appreciative of Little Things.

Look for little acts of kindness and kind deeds you have overlooked before. What are some of your husband's good points you have taken for granted? What has he accomplished—areas he has grown in since you have known him? What kindnesses has he done for you or others since you met him? What do other people appreciate in him? As you find opportunity, tell him what you think. Once you start looking for his good points, you will become more and more sensitive and will find much to compliment. Be careful to admire not only his achievements, but also his character.

In *Capture His Heart,* author Lysa TerKeurst tells of boarding a shuttle bus where she met a 60-year-old man who told her, "Everyone is excited to see me pull up to the curb. That's why I like my job so much. People get on the bus and smile so big. They've just been waiting for me, and when I finally arrive, they are happy I'm here. I've often wished I had a video camera to tape people as they get on my bus with the smiling faces and glad-to-see-ya comments. I'd love for my wife to see a tape like that. That's the way I've always wanted her to look when I come home from work."[56] Sometimes a man's surly moods can make it very difficult for you to feel happy to see him. Even so, he needs to see your joy when he arrives. When you stop taking your husband for granted, he will feel noticed, special, and appreciated. According to the book *Sacred Influence,* when a man feels appreciated it makes him more *moldable*: he will be more receptive to not *stay* in a bad mood. When he feels he is taken for granted he becomes defensive and resentful of the mere suggestion of change.[57]

Appreciate your spouse. Don't fall into the trap of never knowing what your husband's plans are, what he is thinking, or what is important to him. If he talks, stop doing what you are doing and *listen* to him. *Look* at him. He will open up when he knows you are really interested. Appreciating and listening to even seemingly inconsequential details will bring down barriers and create love in your relationship, as long as you are willing to give up time and be available.

5. <u>Never Underestimate the Harvest that Comes From Small Seeds!</u>

Because my days have so much jammed into them, I have learned to appreciate the value of a few minutes. I've learned large blocks of time rarely come, and if I wait for the time to do something big, I will end up doing nothing at all. Instead, I make it a practice to do a *little* something with the few minutes of time I find here and there.

I've put this principle to good use in my marriage too. Small efforts show Gary I care about him. Organizing his mail takes me a few minutes but helps him when he gets home. Making a call he wanted me to make or running an errand he wanted shows him he is important to me. Putting a little note in his home office area, bringing him a sandwich if he's working, bringing him a glass of water if he's outside or finishing a run shows him I am thinking of him. Little statements here and there tell him how much I appreciate him or what I appreciate about him.

Little seeds planted end up creating an amazing harvest in your marriage.

In the same way, inconsiderate actions or statements, sarcastic digs, or thoughtless remarks, no matter how small, wear down a beautiful relationship. Never underestimate the power of little termites eating away at a foundation. Over time, the house crumbles.

Look for the many little opportunities you have for doing good for your spouse. Build up your relationship with little seeds of kindness every chance you can.

6. <u>Make Sure You are Really Listening</u>.

I love to visit friends who turn off their televisions and put down their cell phones so that we can have a quality visit. Give your marriage the same courtesy. Put your phone down, stop, repeat ideas back to him, and ask pertinent questions. All these techniques show your husband how you care to hear what he has to say. Your greatest opportunity to admire him will be when he talks, especially when he talks about himself or subjects he is interested in. If you pay close attention, you will discover character qualities to admire when he talks about his life away from home, what he deals with at work, or how he solves problems.

Encourage your husband to talk about himself, especially his hours away from home. Begin by asking him leading questions about his work. This is not to suggest you pry or judge. But steer the conversation to his interests. When you see he is enjoying the conversation, keep it going with your comments and questions. Then learn to listen. Overcome the temptation to finish his sentences; he may need to process information before he speaks, and it may take him longer to express his thoughts. Be comfortable with silence. Give him time.

When my husband speaks, I ask, "What is that person's name?" or "Where did that happen?" More questions help me intelligently converse with him because I know the people and places involved.

Do not listen only to the words your husband is saying, but see behind the words to find the value in who is saying it. Follow this rule and you will be a good listener. You may notice his passion, his frustrations, his loyalty, his ability to handle problems, and his ideas.

When you start appreciating more about him, he will be happy he has you.

Don't become so passionate about subjects he talks about that you start to become critical of him or fail to appreciate how *he* handles things. Don't be argumentative or take sides against him. If you disagree, respect his opinion and allow him the right to it. Learn to keep silent.

Even if you don't understand every detail, stay attentive. See his heart for the subject, and hear what he communicates behind the words. Every man wants to be admired and appreciated. If he is making a subject complicated on purpose, he may be looking for your admiration and respect. Even if you don't thoroughly understand the situation, thoroughly *try*.

Maeterlinck's wrote:

> "...what care I though she appear not to understand.
> Do you think that it is for a sublime word that I thirst
> when I feel that a soul is gazing into my soul?"[58]

If you learn to *really listen* to a man, it doesn't matter if the subject is interesting or dull. You can converse on world affairs or the details of his business career. You will welcome the most tedious discourse, to seek out things to admire.[55]

7. <u>Be Appreciative for Provisions.</u>

When you are able to purchase items for your home, new clothes, and pay for costly medical or dental procedures, be grateful. When I was working, I took pride that I purchased a lot of extra items and paid for vacation rentals, but I knew I could only do that because my husband's income covered all our living expenses. Whether we work outside the home or not, our provisions are a team effort once we are married. In order to provide things, often other things or financial plans must be deterred or sacrificed. A grateful heart is a happy heart. If you work, wouldn't your husband love to hear you say something like, "I am so grateful we were able to..." or "I'm so glad we could make it happen. Thank you for caring about our home." Since I currently don't work, my husband loves when I say something like, "Thank you so much... I know this represents a good deal of your life and a lot of hard work."

8. <u>Compliment Your Husband in Front of Others</u>.

There is no better way to show your husband how much you appreciate him than to compliment him to others in front of him. He loves to hear you make positive remarks about him to others. Make compliments part of your normal conversation. When you say something like, "If you show Gary anything, he can learn it—he is so quick to pick new things up," you show how you feel about him. Try it and see what happens.

In the same way, tell your children how hard their Daddy works, both at his job and around the house. Be loyal to your husband. If you can't be loyal to him, who are you truly loyal to? Don't *ever* trash-talk him nor any one with whom you want a good relationship. Negativity says more about who *you* are than about who *they* are. Disloyalty becomes part of your spirit and nature and ends up polluting the places you go and people you converse with.

One of my favorite fairy tales is about two girls: one kind, considerate girl that spoke good words, and one rude, selfish girl that spoke evil. One day a woman made it so that whenever they opened their mouths, either physical *good* or *evil* would come out depending on which girl spoke. When the unselfish girl spoke, diamonds, rubies, and pearls came out of her mouth, but when the inconsiderate girl spoke, snakes, toads, and lizards came out of her mouth. No one wanted the unselfish girl around. Listen to your words. If a physical representation came out of your mouth, would people want to be around you?

9. <u>Be Consistent.</u>

Can your spouse count on you? Are you consistently wonderful, or does your spouse have to *wonder* what kind of mood you'll be in?

My children know I'll always stick up for my husband. Even when his rules were harsher than mine, I taught my children by example the principle that they were expected to obey people in charge. Too many children contest authority. I believe this disrespect starts at home with moms challenging dads' authority in their homes.

In the Bible, Joab seemed to be King David's right hand man. Joab came back from the battlefield and got King David to finish off a victory, so Joab wouldn't get the credit for it; he intervened in the matter of Absalom's restoration; he fought for David and seemed totally devoted to him. But I always wondered why Joab was not in the list of David's mighty men. When David's "mighty men" were listed, Joab was glaringly absent. So I looked through every scripture that mentioned Joab. I discovered that Joab obeyed David unless he disagreed with him. You cannot be a mighty employee, wife, partner, server, or student by only following leadership if you agree. Don't allow your children to speak ill of their father, or you will be feeding attitudes that will ultimately poison the way they respond to every authority in their lives.

I shared with my children the attitude I had: "Dad does so <u>many</u> things in such an amazing way, that the few areas you may not agree with you need to not focus on." Later, one of my sons told me the same thing back: he told me that although he didn't agree with all our house rules, because of his respect for us he would abide by them without making an issue out of any of the things he disagreed with.

10. *Think* About Him.

When a husband works hard, attends school, helps at the church, and completes chores, he may not see his own accomplishments. All he can see is the time and effort he is putting into his responsibilities. You are not helping much if the only time you praise him is when he has problems and then you try to lift him up. Seems rudimentary but unfortunately many women have to be reminded: just *think* about your husband. Our thoughts focus on our own concerns—the children, household chores, personal problems, our projects, our job or career. Instead, think about your husband. Think about what kind of a man he is. What problems has he faced or is he facing now? What obstacles has he overcome? What would he like to do in the future? What is he doing to try to help out? Keep your eyes open and observe his life and his heart and you will find much to admire.

★★★★

Appreciation is its own reward. When you are appreciative, you cannot be a complainer. When you are grateful you cannot be a martyr. When you look for qualities or actions to appreciate, you begin to actually make your own dreams come true. You will be easier to get along with because you are more reasonable and realistic. Turn a blind eye to the faults of others and to what you cannot change. Learning to live with imperfections guarantees you will become less demanding and more content. Contentment is a beautiful virtue, but in this fast-paced world that is constantly signaling that more is better, that upgrades are necessities, and that flaws are intolerable, few have it. John Ortberg said, "Gratitude is the ability to experience life as a gift. It liberates us from the prison of self-preoccupation."[59]

Think of when you have given something to someone when you know they needed it. You may have even gone *way* out of your way for them. You may have rearranged your schedule to drive them to the airport, and they casually just say, *Thanks!* and jump out of the car. Or you may have made an entire four-course dinner, and someone comes, eats and runs, and throws a casual *Thanks!* over their shoulder. Do you *really* want to *repeat* that experience; do you *look* for opportunities to give something to a person who doesn't even seem to appreciate your efforts?

Think of other times when you do something for someone and they are *so appreciative* of what you did that you *can't wait* to do something else for them!

If someone appreciates what I do for them, I usually do more to elicit such delight and expression from them. If your husband believes you are sincere in appreciating him, it may motivate him to work harder for the success of your relationship too.

Be a gracious, fun, excited receiver. Marriage is a long-term relationship and the "everydayness" can snuff out the life and excitement. Make it your goal to show how you appreciate him. I get so excited when my husband puts gas in my car or cleans my car that he can't wait to tell me when he does those chores for me. I make sure he has no doubt in his mind as to how much I appreciate getting into a clean car with gas in it.

I taught my children to say three sincere sentences to the giver to communicate they appreciated any gift they received. They grew up learning how to be grateful. Expressing your appreciation is a skill that can be developed and learned.

"Make the most of every chance you get. These are desperate times!" we are reminded in Ephesians 5:16 (THE MESSAGE).

A fun way to make the most of every chance I get is by realizing and investing in what I call the "WOW Factor."

The WOW Factor

What is the *WOW Factor*? It's those times when you do something way out of your comfort zone for the other person. It's learning to play euchre, a card game you may not even particularly like, because the other person loves it. Playing tennis when it's your least favorite game because it's the other person's most favorite. It's learning to love football because your husband loves it. It's the unexpected and amazingly special surprises you do for the other person at a great personal sacrifice. It's hanging around with your spouse on the bunny hills while they learn to ski instead of heading for more advanced territory.

1. Realizing the *WOW Factor.*

When my husband or boys mowed the lawn, I'd take a minute to run out with some lemonade. When they shoveled the snow, I made hot chocolate. I'd often tell them, "I love seeing you work so hard. Whatta guy!"

To realize the *WOW Factor,* you need to look for and notice those times when your husband goes out of his way for you. Then make a big deal of it. I tell my husband "WOW, this is going to really make it hard for me to get irritated with you for a while! Whatta guy!" He beams with pride.

When you are irritated over something your husband does, cutely recall his last WOW-Factor gesture. When my husband and I make plans to do something fun, such as go to dinner or play tennis, often he runs late. Because he is rarely home, it is easy for him to get caught up in doing jobs around the house, time slips by, and he isn't ready on time. I keep checking with him, but busy myself with something I can easily put down while waiting for him to finish up his work. Then I say something such as, "Well, you did just wash my car: how can I possibly be mad at you now?"

2.   <u>Investing in the WOW Factor.</u>

When is the last time you really "wowed" your guy? Can you list the last three times? When you fill his world with extraordinary favors, he will shake his head in amazement: "WOW. Whatta girl!"

Actively look for opportunities to WOW your husband. Even make a little list of ways you can continually WOW him. If you aren't looking for opportunities, time will squeeze the chances out of your life. I love to bake, and often when we have guests or go somewhere I make a tempting dessert. My husband can't resist wanting to try it out as soon as it comes out of the oven. After shooing him away, I thought, "Why shouldn't my *husband* be the one that gets the special first piece?" Now when he comes into the kitchen wanting to "taste test" my desserts, I cut him a piece from the back and put it on a plate. When I tell my guests that my husband had to taste test the dessert, it demonstrates that I am willing to go outside of the box for him. I tell my guests something like, "How can I say 'no' to this guy?" Become that "WOW: whatta girl!" that makes your spouse amazed continually! You will not be sorry!

In the Midst of a Storm

Some of you may be dealing with big issues and difficulties. Your husband may have turned to alcohol, drugs, gambling, or pornography. Never live with abuse of any form—mental or physical—because you do not deserve to be hurt purposefully or continually.

When your husband has destructive abusive habits, be sure you do not let his problems become a convenient scapegoat for your own shortcomings. You are still responsible to do the right thing even in the face of hostility or abuse. Without blaming his problems for your attitudes and responses, you must avoid co-dependency traps. Part of the emotional abuse might be making you feel responsible for his actions. In order for your husband to make you feel responsible for his behavior, you have to take on that responsibility. You may not even *recognize* the emotional damage caused by living in an abusive, co-dependent relationship. If you find more than a few of the following detrimental effects of emotional abuse being acted out in your home, it is wise to seek professional Christian counseling to work through the reasons why you are taking responsibility for someone else's bad choices. It is wise to remember that as much as the Lord desires your marriage to succeed, He also wants each individual part of the marriage to be victorious and glorify Him as well.

A few warning signs you should look for are: feeling bullied or pressured into doing things you are not comfortable with, being blamed for lapses and expected to lie or cover up for someone else's character or decisions, being harassed, threatened, or lied to habitually, or being over compensated for taking abuse or being wrongfully treated.

When someone close to you manipulates you emotionally, you need to take steps to break the cycle for good, and you may need professional help to do so. In the book *Emotional Blackmail: When the People in Your Life Use Fear, Obligation and Guilt to Manipulate You,* the authors give a few tag phrases to look for to spot threatening manipulation: "If you really loved me, After all I've done for you…, and How can you be so selfish… These are all examples of emotional blackmail, a powerful form of manipulation in which people close to us threaten to punish us for not doing what they want. Emotional blackmailers know how much we value our relationships with them.

They know our vulnerabilities and our deepest secrets. They are our mothers, our partners, our bosses and coworkers, our friends and our lovers. And no matter how much they care about us, they use this intimate knowledge to give themselves the payoff they want: our compliance."[60]

You may need to take protective steps to protect yourself, but even if you do, continue to work on being the person you need to be. Your husband may be able to find peace, love, acceptance, and a safe place in you instead of finding you a hard place he needs to escape from. Refuse to cover up or lie for him. Make him be accountable if he is addicted to damaging substances. Always be part of the solution without piling guilt and blame onto his other problems.

Since God designed marriage, we should look first to Him about how we can best encourage, inspire, challenge, and appropriately influence the man we married or are going to marry. God wants you to feel loved, to be noticed, and to be cherished. He didn't create you and cast you adrift on a sea of happenstance or circumstance. He has watched you every day, and He is watching you even now, catching even the tear you might be shedding this very moment at the thought of a God so involved in your life that he put your thoughts on paper for you to read. (Gary L. Thomas, *Sacred Influence: What a Man Needs from His Wife to Be the Husband She Wants*, Zondervan Publishers, 2006.)

I love the quote from 1 Corinthians 7:17 (THE MESSAGE): "And don't be wishing you were someplace else or with someone else. Where you are right now is God's place for you. Live and obey and love and believe right there. God, not your marital status, defines your life."

Leslie Vernick, author of *How to Act Right When Your Spouse Acts Wrong,* once asked a husband in a counseling situation what he would most like from his wife. He responded, "There was a guy at work who was clumsy and never did the job quite right. None of us guys thought much of him, but when his wife came in one day, she looked at him like he could do no wrong. All of us guys were jealous of him from then on, because we knew he wasn't perfect, but his wife treated him like he was. I would love for my wife to look at me like that."[61]

Wives impact and influence homes. We don't simply hope for the best. We may make mistakes; but when we appreciate, love, care, and communicate, we can inspire and encourage our husbands.

When someone who seems to have no respect or admiration for me tries to give input into my life, I have little or no interest. That person's opinion doesn't matter even if they communicate clearly, honestly, and practically. But when your husband believes you respect him, you will influence and support him.

Chapter 8

Choices and Changes

The way we respond involves choices. In Chapter 1 we saw the need to choose who we want to be, in Chapter 2 we learned to choose character, in Chapters 3 and 4 we realized that we need to relinquish control. In Chapter 5 we discovered how to make right choices in face of opposition, and in Chapter 6 we made the choice to be reasonable and realistic. Chapter 7 taught us how to show our husbands they are admired and appreciated. In this chapter, we continue to look at the choices we make, and how choices and changes impact our relationships.

What we believe determines our choices. First, what we believe about God determines how wise we are about life. Our relationship with God gives us a different perspective on life. We know what matters. We know what lasts and what passes away, and we are able to choose based on eternal rather than temporal values. We bring our perspective to every choice we make, whether or not to be trustworthy, to plan ahead, to work diligently, to show compassion, to pursue our goals with diligence, or to control our tongues. The fear or reverent awe of God motivates us to manage our time wisely in the light of eternal values. The fear of the Lord motivates us to use our resources wisely to benefit others. The fear of the Lord helps us evaluate every choice we make each day.

A hundred years ago Ella Wheeler Wilcox published a short poem with lines are as true today as they were a century ago when she wrote them.

> One ship sails East,
> And another West,
> By the self-same winds that blow,
> 'Tis the set of the sails
> And not the gales
> That tells the way we go.

It's the set of the sail and not the gale. It's your choices. Men and women, singles and marrieds, learn from Proverbs 31. Choose to live your life wisely, in the light of what lasts forever. If you do, you will be characterized by a strong commitment, by trustworthiness, by shrewdness (which is someone intelligent or clever; someone who does not take advantage of other people but who takes advantage of opportunities), by generosity, by diligence, and by a controlled tongue. Even more, you'll know the difference between what passes and what lasts, and you'll devote your energies to what lasts for eternity. That's God's formula for living life with skill. Be wise. Be a person of strength. It's your choice.[62]

Choice Number One: What is number one on my list?
Goal: To be sure my actions show my children and my husband that my husband comes first.

Each day we choose our priorities. When the children cry louder, or are more demanding, we allow their needs to take precedence over our husband's needs. This choice is a huge mistake. When your children see the honor that you give your husband as the head of your family, they will also honor him. I believe that the sooner that your children are taught that they are not the sun and every one else the planets that rotate around the sun, the better! This errant idea usually is planted in children's heads by their parents unintentionally, and if this lifestyle is not changed it will result in mass chaos when they become teenagers.

You probably feel a sacred responsibility for your children—an obligation to nurture them in body and spirit and provide them with every opportunity to grow to their highest potential. This noble feeling of motherly devotion, when moved by a strong feeling of motherly love, can cause you to focus on the care and training of your children so much that you automatically make them your first priority. By making them your first priority, without realizing it you are damaging their perspective of authority, respect, appreciation, and honor.

A man wants a woman who will place and keep him at the top of her priority list. Being placed in an inferior position can cause a man to form bitter resentments toward his wife and even his children. Your children should never replace your relationship with your husband as your best friend and confidant. Your children began as a reflection of your love, but they should not replace it.

Parent your children together with your spouse. It is a firm foundation for a strong effective family. Eventually your children will leave and it will be you and your husband again. If you have put your children first, not only will it cause difficulties for you and your husband when they leave your home, but it will cause problems with them establishing their own homes soundly as well.

To demonstrate this concept visually, for a season I kept a Burger King crown at our house. When my husband came home, my children learned he was the "King!" The crown would come out, and I would playfully and dramatically inform them that Daddy is "King" around here. Helping your children put your husband in his rightful place of authority and honor in your home will result in children who know how to respect and be grateful for those entrusted with their care.

Firm boundaries teach your children that your relationship with your husband is top priority to you. My mom said that children are like wild horses: they will keep running unless you put fences up! Put those fences up and be sure that you keep re-establishing them. Firmly establish routines such as cleanup time and bedtime. Once your children are in bed, don't allow them to control the evening from their beds. Establish boundaries that bring peace and eliminate chaos from your home. When your children are teenagers, allow guests but establish boundaries for cleanup and curfews as well. I loved when my teenagers' friends took responsibility for cleaning everything up because they knew if they didn't the get-togethers at my house were going to stop.

A man should not expect his wife to neglect important duties. He is aware of the demands of her life and wants her to give each responsibility the attention it requires. He does not want his children to suffer. Most men realize that wives are entitled to other interests and diversions. But your husband doesn't want to be regarded as a convenience, a paycheck, an escort, a social asset, a ticket to security, or even just a sex partner. Your husband wants to know that you married him for who he is and not as a means of fulfilling your needs or reaching your objectives.

Making your husband number one does not diminish your sacred duty to your children, nor does it indicate lack of love for them. You can be both an amazing wife and mother without conflict. Your husband will love you even more when you are a wonderful mother, but he needs the assurance that your love and devotion to him always comes first. Your husband should not need to compete with his children for your time and attention.

Children miss nothing when their father comes first, but rather feel more secure and happy. Your happy marriage will be the foundation of a happy home, and the entire family benefits. If you find it hard to make your husband number one in priority, without neglecting your children, remember, the best gift you can give your children is a happy marriage. When your children leave to make their own homes, they will see you and your husband side by side loving each other.

How do you handle your children's needs? Do you pamper them by giving in to every little thing they want? Overindulgent mothers not only harm their children; they set them up for unrealistic feelings of entitlement later. And this excess adds strain to their husbands caused by the children's unrestrained desires.

When your son or daughter has a special event coming up, give him or her a budget to work within. For proms, I allotted a certain dollar amount; each person would then set priorities and limits for the amounts they would spend on the event: whether it was for clothes, dinner, flowers, hair, nails, or makeup.

Your children need to see that you consider your husband first, and you will not cater to them at your husband's expense. Show your husband he is your top priority: keep an open ear for his small requests, what he likes for dinner, how he would like to spend the evening. Your house is made to serve the family, not the family to serve the house. Create a home and not a showplace. A castle is not more important than the king that dwells in it!

Even when you have a career and you need sleep or help around the house, the job must not have top priority over your husband. If your job requires you to work at home, plan time and activities with him when you can so when you are required to focus on work he will understand. My husband's work schedule is demanding and requires much of his time at home, but as long as when he is with me he is trying to be there 100% I have to accommodate and understand his taxing work schedule may require him to take phone calls or do text messages. Also, my husband has let me know that, even though his job makes incredible demands on his life, if I need to interrupt him for something important or I really need something, he attends to it as soon as possible to show me that I am his top priority,

Choice Number Two: *Good* or *Bad* Attitude
Goal: To choose a good attitude.

If you're having a bad day, you may have no control over the situation. Often, you have only one choice: to respond with the right attitude or not to respond with the right attitude. That choice is yours.

Realizing my attitude is a choice helps me pick the right one. You have the opportunity to change your attitude. As sure as you hit the light switch and a dark room is flooded with light, you can *flick the switch* to change your attitude to the right one instead of the wrong one. Teach and show your husband and your family that you can change your attitude that quickly. I tell my family, "This is the only _____ (whatever the date is) that I'll ever have, and I want to make it a good one on purpose."

It helps to post a trigger or reminder to change your attitude. For me having visual reminders help: a sign by my bathroom: *Do Everything in Love*, or a wrapped present on my nightstand, which reminds me to *Enjoy my Present* or a geode on the counter that reminds me about the importance of inner beauty.

Choice Number Three: Accept or Reject
Goal: To have my husband know that he is accepted by me and to be free in that acceptance to be himself.

Without feeling appreciated, admired and genuinely respected, your husband probably will never change. If you notice a lot of tension in your home or if you notice a high level of frustration and anger in your husband or if you sense a discouragement leading to passivity (where he underachieves) or if you notice an "escapist" mentality (where he spends his free time playing computer games or watching sports or escaping from the home and spending inordinate amounts of time with recreation)—then, more times than not, you're looking at a man who doesn't feel loved, appreciated, and respected. He's a man who is coping, not truly living. And men who merely cope don't change nor are they looking to improve: they just pass time.

Sacred Influence, written by a man to help women understand men, postulates that acceptance and encouragement are biblical requirements, not just men's desire.[63]

"Therefore, accept each other, just as Christ has accepted you so that God will be given glory." (Romans 15:7 NLT)

"So, encourage one another and build each other up, just as you are already doing." (1 Thessalonians 5:11 NLT)

"Encourage each other every day while you have the opportunity. If you do this, none of you will be deceived by sin and become stubborn." (Hebrews 3:13 GW)

Even if your husband never changes, even if every bad habit, every neglected responsibility, every annoying character trait, stays exactly the same—even then—for your own spiritual health, learn how to love this man *as he is*. Too many books and articles ignore this point. Your first step, the primary one, is to love, accept, and even honor your imperfect husband.

In *Steel Magnolias,* I love the quote "I would rather have thirty minutes of wonderful than a lifetime of nothing special."[64] Work on making your married life *wonderful* instead of *nothing special* by accepting your husband.

You may not want to accept your husband, but if you do not accept him, then you reject him. There is no middle ground.

The disciples didn't realize this principle, but Jesus affirmed it by saying, "He that is not with me is against me; and he that gathereth not with me scattereth abroad." (Matthew 12.30 KJV) If your husband senses you don't accept him, you can be sure he feels you reject him.

Choice Number Four: Affirm or Negate
Goal: To establish and strengthen your relationship instead of nullify and make ineffective.

I love the word "affirm"—the word is from the Latin words *ad* or "to" and *firmare*, "strengthen, make firm or strong." When you *affirm* your spouse you are strengthening, making firm or strong, confirming, establishing as valid or genuine, vouching for, verifying, demonstrating, proving, and establishing. You are validating, asserting positively, and upholding.

The opposite of *affirm* is *negate*. Invalidate, nullify, neutralize, cancel, undo, reverse, void, rescind, countermand, or overturn. Plainly, "negate" is to "make negative in meaning." Who would intentionally want to sabotage their marriage relationship with these connotations?

When you don't *affirm* men, they'll seek affirmation elsewhere. Jim Burns, from HomeWord.com, said that the antidote to men's vulnerability is affirmation. To "men, affirmation from their wives is everything! ... When they receive regular and genuine affirmation from their wives (not flattery, by the way), they become much more secure and confident in all areas of their lives."[65] There you have it, from a man.

How are some of the ways you can *affirm* or "make firm" your marriage?

With the words you say. Make sure your words build and that every statement brings life and not death to your love.

By your actions. Strengthen your commitment with deeds. Kiss him when he doesn't expect it. Make his favorite dinner.

With your thoughts. The natural human tendency to obsess over your husband's weaknesses needs to be quelled if you are to affirm his strengths. It's not as if you are choosing to minimize his weaknesses, rather you are just making daily spiritual choices of focusing on qualities you are thankful for. "Obsessing over your husband's weaknesses won't make them go away," Leslie Vernick warns. "Regularly thinking negatively about your husband increases your dissatisfaction with him and your marriage. Affirming your husband's strengths, however, will likely reinforce and build up those areas you cherish and motivate him to pursue excellence of character in other areas."[66]

In *Sacred Influence,* Gary Thomas says that men love how it feels when their wives respect them, and "we [men] will but travel the ends of the earth to keep it [the praise and affirmation] coming."[67]

Choice Number Five: Thermometer or Thermostat?
Goal: To set the temperature rather than register the temperature.

Early in my marriage, I realized that I could be a thermostat instead of a thermometer. I could set the temperature in my home rather than register the temperature that someone else set. Do a test: when you see your husband, be exciting, excited, "UP," fun, cute, and winsome, and watch his attitude lift just by being around you. Then, if you dare, be nagging, ugly, mean, short, abrupt, faultfinding, and just plain miserable, and watch his attitude drop.

You can choose to be the thermostat every day: set the temperature of your home with your attitude. The sum of the whole will be even greater than the sum of each individual part because of the synergy and energy you create. Refuse to "read" others' attitudes and simply register the temperature someone else is setting in the room. If my husband has a bad day, I let him know, "You're home now; let's just enjoy our evening and leave that hard day behind you." When my children had a difficult day, I encouraged them to make it an *amazing* night then. Work on it. You alone choose your attitude! Watch how magnetic a buoyant attitude can be.

Choice Number Six: To Add Value or Subtract Value
Goal: To be sure that if you are around, it's Value Added.

My dad taught me to leave a place better than it was before I came. So if I stay in someone's home, I clean up after myself and leave a gift. If I go to a party, I help the host tidy up. I also want my life to affect people positively so I focus on *adding value* to others' lives.

When I eat at a restaurant, I thank the server for good service. When I am running, I tell other runners, "Good job!"

Unfortunately, the new "norm," that has infiltrated job hunting, playing sports, and a variety of other relationships is that individuals are more worried about what's in it for them than what they are bringing to the relationship. This attitude has seeped through to the church, too. Some people are more concerned and preoccupied with what a church offers than they are about what their particular gift can add to the church. This selfish attitude is not living a life that adds value to others.

How did we go from the marriage altar where we pledged all the things *we* were going to do for our spouse to whining and complaining about all the things our spouse *is not* doing for us?

In the workforce there is something called *Value Added Proposition* that I challenge you to incorporate into your relationships. R. M. Salley, business writer, describes *Value Added Proposition* as follows, but I have emphasized how it relates to our relationships in the underlined parts:

"Succinctly, the Value Added Proposition is what you bring to <u>your husband</u> that the next person doesn't. What makes you or what you have to offer unique and worthwhile? You should be able to sum up your VAP in as few words as possible … preferably ten words or less, although some will argue that it should be even fewer words. Your VAP is a personal version of a mission statement. In much the same way that a mission statement should be clear and concise, so should your Value Added Proposition. In effect, <u>what is it that makes you different, the reason your husband was sold on you?</u> As your experience changes, so will your VAP. <u>If your husband asked</u> the age-old WIIFM factor…'What's in it for me?' <u>why would he want you to be his wife, what are you going to provide to him?</u> So, I ask each and every one of you to sit down and figure out your Value Added Proposition."[68]

Why do so many people make it easier to live without them than with them? Do not let that person be you. Make sure that when you leave the room, your absence is felt, your presence is missed, and it's just not the same (in a good way) than if you were around. Think of some of the people you know that make a positive impact on you whenever they are around. It can be just their sweet presence, the fact that their conversation is interested, interesting, and uplifting, their ability to draw people into a conversation, or to connect with people one on one. Think of other people that have the adverse effect: it is as if they are Eeyore walking around with a cloud over their head, finding the negativity in everything. I've been around people that complain so much that I feel like I am carrying a burden once they leave the room.

I learned a valuable lesson that changed me from a complainer to an uplifter. My Uncle had taken me out on his speedboat. It was a beautiful day, but I found enough to complain about that he felt I was a cloud over the sun. He pulled the boat over at the nearest dock, which was about 20 miles from my car, and dropped me off. He let me know he couldn't let me ruin his day by my complaining. I was stuck finding a ride back to my car. Although his actions were extreme, it made an indelible impression on me to not spoil a beautiful day by my negative attitude.

Choice Number Seven: Look for Good vs. Look for Bad
Goal: To find the good in others and situations.

You will find what you are looking for. Once I taught my daughter Christa's class using a bouquet of gorgeous irises (my favorite flower) to illustrate this concept. I asked half the group to come to the front of the room, examine the irises, and tell everything good about the flowers. They noticed how vibrant the flowers were, the intricate details of the double flower, the contrast of the pistils, and the interesting little fuzzy beard on the sepals. Then I asked the other half of the class to tell me everything wrong with the irises. They noticed that some of the sepals were discolored, a few leaves were broken and brown, a few petals were broken off or bent, and some of the double flowers were wilting and shriveling. Each half of the group found what they were looking for.

I told my children that if they wanted to find reasons why I am a wonderful mom, they'd have plenty to list. However, if they wanted to find reasons why I *wasn't* a wonderful mom, they'd be able to do that as well. You will find what you are looking for.

The concept is true with your husband. What are you looking for? Observe the good qualities and you will find them. Examine his faults and you will uncover all. Appreciate the wonderful qualities

151

in your husband, and *celebrate them*. Be sure that these are the things you talk about with family and friends.

Focus only on the good; refuse to focus on what is lacking. Write your own love story. Verbalize everything you appreciate. Flirt by saying what you love about your spouse out loud.

Choice Number Eight: Choose Joy or Choose Misery
Goal: To cultivate a life of joy.

Choose joy. Joy is a choice. In spite of your circumstances, choose joy. It is not the abundance of things that will make you happy. I call that idea the Hollywood principle—there are multitudes of people in Hollywood whose misery proves that even if you have material things, those things don't make you happy.

Learn to laugh. Joy can be expressed with laughter, but also laughter can expand your joy. Laughter is like medicine. "A cheerful heart brings a smile to your face; a sad heart makes it hard to get through the day." (Proverbs 15:13 THE MESSAGE)

"A keen sense of humor helps us to overlook the unbecoming, understand the unconventional, tolerate the unpleasant, overcome the unexpected, and outlast the unbearable." (Billy Graham)

Laughter, said Dr. William F. Fry of Stanford University, "stimulates the production of the alertness hormones catecholamines. These hormones in turn cause the release of endorphins in the brain. Endorphins foster a sense of relaxation and well-being and dull the perception of pain." Laughter's benefits include, "Decrease in stress hormone levels, Strengthening of the immune system, Muscle relaxation, Pain reduction, Lowering of blood pressure, Cardiovascular conditioning, and Natural anti-depressant."[69]

Do you know how to make your spouse laugh? Do you laugh at his jokes? Train yourself to see a bit of humor in tough situations. Develop a sense of humor. Sometimes it helps me keep my sense of humor by pretending I'm in a sitcom; I find stressful situations much more comical. Once when my five children were ages four through nine, they had upper respiratory infections, and I had to give them each a teaspoon of medicine. I had a new larger medicine dispenser, and because I was suffering from lack of sleep, I gave them a tablespoon instead of a teaspoon. When I realized it, I telephoned my pediatrician, who told me I had to give each of them syrup of ipecac to make them throw up the medicine. As I went child to child, knowing I was in for a rough time, I mentally removed myself from the situation and imagined watching the scene on a sitcom. It enabled me to see the humor in a terrible circumstance.

I quite often imagined our lives as a sitcom: I then saw the humor in a cartful of children ahead of me and grocery cart behind me while a potty-training toddler was unable to make it to the bathroom and went all over the aisle. I simply opened my paper towels from the cart and didn't miss a beat. I knew first hand some of the situations that sitcoms with many children would thrive on.

During the most stressful times of our lives, a sense of humor has brought us through. My husband is a very intense person, and over the years I have discovered little things that make him laugh and lighten up his intensity. Once we took a road trip to Disney when our children were ages four through eight. We had scrimped and saved, and had enough money to stay in the campground there. Our trailer suffered a flat tire. With difficulty we found a tire, but we waited hours to have it fixed in the heat of the day. We finally straggled into the campground well after midnight. We went right to work putting up our large tent and blowing up air mattresses. Then we discovered we had put the tent up backwards, and we had to cut a path in dense woods to jump into the tent. Although our nerves were frayed, I looked at my husband and opened my eyes widely and said, "Ummmm," and rolled my eyes. We both burst out laughing.

Sometimes, if my husband gets upset, I will open my eyes widely, put my four fingers between my teeth and look scared, and it is often enough to make him start laughing. Sometimes I will say, "Scary!" in a child's voice.

There are many gestures I have learned over the years to lessen intensity, and I have found that these gestures are much more effective than a shouting match or spouting off to diffuse an impassioned situation.

It is wise, though, to avoid sarcasm in your sense of humor, because often sarcasm has a *bite* to it. Although it takes a little work and effort to live with and practice a good sense of humor, a well-developed sense of humor is the *sunshine of the mind*.

"Those who bring sunshine to the lives of others cannot keep it from themselves!" (J. M. Barrie)

A sense of humor is a very developed sense of perspective that allows you to access joy even in adversity. In his article, *Developing Your Sense of Humor*, Joe Love states a few key elements:

> "Most of us have a tendency as to believe that any problem we are confronting and facing at particular moment is the most important thing that is going on in the world.

> "This way of looking at problems is a very heavy responsibility. It makes you feel as if the problem is everywhere and it becomes the focus of your being. This is why a developed sense of humor is so important, because it allows you to see

yourself in the scope of things rather than always at the center of things.

"When you look at things with a sense of humor perspective, it enables you to have a remarkable capacity to control how you see the things that are going on in your life. You cannot control the external events in your life, but you can control how you look at them.

"An important part of a developed sense of humor is the capacity to take yourself lightly, even though you may take your work or your problem very seriously. A sense of joy in being alive is an intimate component of the human will to live. It's not abstract, but it's not easy either, <u>you have to work at it</u>.

"The root form of humor is umar in Latin. It means to be fluid and flexible like water and that is what humor is about. It's staying flexible so you don't become broken by the difficulties you confront. Being flexible enables your creative mind to stay open so that you can still come up with solutions even in painful situations.

"...[M]ost adults over the age of 35 cannot write down more than three things that give that make them happy. They will invariably start off with something such as, my work, I love my work.

"Misery is not subtle. Pain is not subtle. Joy, humor, and laughter are very often subtle. So you have to pay attention to them to start activating them into your life and that's what this list will help you to do.

"Making a list of all the things that you enjoy and put a smile on your face will not only help develop your sense of humor but it also gives you the opportunity to find out more about the people in your life and what makes them happy and this will enable you to help them develop their sense of humor. When you are able to give other people joy and put a smile on their face, especially when they need it most, you will be giving them the greatest gift you can give."[70]

Develop your sense of humor. Bring humor into your life. Spread it to others. Give your spouse joy and put a smile on his face, especially when he needs it the most. When my husband is overworked and overdone, I will tell him, "You're not a *man,* you are a *machine!*" If he or someone starts lamenting on their problems, I recite a few lines from "Me Monster" by a favorite comedian that we watch on YouTube, Brian Regan.[71] When I fell and broke my arm in three places the day before our family was flying to Florida, I put a bright pink cast on and had Tigger autograph it. Laugh and look for the bright side, or even the other side of problems: deal with the problems and then put the positive spin of a good sense of humor onto them whenever possible.

Choice Number Nine: To Encourage Yourself or Become Discouraged
Goal: To learn how to find strength to overcome trials in your life.

In the Old Testament, when David and his men returned to the city of Ziklag, they found that their wives and families and all their goods had been taken captive. On top of that, the men wanted to blame and stone David. David did what we need to do when we feel we're losing the battle:

"But David encouraged and strengthened himself in the Lord his God." (1 Samuel 30:6 AMP)

After he encouraged and strengthened himself in the Lord, David had the courage and strength to go to battle, and he took back everything the enemy tried to steal from him. The word *encourage* comes from an old French word, and means to literally "put in strength," while *discourage* means to "take strength away."

Whenever I am discouraged, don't have the right answers to get through to the other side of the storm, am distressed, or am sad, I encourage and strengthen myself in the Lord.

The Word of God is true; in His presence alone is fullness of joy found, and in His presence is strength.

"You will show me the path of life; in Your presence is fullness of joy, at Your right hand there are pleasures forevermore." (Psalm 16:11 AMP)

"Honor and majesty are [found] in His presence; strength and joy are [found] in His sanctuary." (1 Chronicles 1:27 AMP)

God is there to impart wisdom: He is the *only* the *true source of wisdom*. He has the answers for my situation, and will guide me through to the victory side.

"If any of you needs wisdom to know what you should do, you should ask God, and he will give it to you. God is generous to everyone and doesn't find fault with them." (James 1:5 GW)

Too often, we lean on our own understanding rather than seek the Lord's ways. When we let Him come into our situation, we not only find joy and strength in His presence, but the wisdom and grace to do His will. Be of good cheer as you face trials and tribulations, He has overcome the world.

"I have told you these things, so that in Me you may have [perfect] peace and confidence. In the world you have tribulation and trials and distress and frustration; but be of good cheer [take courage; be confident, certain, undaunted]! For I have overcome the world. [I have deprived it of power to harm you and have conquered it for you.]" (John 16:33 AMP)

What trials and tribulations do you face today? Are you losing strength to deal in any areas of your life? Are you losing your joy? Encourage and strengthen yourself in the Lord. Spend time in His presence as much as possible and seek His wisdom above all else. Let His peace keep your heart and guard your mind. Take back what the enemy tried to steal from you.

Choice Number Ten: To Work Hard or Hardly Work
Goal: To know that in order to enjoy the fruit of your labors, you must labor.

Ecclesiastes 4:9 (KJV) tells us that, "Two are better than one because they have a good reward for their labour!" The reward comes from *their labor.* Psalm 128:2 (AMP) tells us, "For you shall eat [the fruit] of the labor of your hands; happy (blessed, fortunate, enviable) shall you be, and it shall be well with you."

I have a plot in my back yard for my garden. If I do nothing, weeds and garbage will drift in and overpopulate the ground. I need to till the soil, fertilize the ground, plant the right seeds, and get rid of the weeds and pests in order to grow anything worthwhile. The Bible says, "Farmers who wait for perfect weather never plant. If they watch every cloud, they never harvest." (Ecclesiastes 11:4 TLB)

If you are planting seeds of misery, discontent, boredom, complaint, criticism, and fault-finding, your harvest is not going to be a good one, because nothing good will grow from these seeds. You can't plant one seed and expect to grow a different harvest. This is such a simple law of the land, but it stymies so many people. Be aware of the seeds you plant today in your relationships, because those seeds are tomorrow's harvest. Assuredly.

Be ready to work. If you think you are coasting, you're either losing momentum or else you're headed downhill.

Choice Number Eleven: To Commit or Disavow
Goal: To show the diligence of commitment in your life.

Commit is from the Latin word *committere,* which means to unite, connect, bring together. So what does *commitment* in a marriage mean?

Mitch Temple, from *Focus on the Family,* gives a way to consider your level of commitment.

"Ask yourself the following:

- Has your marriage been on auto-pilot for so long that neither you nor your spouse have a clue where you're headed?
- Where would you like to see your marriage go this year?
- Are you committed to making positive changes?
- Do you expect your marriage to get better by doing the same things you did last year?
- How committed are you to your marriage for the long haul?
- How committed is your spouse to your marriage?"[72]

What does *commitment* really mean? Mitch Temple goes on to define commitment as three levels:

"...Dr. Michael P. Johnson, Sociology Professor at Penn State University, views the decision to continue in a relationship as a function of three different experiences, or levels, of commitment — personal, moral and structural."[72]

The three levels of commitment are personal (I want to), moral (I ought to), and structural (I have to). Temple states that our marriage benefits from having all three levels of commitment in place, as Ecclesiastes 4:12 (NKJV) states, "A threefold cord is not quickly broken."

Consider ham and eggs; the chicken was *involved*, the pig *committed*. Commitment is laying down your life continually. It is not a decision made at the altar and then forgotten about; rather, it is a decision that must be made daily. Commitment rises above emotions and feelings and is not situational. Your heart needs to be dedicated to it, your words need to showcase it, and your actions and priorities need to prove it.

Commitment can be undermined or devalued by words and actions. Are your words and actions are in line with your commitment? If you are struggling, seek wise counsel and accountability from someone who is strong and victorious in this area.

When you have no strength or will to stay committed, when all three levels of commitment are missing, you need supernatural strength and love from the Source to live out your vows. "I have strength for all things in Christ Who empowers me [I am ready for anything and equal to anything through Him Who infuses inner strength into me; I am self-sufficient in Christ's sufficiency]." (Philippians 4:13, AMP) When you don't even have the *will* to live it out, ask God for it, knowing that it is "[Not in your own strength] for it is God Who is all the while effectually at work in you [energizing and creating in you the power and desire], both to will and to work for His good pleasure and satisfaction and delight." (Philippians 2:13 AMP)

The opposite of commitment is *disavow,* which means to deny any responsibility or support for, to disclaim, repudiate, disown, renounce. It comes from the Latin words *dis-* meaning opposite of and *avoer,* which means accept, acknowledge, recognize. Commitment is like cement that solidly holds your relationship together; if it isn't solidly in place in your relationship, you are renouncing, or repudiating, your husband.

When you deny support, you disassociate. Commitment links you, and disavowing unlinks you. I like to picture a circle made with a rope to determine whether my actions, words, and thoughts bring my husband *into* the circle or keep him *outside* of it. If you find yourself belittling, correcting, and undermining your husband's work, hobbies, actions, or character, you are breaking down the cement of commitment that links you together.

Choice Number Twelve: Selfish or Unselfish
Goal: To live with your husband preferring his needs above your own.

Are you selfish or self-less? God made us in His image and likeness. We are made to give. Unfortunately, our society has bent and molded and shaped us to get all you can, look out for Number 1, and go for the gusto. We need to be re-trained to think as the Lord thought: to humble ourselves, to deny ourselves, to consider others better than ourselves, and to love without expecting anything in return. (See Philippians 2.)

This type of unselfishness looks for ways to daily deny ourselves, consider our mate's needs above our needs, and sacrificially love, with supporting and convincing actions, without expecting anything in return.

Being selfish is being concerned only with yourself and your advantage to the exclusion of others. Being unselfish is disregarding your own advantages and welfare to consider those of others. It is the life of a champion: the denial of your present day do-whatever-you-feel-like-doing for the greater good, with the ultimate goal in mind. Olympic athletes sacrifice and commit to achieve what others cannot because the ultimate treasure is the gold medal. Wives and husbands sacrifice and commit to achieve success and victory in marriage and to reach the golden anniversary and beyond.

Your marriage will not be truly successful unless you learn to be unselfish. I wonder if the Lord thought something like this: "It is such a short life for my children to decide their eternal destiny. They need to take on my character, which is supreme love, and to walk with Me. What is the best way to accomplish that goal: hmmm, I'll institute marriage. They'll need to be unselfish or their marriage simply will not work."

Choice Number Thirteen: Leave Him Out or Let Him In
Goal: To make it easy for your spouse (or any one) to come "back in" after a problem.

When your spouse acts stupidly, is crabby or angry, it is easy to shut him out. When he realizes he was wrong, he may opt to change his mind and attitude, but you won't let him "back in." Give others a chance to change their minds or change their moods without closing them out. My husband can get very passionate about things that go wrong. Being very solutions-minded, he gets frustrated quickly if solutions fail. Because he is used to accomplishing a lot in small fragments of time, he can pepper statements like a machine gun. After he settles down, he wants to make the most out of his free time. I need to allow him to change downshift without hanging his earlier displays of frustration over his head. If I held grudges for the way he hammered statements out earlier, I would lose a great many memorable evenings.

Make it easy for someone to come back in to the night after he has been acting unreasonably. A lot of times someone will realize how he or she has been acting, but by then the night is ruined because the other person won't capitulate, or they have to make (or stress) a *point.*

Be gracious, and make it easy for your spouse to change his mind or heart if he needs to: make it easy to come back in to your happy relationship so that you can enjoy the rest of the day or night and have a great time together.

"We all make choices, but in the end our choices make us."[73]

Chapter 9

Changing is a Work of Heart

A famous prayer attributed to Reinhold Niebuhr says, "God, grant me the serenity to accept the things I cannot change, the courage to change the things I can, and the wisdom to know the difference."

Change takes courage. Change is difficult for me, yet I force myself to live outside my comfort zone and constantly change and tweak my behavior and my mind. The Bible says that if in me "there has been no change [of heart],… I …do not fear, revere, and worship God."[74] If we are to go from "glory to glory"[75] and my path is as one "that shines more and more (brighter and clearer) until [it reaches its full strength and glory in] the perfect day,"[76] then change is mandatory.

Using the acrostic Work of Heart, let's look at a few dynamics of change.

W – Walk the Talk.

You cannot give what you don't have. If you find that you are out of love, patience, joy, or any other character quality you need to give, what do you do?

Many women dedicate themselves to pursuing excellence and beauty physically, socially, emotionally, academically, and in careers.

Unfortunately, as they achieve these high objectives, these same women fail to make time to develop spiritually. Since your spirit is something that cannot be seen, it is easy to overlook. Yet our spiritual well being not only determines our eternal destiny, but also determines our vision, pursuits, and priorities in life.

When God chose a word picture to describe our role, He chose to describe life as a battlefield and to describe us as soldiers. We are in a battle, and the battle is for our souls and our eternal destiny.

"Fight the good fight of the faith; lay hold of the eternal life to which you were summoned and [for which] you confessed the good confession [of faith] before many witnesses." (1 Timothy 6:12 AMP)

Maybe you can't imagine yourself as a soldier. Maybe you feel your life is more like a merry-go-round with nothing but blue skies, rainbows, and cotton candy. Or you realize that you need to be equipped to fight for your family, but you are unaware of how to be trained and feel ill equipped and insufficient. Maybe you feel as if you are in a losing battle and there is no way you can be victorious.

The One who created you longs to have a deep relationship with you. Our sin separated us from God, and the wages of sin is death. But because of God's love, He sent Jesus, His one and only Son, to pay the penalty for our sin. Whoever believes in Him and accepts His forgiveness has the gift of eternal life. When we receive and believe in Him, then we become His children.

He longs for a relationship with us, and waits for your response to His sacrifice and invitation.[77]

When we walk with Him, …His "divine power has bestowed upon us all things that [are requisite and suited] to life and godliness, through the [full, personal] knowledge of Him Who called us by and to His own glory and excellence (virtue). By means of these He has bestowed on us His precious and exceedingly great promises, so that through them you may escape [by flight] from the moral decay (rottenness and corruption) that is in the world because of covetousness (lust and greed), and become sharers (partakers) of the divine nature." (2 Peter 1:3-4 AMP)

His divine nature becomes yours as His child, your sins are forgiven, and you are a new creation. His truth sets you free, and you have peace. Although you have trials, you become an overcomer and even *more* than a conqueror. You can do all things through him, and He strengthens you and equips you.[77] We can then, as part of His army, "Be strong and courageous. …Someone greater is on our side. …the LORD our God is on our side to help us and fight our battles." (2 Chronicles 32:7-8 GW)

God says, "They're mine, all mine. They'll get special treatment when I go into action. I treat them with the same consideration and kindness that parents give the child who honors them. And know that Jesus has the last word on everything and everyone, from angels to armies. He's standing right alongside God, and what he says goes." Because of His power in us, and at work in us, He will "do superabundantly, far over and above all that we [dare] ask or think [infinitely beyond our highest prayers, desires, thoughts, hopes, or dreams]…"[78]

Accepting God's forgiveness and having a personal relationship with Him is the biggest decision you will ever make in your life. As we apply ourselves to the disciplines required for extraordinary relationships, it needs to be acknowledged that the Source of everything we need is found in God through Jesus Christ. When you receive His love and forgiveness, He empowers you to love others as He has loved you. If you have accepted his forgiveness and love and desire to walk through life with the One Who created you, I would love to know about it and celebrate with you.

We need tools to build strong marriages and other relationships, and to make them strong. Our tools include forgiveness, humility, patience, and self-restraint. When a carpenter needs a certain tool, he gets it. He doesn't abandon the building project. When you realize you lack the necessary tools to build better relationships, you need to find out how to get the tool(s) you need.

Physically, this concept is easier to comprehend than spiritually. For example, when my baby cried because he was hungry, if I didn't have anything to feed him, I had to go get something right away.

The same principle applies spiritually and in character attributes. When my toddlers began to become impatient or easily angered, I realized that in order to equip them with the character attributes they needed to get through their frustrations, first I had to *demonstrate* the attributes I desired to pass on to my children in my own life. This was particularly fun with toddlers and younger children, because I could get so dramatic with them. I'd ask them, "Is this what I do when I have to wait for something?" and then I'd over-react as they had. I'd then elaborately demonstrate the correct way to react. As I taught them how I walked in victory in the areas they struggled with, I saw that if I had not learned how to deal with my frustrations correctly, there would be no way I could teach my children how to deal with *their* frustrations correctly.

Picture a toolbox at the end of your bed depicting the tools you need to handle tough situations. Purpose to add to your toolbox what you need for successful relationships. Tools such as forbearance, forgiveness, patience, understanding, kindness, and believing the best are qualities that help you navigate rough waters in relationships. If you are not sure of the tools you lack, don't worry... the situations in your life that are handled incorrectly will quickly let you know what you are missing. For example, when someone cuts me off in traffic or I have to wait longer than expected in a checkout line, I see by my response that I need forbearance and patience. It is important when you notice that you need this positive character that you purposefully "pick up that tool" and use it! No excuses.

Picture each of your children having a large empty toolbox at the end of their beds. Throughout the day, you fill their toolboxes with the same tools you use for life situations. When your children leave your home, they take their "toolbox" with them, equipped for their lives and their futures with what you have given and demonstrated to them. In *Time to Be in Earnest,* P.D. James said, "What a child doesn't receive he can seldom later give."

Are you equipped with the right tools to handle troublesome situations? This week, count each situation you come across as a training ground: every little frustration, every set-back, every time you don't get your own way, see an opportunity to find out what tools you need to be more successful in relationships. Challenge yourself to grow into a higher level of maturity so you can live your life using the tools you have and getting the tools you need.

O – Outer vs. Inward Appearance

In the book of 1 Samuel, the prophet Samuel was looking for a king for Israel. Jesse gathered all his older sons together. When Samuel saw Eliab, he thought for sure this good looking, strong man was the one chosen to be the next king. But the Lord said to Samuel, "Look not on his countenance, or on the height of his stature, because I have refused him: for the Lord seeth not as a man seeth; for man looketh on the outward appearance, but the Lord looketh on the heart." (1 Samuel 16:7 KJV)

We see outwardly, yet the Lord looks at the heart. I have learned that there is always more than meets the eye when it comes to relationships. When I was younger, I was impetuous and often acted or spoke before I thought. There were many repercussions. My parents did not let my actions undermine their love for me. Because of their response, I felt truly repentant. If they had only seen the outside, they would never have known my heart. My parents gave me a chance to change my mind and my attitude, believing in the better part of me that couldn't yet be seen, except through eyes that chose to believe the best.

I see potential as a part of who I am, because as I am inspired to live up to my potential—it becomes a part of me. I see potential as part of who my husband is too, for the same reason.

I was inspired by my parents' belief in me. When my mom told me her perspective on something, she would also say, "I know you will make the right choice." Even though I didn't always make the right choice, her belief in me inspired me to choose more carefully and wisely. She inspired me by not seeing only my actions, but appealing to my *heart*, which is where my actions originated.

Because we know that we can't see someone's heart, we need to act on what we *do* know about the unseen heart: that our husband or children or even we ourselves can't be happy when we are unforgiving, ugly, or mean to others. You can say to your husband "I know you can't have a happy heart when you talk to me like that!" This is such a great appeal while training children when they are unkind: teach them to pay attention to how their heart feels, and let them recognize the feelings of not having a happy heart—and conversely how good your heart feels when you do the right things.

Expect the best from your husband and your children. Let your husband know what you believe, and tell him, "You are a good man; I trust you will choose correctly."

There is something incredibly significant about someone who believes in us. These are the ones who inspire us to chase a dream and run after the seemingly impossible. Marlo Thomas compiled a book titled, *The Right Words at the Right Time*[79] that recounts moments in people's lives when just the right words said at the right time became life changing. Sometimes a family member said the words, sometimes a teacher or coach, sometimes it was words on the radio, or even words spoken in passing by a stranger.

Why don't you remind your spouse of his successes and choose to cheer him on, despite his weaknesses? Why not become his inspiration and the person who inspires him? When you inspire him, he will aspire to more. Words kill, words give life; they're either poison or fruit—you choose.[80]

If you choose to believe in your husband, you can inspire him to achieve more than he thought he could. When I am running, spectators cheering on the sidelines help me pick up my pace. I lift my head and run faster than I normally would. In the same way, you can remind your husband of strength inside of him that he hadn't remembered or realized was there. You can remind him of who he was created to be just when he needs to hear it the most.

Focusing on the best in your husband helps him see his potential, capture a vision, develop a mission statement, or see the possibilities. Mediocre lives are lived by those who don't believe they have what it takes to live extraordinary lives—someone in their corner cheering them on, encouraging them, and believing in them.

Who are the people who believed in you, and what effect did they have in your life? Can you believe in your husband and change his life for the better?

"I learned from my grandfather that when someone believes in you before you deserve it, it transforms you." – Kris Vallotton[81]

In 1 Corinthians 13, God calls us to this kind of love: "Love bears up under anything and everything that comes, is ever ready to believe the best of every person, its hopes are fadeless under all circumstances, and it endures everything [without weakening]. Love never fails [never fades out or becomes obsolete or comes to an end]…" (1 Corinthians 13:7-8 AMP)

I thought the best line in the movie *Divine Secrets of the Ya-Ya Sisterhood,* came from Sidda Walker (played by Sandra Bullock). She asked her dad, "Did you get loved enough?"[82] That question made me wonder if my husband had been loved enough. If he hasn't, the lack is from me. I prayed for my sons' future wives—that they would love my sons like I do—the way they may lift an eyebrow when they are wondering something, the passion they speak with, their expressions, the way the interact with people, the hair that falls into little curls on their forehead: the little quirks and habits I love so much about them. Have you loved your husband enough? Do you notice his cute idiosyncrasies any more? The busyness of life can keep us from delighting in our husband.

My mom always loved so many cute little habits and actions of my Dad. My mom used her special gift of making everything seem way better than it is to appreciate my Dad. There were many times when she would call our attention to how precious my Dad looked when he would lay his head in his crooked arm to sleep. She would constantly recite how he went to the store for her and then came home and worked alongside her to cook and clean. She impressed on us how my Dad didn't want her to scrub the pots and pans so he always did it. A week couldn't go by without my Mom letting us know something good about my Dad. Now that my Dad has passed on, she tells us over and over that no one ever had such a husband as hers. Look for your husband's special quirks; it will help you to love your husband "enough"… or even more than enough.

> "While we may not be able to control all that happens to us, we can control what happens inside us." Benjamin Franklin[83]

R – Respect and Respectable

Respect for the other person is essential in a relationship. Even when you can't respect someone's actions, you can respect the position they hold. I have chosen to respect my husband and children. If you want your marriage to get better, you need to look for the attributes in your husband that you can, and do, respect. Is he a good father? Does he help around the house? What do you admire? If you always have some positive feelings for him, it will be an incentive for him to become a better man.

Don't forget that if you look down on him, most likely he knows, whether you verbalize it or not. Often, when we feel that another person thinks poorly of us, we don't even *want* to try to change their mind. We may even feel that it would be impossible, or not worth the effort, to try to win the other person over. If your husband feels that no matter what he does you won't be happy, then he won't even bother trying. "It's important for women to realize that for a man to be in a marriage where his wife isn't happy, that has to be the most crushing thing in the world. He feels like he is the source of her happiness. When she's not happy, then he must be failing..."[84]

Respect for your husband and for your children is reinforced when you can show them that you respect others in general. Respect the teacher who is sending home a bad report about your child, and respect that teacher in front of your child, showing your child the great deal of respect you have for those in authority over them. Respect people that make a mistake while driving alongside you. Respect people you disagree with. Respect people in general, and your family will clearly see that you don't have to think people are perfect or without mistakes to give them respect.

What is *respect?* It is showing honor, regard, esteem, and deference. It is being considerate.

> 1 John 4:20-21 (THE MESSAGE) says, "If anyone boasts, 'I love God,' and goes right on hating his brother or sister, thinking nothing of it, he is a liar. If he won't love the person he can see, how can he love the God he can't see? The command we have from Christ is blunt: Loving God includes loving people. You've got to love both."

When you respect others and yourself, you will earn the trust of your family. They will know they can talk to you about anything. Here are a few tips to help you earn your husband and family's trust:

- Do not speak negatively about them to others.

- Do not ever, never, no–matter–what share a secret someone told you. Let it be their secret to share with whom and when they choose.
- Give impartial advice; consider the other person's viewpoint too.
- Give your full attention; showing what concerns them is important to you.
- Have their back—if someone says something about your husband or child, believe the best not the worst. Under no circumstances, even if the problem is true, should you ever trash talk your child or husband. If you "throw them under the bus," they may never get over it.

Earn the trust of your husband and children. It is the best bridge you can build to their hearts.

K – Kindness

Women often are especially careful about what they feed their family, opting for healthy nourishing foods. I wish more wives and mothers would be concerned about how they poison the family's thoughts and minds by the way they talk about other people.

Poisoning hope in your family is destructive. Hearing parents criticize others spreads toxins in the home. Keeping the television on constantly destroys creativity in your family. Polluting love in your family fractures relationships with friends and family. Failing to forgive cripples your family. There are so many examples of ways you can poison your family with wrong attitudes and actions; think of ones that *you* need to address.

Holding grudges and retaliating will not only be like poison ivy that spreads over your heart, but will defile other relationships besides the one you are reacting to. It will also stop you from receiving God's blessing. This principle is so important that it is mentioned three times specifically in Scripture (1 Thessalonians 5:15; Romans 12:17 and 1 Peter 3:9).

> "Summing up: Be agreeable, be sympathetic, be loving, be compassionate, be humble. That goes for all of you, no exceptions. No retaliation. No sharp-tongued sarcasm. Instead, bless—that's your job, to bless. You'll be a blessing and also get a blessing. Whoever wants to embrace life and see the day fill up with good, Here's what you do: Say nothing evil or hurtful; Snub evil and cultivate good; run after peace for all you're worth. God looks on all this with approval, listening and responding well to what he's asked; But he turns his back on those who do evil things. If with heart and soul you're doing good, do you think you can be stopped? Even if you suffer for it, you're still better off. Don't give the opposition a second thought. Through thick and thin, keep your hearts at attention, in adoration before Christ, your Master. Be ready to speak up and tell anyone who asks why you're living the way you are, and always with the utmost courtesy. Keep a clear conscience before God so that when people throw mud at you, none of it will stick. They'll end up realizing that they're the ones who need a bath." (1 Peter 3.8 – 16 THE MESSAGE)

Be careful of what you feed your family on the table, for sure, but be extra careful of how you poison your family's character by how you act. If you have allowed poison to creep into your home, detox immediately and instead, offer kindness and gentleness and grace.

In bringing kindness into your homes follow these guidelines:

- Choose to believe the best about people.

Believing the best in others pulls the best from them. Human capacity and potential is underneath the surface. James E. Faust said, "It is a denial of the divinity within us to doubt our potential and our possibilities."[85] I am intimately acquainted with many people that have overcome extreme abuse as children and have "reversed the curse" with their own children. Instead of using past torment as an excuse to fail, they have made it a reason not to fail. Knowing these successes strengthens me to continually try to see potential in lives I touch.

- Go the extra mile for the people you love the most.

When I was working in the corporate world, my husband asked me for a cup of coffee one night. I was indignant. We were both equal distance from the coffee, and we had both worked hard all day. Why should I get coffee for him? I told him that while he was getting his, maybe he could get one for me. The next day at work, my selfishness surfaced. I was a legal assistant with two assistants working directly for me, and we were holding a large closing. I had the two girls scurrying around making copies and putting closing packets together. I had a lot of important things to do, but my boss asked me to get coffee for the entire closing group. Without hesitation I took orders and got the coffee and served it. Then it hit me: what kind of person was I that I would do something for money but would not do it for love. I made a decision then and there that if I would do something at work to accommodate my boss or a client then I most certainly should do that and even more for the one I love!

- Let others have the freedom to speak and be listened to.

When others are speaking, allow them to express their feelings without contradicting them. I have been with people who have interrupted me to tell me I don't really feel a certain way. How does someone actually know my feelings better than I do, and, even if they did, why is it important enough to interrupt and contradict me in a casual conversation? Also, allow someone to share his or her experiences without "one-upping" them. If someone is sharing about his or her family vacation to Florida, rejoice and be interested; don't jump into the conversation to tell about your family's trip to Belize. If someone is telling how they had to get five stitches, don't overpower the conversation with your story about when you needed twenty stitches.

- Learn to give and take.

Let your husband know you will let him pick the restaurant, movie or game sometimes. You pick the game every other time instead of every time. Before you make dinner, ask your husband what he would like to eat. I asked our five of our children to chart their favorite foods and we took turns. On some nights, the family knew the food or activity someone else chose had to be tolerated. If you want to go see a movie, but your husband wants to see a playoff game at home instead, be considerate of his feelings. Learn to walk a mile in someone else's shoes. Allow your husband to enjoy his sports; and even better, enjoy them with him. Because your husband likes it is reason enough for you to choose it. Learn the joy of putting your husband's desires first.

- Let others make a mistake.

We all need grace, so we should be better at giving it. If your husband is talking about something and refers to last "Friday" when you know it was "Saturday," is it really that important to keep insisting that it was actually Saturday? If you already told him something before, is it really that important to announce it so everyone knows he wasn't paying attention or forgot the conversation? We have all heard a couple arguing about details totally irrelevant to the point being made. The awkwardness of the couple arguing eclipses the conversation. It is awkward for everyone when two people start correcting each other about insignificant details in a conversation. Learn to allow others to tell their version of something without correcting them.

- Live so you're missed when you're not there.

Would your husband really miss you when you're not home, instead of saying, "Whew, I finally have a break because she's busy tonight!"? One of my favorite sayings I recite to my family is: "You should be a 'plus' sign, not a 'minus' sign." When my husband is home, he is constantly putting things away, fixing burnt out light bulbs, oiling squeaky doors, snaking clogged drains, and other behind-the-scenes niceties. He meets me at the car to bring in groceries and carries bags when we shop. When we go to the airport, he handles his luggage and some of mine. When I'm not with him, not only do I miss his company, but I also miss how much he considers and helps me. I like to keep uplifting music on, a cheerful attitude, and a helpful hand ready so that when I'm not there I know my husband misses me. I taught my children to be sure if they missed a day at school, and later work, that they would be missed because their upbeat, encouraging and helpful attitude was such a "plus" sign.

There is another side to kindness too. Romans 2:4 reminds us that it is the goodness or kindness of God that leads us to repentance (real change). If you ever want your husband or children or any one to change, it will not be as a result from your nagging, obsessive demands or ugly behavior. That kind of behavior tends to justify others' improper behavior.

When teenagers break family rules, many parents scream, call names, and carry on. The teens roll their eyes and think, "I have a psycho parent." Why should they change their behavior? It costs them nothing for you to carry on. When you calmly inform them they have lost privileges because of their behavior, it is much more effective. When they can't focus on your erratic behavior, they must focus on their behavior.

To illustrate, I know that whenever someone yells at me, or gets out of control trying to communicate to me, I pay more attention to how *they* are out of control rather than listening to what they are saying about *my* wrong actions. When I want to effectively communicate, I communicate in such a way that the other person has to look at the way they handled the situation without being distracted by the way I communicate the problem.

It is as if you are both on even ground and the one person falls short. The other person says, "I'll get even with you," and virtually falls short to the lower level! It is better to hold your ground and character and bring the other person back up to a solid communication level!

When you desire change for your husband or child, be sure you don't communicate it in a way that distracts because they have contempt for the way you communicate. Remember that it is your kindness that will lead to true repentance and change.

H – Hear the Heart Behind the Words

> "The things people say come from inside them."
> Luke 6:45 (GW)

What our husband talks about and the way those words are said should become a gauge, giving us cues for where to target our heart work.

Proverbs 20:5 (NASB) reminds us, "The purpose in a man's heart is like deep water, but a man of understanding will draw it out."

A woman should have a great propensity to draw out her husband's purposes and discover his inner feelings. Pay attention to the words he says, and see if you can creatively discern what his heart is saying underneath the words. A woman who only takes words at face value will not only miss out on many opportunities to know and understand others, but will also miss out on knowing what direction and role to take.

E – Evaluate

Continuous improvement requires systematic and unfiltered evaluation. Evaluation is stepping back to gather information that will provide useful feedback and equip you to assess the worth or merit of what is being evaluated.

Evaluation gathers pertinent facts in order to make a balanced assessment. If you step back to evaluate your marriage relationship, you should be able to see what temporarily adversely affects your relationship. Your assessment will be more realistic in reflecting the short- or long-term challenges facing you as a couple. You will be able to better interpret challenges and barriers and know how to address them more realistically.

In an effective evaluation, after you gather the information, you analyze it and conceptualize alternative actions or strategies to deal with any problems, issues, or concerns. Evaluations are put into place for those who are forward looking and desire changes in order to achieve a desired outcome.

- Do you know what your husband is wrestling with; what is he challenged by?
- Are there steps that need to be put in place to help your husband with accountability or help to get through a problem that he is not able to solve alone?

- Is there anything *you* need to work on to improve your understanding or strengthen your relationship?
- What can you implement to get you to your desired outcome of oneness in your relationship?

A – Action Plan.

If you're not getting better, you're getting worse.

The plan of God is for us to get better and better: "All of us! Nothing between us and God, our faces shining with the brightness of his face. And so we are transfigured much like the Messiah, our lives gradually becoming brighter and more beautiful as God enters our lives and we become like him." (2 Corinthians 3:18 THE MESSAGE)

Develop measureable steps of action that will make you accountable to keep working on challenges and problems.

Remember that changing bad habits into good ones takes time and effort. When Psalm 119:105 (GW) refers to God's Word being a "lamp for my feet and a light for my path," it is referencing a foot lamp that illuminates the next step on the path in the darkness. After you take that step, then the next step becomes illuminated. Too often when we decide we need change, we want to get dropped off at the destination instead of heading there step-by-step. Be patient in the process and handle change one step at a time to get to the desired outcome.

R – Remember

One of the best parts about long-term relationships is walking through different seasons of life together. My siblings and I grew up in the same house, had the same beginning, and have experienced all life's situations together side-by-side. I have years of memories stored in my heart with my parents.

I've been with my husband through the three-piece suit and mustache phase, the excited but unsure new father stage, to the senior executive he is now. I appreciate the history we have together. Do you? Remember the good times. Remember the tough situations you've made it through already. Remember the challenges you faced together. Let those memories make you strong for today and the future.

T – Time

Building good relationships takes time. A lot of time. If you and your spouse have drifted apart, you can definitely track it to the lack of time. When have you taken a walk together? When have you talked without interruptions? Quality time is only found in quantity time.

It takes a lot of talking to stay on the same page with your husband. Iron sharpens iron, and when it does, sparks can fly. Do not try to take the easy way out and avoid discussion because you disagree; instead talk through every tough situation. Until you come to terms together. Maybe sparks will fly. If so, let them. Discussion will help you find solutions.

Change Requires Consistency

Consistency is day-to-day habits. Daily you must conceptualize that you are sowing seeds that will yield your tomorrows' harvests. Sowing the right seeds daily yields the right harvests. Ecclesiastes 11:4 says, "He who observes the wind [and waits for all conditions to be favorable] will not sow, and he who regards the clouds will not reap." Instead of making excuses, apologize quickly, and give lavish appreciation.

What are your most consistent habits? If you find yourself consistently criticizing or finding fault, ask God to help you overcome these tendencies; bask in His forgiveness for your many sins, and then freely give that kind of forgiveness to others. If you find yourself calling names, being sarcastic, or being insincere, examine what you are feeding yourself about relationships by way of the media. Television shows, sitcoms particularly, movies, songs, and plays undermine the value of relationships and the ability to nurture and maintain long-term relationships. If you are flooding yourself with such adverse media input, it will be more difficult for you to rise above the negative statistics to live differently.

Your life should be a consistent example of how love looks. Our love for one another proves that we are followers of Christ.[86] When we receive the grace God showers upon us, we will show His love to others. Fine-tune your people skills. Read good books on relationships. Listen to sermons. Fill yourself with good information, and then purposefully live it out.

> "When we are no longer able to change a situation – we are challenged to change ourselves."[87]

Chapter 10

Rules for Effective Communication

"A marriage can be likened to a large house with many rooms to which a couple fall heir on their wedding day. As we do with the rooms in a comfortable home, their hope is to use and enjoy these rooms, so that they will serve the many activities that make up their shared life. But in many marriages, doors are found locked – they represent areas in the relationships, which the couple is unable to explore together. Attempts to open these doors lead to failure and frustration. The right key cannot be found. So the couple resign themselves to living together in only a few rooms that can be opened easily, leaving the rest of the house, with all its promising possibilities, unexplored and unused.

> "There is, however, a master key that will open every door. It is not easy to find. Or, more correctly, it has to be forged by the couple together, and this can be very difficult. It is the great art of effective marital communication."[88]

Communication is the skill of sending and receiving messages. Communication is the process of sharing yourself, both verbally and nonverbally, in such a way that the other person can both accept and understand you. As you send and receive messages, you are able to climb inside someone's skin and get to know people from the inside out. A good communicator observes that feelings, attitudes, listening, and understanding all are an intrinsic part of communicating.

Communication is one of the most important factors for a successful marriage. If your marriage is a typical one, it's safe to say that you spend fewer than five minutes a day in real communication.

We want to become better communicators, but few people realize the efforts involved in accomplishing this noble goal. Our goal is *not* to make our spouse into a better communicator, but to become a better communicator.

Communication between husband and wife usually goes something like this. Husband walks in the door at night and greets wife:

"Hello! I'm home. How was your day?"

"Good," the wife responds.

"What time is dinner?"

"Half an hour."

Now what was really said in this conversation? "I don't want to talk about my day. I don't want to share my feelings. What I am concerned about is when I can eat dinner."

Generally, the amount and quality of communication between married couples reveals a lot about their marriage. Why aren't we better at communicating with each other?

Why We Don't Communicate

A. <u>We Don't Know How</u>.

Perhaps the most prevalent reason for non-communication is that we haven't learned the skill of communication. The husband who walks in the door with "Hi, honey! I'm home. What's for dinner? Where's the mail?" is showing that he isn't skilled at meaningful communication, nor does he really care. If we are not really interested in our mate's feelings, we aren't going to communicate with him or her.

Too much of the time, we marry and then communicate as we saw our parents, others' parents, or people on screen communicate. If we haven't seen many examples of good communication, we don't have anything to emulate, and we fall short of true interaction.

Large companies require employees to attend several classes, courses, or seminars on effective communication. No successful company takes the area of communication lightly. We, too, must realize the importance of communication in our marriage and learn how to more effectively communicate with each other.

God has made provision for us to relate openly and honestly with each other. He tells us in James 1:5 (GW), "If any of you needs wisdom to know what you should do, you should ask God, and he will give it to you. God is generous to everyone and doesn't find fault with them." Look to the Lord and the principles of His Word for effective communication precepts. When I felt my joy was waning, I studied Philippians because the word "joy" is listed in that small book of the Bible more than anywhere else in the Bible. When I felt I needed patience, I did a word study on "patience" with a Bible concordance to see what the Bible had to say about it. When you go to the Word of God for answers, you know that His Word will "not come back... without results" (Isaiah 55:11 GW). God will be faithful to do as He says in Psalm 32:8 (GW), "I will instruct you. I will teach you the way that you should go. I will advise you as my eyes watch over you."

B.   <u>We are Afraid.</u>

A second reason for not communicating in marriage is a fear of sharing what you really feel with your mate. If you tell your husband your deepest feelings, you may be concerned that he would somehow reject you, get upset, devalue your opinion, or just not care. Your spouse deserves to know your true opinion when he asks. You should be able to tell him if you disagree with a decision that will affect you or your family. You should not be afraid to open up to him and share who you really are and what you really feel. Many decisions should involve both of your opinions, and it's worth the effort to give your input and have it considered before decisions are made.

When you are afraid to communicate who you really are to your husband (the person closest to you), you run the risk of carrying this same errant communication roadblock in your other relationships as well, even your relationship with God. We act as if God wouldn't be able to forgive us if He knew who we really are. God is the God *He* says He is, our Creator, and He already knows who we really are. Instead of confessing to the One that knows us and loves us even in our weaknesses, we try to hide our feelings, fears, needs, frustrations, and apprehensions because we fear He will not be able to forgive us. God knows our weaknesses. He knows how we are tempted and our struggles, but His strength is strongest when we are weakest. We should glory in our weaknesses and infirmities because that's when His strength and power is the most: when we are weak in *human* strength we are most strong and powerful in *divine* strength![89]

It is important to reiterate that a weakness is sometimes a positive character trait that needs to be tweaked because it is being expressed in a negative form. For example, when we are nit-picky about others, it could be that we have a keen sense of discernment that needs to practice the *positive* side of that trait. If my feelings are hurt easily and I find myself getting offended often, it could be that I am sensitive, but I should be directing that sensitivity more to feeling for others instead of focusing on actions or words directed at me. My little kindergartener would break down if her printing went outside the lines; redirecting that attention to detail positively makes her an incredible dentist. Just look beneath any annoying personality lapses to see if they are strengths "in disguise."

If we are going to communicate openly and honestly, we must first be open and honest with the Lord, and then we can be more transparent with others. The Lord knows we are imperfect, and, believe me, so does your husband.

C.   It's Too Much Trouble.

Sometimes it is easier to avoid, suppress, and repress our thoughts and feelings than to take the time and effort to communicate them. We need to go through the trouble to communicate and to learn to communicate. The most childish and immature misunderstanding about marriage is simply that love is self-sustaining and that a good marriage comes about automatically because two good people marry one another. Once you get rid of that false notion, then you can make progress. Communication is a lot of work, but it is one of the most important keys for a successful marriage. Although communication is time consuming and requires a lot of effort, you can enjoy it. You will find that the work is worth it, because the one thing you will do for eternity is love, and one of the best ways to show your love is communicating.

D.   Our Self-Esteem is Low.

Some believe their opinions aren't worth expressing, especially if their opinions have been disregarded or devalued by people they cared about in the past. It is easy then to become turtle-like and pull back into your protective shell—if you don't communicate, your ideas can't be rejected or ignored. Your husband may feel the same way, if you have ridiculed, corrected, or ignored his ideas or comments. This kind of hurt can be buried inside and cause emotional and psychological problems. Eventually, resentment will surface in some ugly way.

Think of yourself as a teakettle on a stove with the steam being your emotions and feelings. If you don't have the opportunity to let out your emotions and feelings in a constant and free-flowing manner, then sooner or later you get to the point where you blow your top. Then, your communication becomes destructive. This smoldering is a very dangerous situation for marriage. Know your value and worth and let your husband know his. Take the time and effort to go through the trouble to communicate with your mate.

In order to communicate with someone else, we really must be able to be in touch with our own feelings and thoughts. For us to be secure enough to take the time to listen, we need to have an honest view of our self worth and be secure enough to consider someone else's posture. A friend of mine learned this first hand after she vehemently opposed her husband being involved with a church group. She was defensive because she didn't want him to be away from her one night a week. When she stepped back and realized the value of his decision, she realized that her insecurity of not having him home that one night each week was a small price to pay for the benefits her husband and the group he was involved with would receive from the commitment.

E.   <u>We Don't Think It Will Change Anything</u>.

Many times I choose to endure situations because I don't think my input will change the circumstances. If you ever feel this way, you must determine whether it is worth the effort to keep trying or if you need to let some matters go.

What is a Good Communicator?

1.   A Good Communicator Prays for Wisdom.

When you seek God's wisdom, you may find that your objection to your partner's behavior is not really valid. Or, you may sense the leading of the Spirit of God to communicate your problem. I often give myself at least a day to think it over and the problem doesn't seem as monumental after waiting.

2.   A Good Communicator Listens Carefully.

Communication usually breaks down when you fail to listen, to really hear, others. "He who answers a matter before he hears the facts, it is folly and shame to him." Proverbs 18:13 (AMP) What is *listening*? Paul Tournier said, "It is impossible to over-emphasize the immense need humans have to be really listened to. Listen to all the conversations of our world, between nations as well as those between couples. They are, for the most part, dialogues of the deaf."[90]

"The wise learn by listening;..." Proverbs 21:11 (AMP)

"Let every man be <u>quick to hear (a ready listener)</u>..." James 1:19 (AMP) God gave us *two* eyes, *two* ears, and only *one* mouth. Is it possible that listening is twice as important as speaking? True listening means that when another person speaks, I am not thinking about what I'm going to say when he stops talking. Instead, I concentrate on what he says. Listening is also complete acceptance without judgment of what is said or how it is said. Often you fail to hear the message because you don't like the choice of words or the tone of voice being used. You react and miss the meaning completely.

By acceptance, you do not have to agree with everything being said. Acceptance means that you understand that what the other person is saying is something he feels or thinks. Real listening means that you should be able to repeat what the other person has said and what you thought he was feeling when he was speaking to you.

Sperry Rand Corporation "brought to the attention of millions of people around the world the fact that most of us have never been trained how to listen. Because we do not listen, or we listen poorly, we frequently have breakdowns in communications."[91] The company developed an eight-hour listening workshop as a device to train their employees. The first agenda on the program is to convince people that they need help with their listening skills, because most people "believe that they listen much better than they actually do."[92] Some key barriers to listening are not being tuned in on someone's response, lack of sensitivity to feelings or emotions expressed, jumping to conclusions, personal pressures, prejudging the subject, and judging delivery and not content.

When big business learns that it pays to listen, we ought to take note. The bottom line for business is the increased productivity as a result of good listening habits. Because of their listening program, they create an awareness as to the importance of listening, make people more aware of the barriers to listening, so that they can be on guard to avoid or overcome them, help people identify their own personal, poor listening habits, and improve responsive listening skills.[92] We could revolutionize our marriages by simply listening to our husbands. Increase your productivity in your marriage and take the time to really listen.

3. A Good Communicator is Mature.

    a) <u>Plans a time that is good for her **husband**</u>**.** Usually you should not discuss anything serious or negative after 10:00 p.m. Life seems darker and problems loom greater at night. However, if you and your spouse are not both early risers or are rushing to meet deadlines in the morning, then the morning is not the best time either. Many couples find that after dinner is a good time for communication. Small children can make this time more difficult, but each couple needs to find a time when they are best able to look objectively at themselves and situations and work through issues. With busy schedules it helps to considerately ask the other person when a good time to discuss something important would be. Not only does this help schedule a convenient time for both parties, but it also prepares the other person that something is important enough for you to schedule a special time to discuss it.

    b) <u>Speaks the truth in love</u>. "The tongue has the power of life and death, and those who love to talk will have to eat their own words." (Proverbs 18:21 GW) Did you ever hear how people without a filter communicate truth? Sometimes they say something that may be true yet shouldn't be said quite the way they say it and at the time they say it. Words can be cruel, sharp, and hurtful. Consider what you want to accomplish before speaking. I get so upset when I hear someone blurt out hurtful or accusatory comments or negative things about people and there is no possible way anything good can come out of the situation. It's like air pollution.

Paul said "When I was a child, I talked like a child, I thought like a child, I reasoned like a child. Now that I have become a man, I am done with child<u>ish</u> [not "like"!] ways and have put them aside." (1 Corinthians 13:11 AMP, emphasis added.) In the verses before verse eleven, Paul listed the attributes of real love, and he closes those thoughts by saying, "If I am really going to love I cannot be childish; I need to be mature."

There is no way a child can know how to communicate love as described in 1 Corinthians 13. "Love is patient, love is kind, love isn't jealous, love doesn't sing its own praises, love isn't arrogant, love isn't rude, love doesn't think about itself, love isn't irritable, love doesn't keep track of wrongs, love isn't happy when injustice is done, but is happy with the truth, love never stops being patient, love never stops believing, love never stops hoping, love never gives up."[93] Can you imagine if all our communication followed those principles?

We need to "...<u>grow up</u> into Him in all things..." (Ephesians 4:15 KJV) We need to be mature and be considerate and careful of what comes out of our mouths. Be kind, and in kind words say what is on your heart. If your heart is ugly, go clean it up before you try to communicate from it.

c) <u>Is Sensitive to the Other's Feelings</u>.

Feelings are an important part of the messages you send and receive. They often communicate as much as your words. Communication improves when you share feelings as well as facts. Don't be afraid to share your innermost feelings with your spouse. You may say,

"Would you please get gas for my car?" or if you were to share your feelings you would say, "I am extremely uncomfortable getting gas alone at this time of night. Would you mind getting gas for my car?" Another example would be if you were hosting a party. Instead of asking your husband, "Would you please pick up a few things at the store?" you may share your feelings by saying, "I feel the burden of having guests over is all on me. Would you mind chipping in by picking a few things up from the store?"

When you share feelings, you must be open to the other person's viewpoint. There are many different ways to perceive the same situation. Think of how hunters, botanists, pilots, weather forecasters, vacationers, golfers, farmers, and fisherman perceive the weather so differently. Each person understands the weather's effect through his or her perspective. Be sensitive to the way your husband feels about things, especially if it is vastly different from the way you feel. If he is not in the habit of communicating his feelings with you, try to ask him how he feels about what he is communicating so he can get more used to telling you his feelings.

d) <u>Allows for reaction time</u>. Don't be surprised if your communication is met with an explosive reaction. You have the advantage in that you know what you are going to say; you have prayed over it and have prepared yourself. Your partner is taken by surprise. Don't defend yourself, but let your spouse think about what you have said.

4. A Good Communicator Knows Tone of Voice Influences Message Being Communicated.

Tone of voice expresses different messages using the same word, statement, or question. Our tone of voice is an essential part of how we communicate. If you are not aware of your tone of voice, use your phone to record some of your conversations. Play them back and pay attention to your tone of voice and what it implies.

Address your heart issues before you open your mouth. If your heart is right and your motive is right, your communication will most likely have the right tone necessary to communicate the message correctly.

5. A Good Communicator Asks for Clarification if the Problem or Solution is Unclear.

Clarify your message until it is understood, and ask for clarification of others' messages until you understand them. You must check the accuracy of the messages you receive. Try responding with, "Here's what I heard you say…"

The telephone game is fun to play because it helps you to realize that messages are distorted between the speaking and the hearing. When I photograph a scene, I use various filters that affect the way the photograph turns out. Sometimes I may shoot a photo but the result is different from what I expected. When I check the camera, I discover that I left a filter on the lens that shouldn't be there.

In the same way, we see and hear based on a filter we have left on our hearts. If we internally believe someone is inconsiderate, for example, we will see and hear everything they do and say through that lens and begin to build a case on how inconsiderate they are. It is very important for us to continually examine our hearts to be sure that we have the kind of love that "…isn't rude. It doesn't think about itself. It isn't irritable. It doesn't keep track of wrongs. It isn't happy when injustice is done, but it is happy with the truth. Love never stops being patient, never stops believing, never stops hoping, never gives up. Love never comes to an end."[94]

Examine your heart to be sure you aren't seeing and hearing through a filter you may have inadvertently left on your heart from a prior situation.

In Richmond, British Columbia, when a terminal was struck by a bulk carrier ship, the investigation found: "Without effective communication regarding their shared mental model during the approach, the master and the pilot did not identify the developing risk as the manoeuvre (sic) progressed, and did not take timely corrective action."[95] It was determined by the Transportation Safety Board of Canada that because neither the pilot of the ship nor the master had properly communicated their positions, a crash resulted. We need to have effective communication to share our "mental models" so our relationships don't crash. Be sure you are clarifying each other's positions so both people correctly understand both perspectives.

Some examples of a direct approach to clarification:

"Did you just say…?"

"Here is what I just heard. Is this what you meant to say?"

"Are you saying I need to <u>do</u> something about this?"

"Here is the picture I am getting. Is it accurate?"

"Let me tell you what I think; then you tell me what you think."

6. A Good Communicator Knows that Communication is Not Only Verbal; It Involves Actions as Well as Words.

Every message we send has three components: the actual content, the tone of voice, and the nonverbal communication. Nonverbal communication includes facial expression, body language, and actions. An example of a nonverbal facial expression is rolling your eyes, or engaging your eyes to look into your husband's eyes. Body language can be an impatient foot tapping, your arms crossed defiantly, or putting your hand on his arm. Communicating with actions can include holding a book or phone in front of your face while talking (which should be avoided), or sitting next to your husband and holding his hand while listening.

Addressing the importance of nonverbal communication, Albert Mehrabian suggested the following breakdown of the importance of the three elements of communication when the content, tone and nonverbal contradict each other in expressing feelings:

Content 7%
Tone 38%
Nonverbal 55% [96]

Take a minute and think about how you communicate nonverbally. Then think how your spouse communicates nonverbally. Think of what your nonverbal communication means to your husband and what his nonverbal communication means to you. Take a minute to compare and discuss responses with your husband.

7. A Good Communicator Disagrees Without Getting Angry.

Ephesians 4:26-27 (KJV) says, "Be ye angry, and sin not: let not the sun go down upon your wrath: Neither give place to the devil." If you have a temper, you know that anger is not just a state of mind.

It is a physical feeling as well. If allowed to remain, it can and will do you much harm.

Amongst other things, anger has been shown to cause teeth grinding, flushing, paling, prickly sensations, numbness, sweating, muscle tensions and temperature changes. Anger can increase the risk of coronary artery disease and result in three times the risk of heart attack.[97]

Anger has the propensity of a volcano. In a few minutes time it can destroy what took years to grow. Anger renders the most educated person irrational and illogical. This is a biological response that is the same response that stress produces. It causes the hypothalamus-pituitary-axis to be set off, sending a message to your pituitary gland, which sends the message to your adrenal glands to kick in your fight, freeze or flight responses. Your body changes the way blood is sent to your body and brain, shutting down certain parts of your brain and pushing extra blood to other parts. Your forebrain that controls logic and reasoning works far slower than your subconscious mind because in an emergency you need to act quickly without thinking and processing information. You can't think. Your IQ drops.[98]

Proverbs 14:29 (GW) says, "A person of great understanding is patient, but a short temper is the height of stupidity." Ecclesiastes 7:9 (AMP) tells us, "Do not be quick in spirit to be angry or vexed, for anger and vexation lodge in the bosom of fools." It is futile to try to be rational when you are angry, or try to rationalize with another person when they are angry.

If you have a problem with anger, know that with awareness, discipline and self-control there are some things you can do and choose to gain mastery over your anger before it controls you. Get a grip on the following anger diffusers, because a good communicator disagrees without getting angry. Remember the goal of our communication is to be "good and beneficial to the spiritual progress of others, as is fitting to the need and occasion, that it may be a blessing and give grace (God's favor) to those who hear it." (Ephesians 4:29 AMP) All bitterness, anger, and wrath grieve the Holy Spirit (Ephesians 4:30-32), probably because it negates effective communication.

Try these things the next time you feel anger welling up inside of you:

a) Breathe deeply. The physical feeling of anger caused by the increase of adrenalin in your bloodstream speeds up bodily processes, and you cannot relax until all the adrenalin is burned up. Breathing deeply increases the oxygen in your body and helps use up the excess adrenalin not used in physical exertion.

b) Try to think objectively. When someone is telling you off, it is hard to think objectively. It helps me to stand back mentally and pretend I'm watching a drama. I try to objectively determine if there is any validity in what he or she is saying. If the person speaks with a right motive and is taking the time to confront me, I look for an element of truth in his or her words. Even if the person is venting his or her emotions and means to hurt me, I may be able to see something in me I need to change. I want to be approachable, so I let the person vent without criticizing or disregarding what he or she says. Listening and thinking objectively shows I realize it is not always about me. When I homeschooled my five children, I had many close friends and relatives confront me about my decision, sometimes criticizing me or challenging our decision to homeschool. I believe that these discussions taught me the importance of thinking objectively and allowing others to voice their opinions even though we felt differently.

c) Consider the source and don't rationalize. When people criticize you, consider who is speaking while you consider what they are saying. Even though you should listen to what any one has to say about you, you must realize that the person may be biased and the accusation may not be true. Actions are misinterpreted; statements are misunderstood. Don't refuse to listen and rationalize away anything he or she has to say. But do consider the source. The Lord will help you to separate what is true from what is not.

In considering the source, consider elements in that person's background that makes him or her act the way they do. Perhaps the person learned this behavior in childhood. Perhaps he or she is insecure or has a bad self-image and that's why it feels better when putting other people down. Even though this conduct is not right, your understanding will make it easier for you to not to take their style or words personally. You will be able to say to yourself, "I don't like the way they are acting, but with God's help I can benefit from this experience." Then ask the Lord's help so you can benefit from the experience. Obviously, if something is being communicated in an emotionally abusive, profane, accusatory, disrespectful, or demeaning way, take positive, tangible steps to stop the damaging conversation.

d) Again, concentrate on listening. Our natural reaction is to defend ourselves, especially when facing criticism. It is sad when married couples cannot communicate because discussion brings on reactions of anger, self-defense, and a quick retort. It is easier to remain quiet. Listen and do not interrupt. An interruption is cutting someone off. It says, "What you are saying is not nearly as important as what I have to say." Stop interrupting just because you think faster. It is like slapping someone in the face or putting your hand over his or her mouth. Keep silent while the other person is speaking, even waiting a few seconds to comprehend it.

e) Don't add fuel to the fire by backbiting and not keeping to the issue at hand. It is a lot easier for someone to acknowledge they were unkind in a situation than to take care of an accusation that is part of who they are. For example, if you say to your husband, "It wasn't considerate of you not to let me know you were going to be an hour late. I could have done things differently had I known and not just been waiting for you," this is addressing a *situation*. If you say something like, "You are so inconsiderate [all the time is implied]," or, "You never think about my feelings," or, "You are so selfish," you have attacked him as a *person*. What do you expect them to say to fix it? Ask yourself what you want to get out of the communication before you start it so you don't make it so open ended that there is no resolution possible.

An argument or tense situation will burn out in a minute if no one adds fuel to the situation by bringing up new subjects unrelated to the subject at hand. Proverbs 26:20-21 (THE MESSAGE) gives some key points on this: "When you run out of wood, the fire goes out; when the gossip ends, the quarrel dies down. A quarrelsome person in a dispute is like kerosene thrown on a fire." Stop adding wood to the fire and don't succumb to arguing and confronting when handling a disagreement.

f) Don't put the other person on the defense. Picture your words packing a punch. If your words make your husband put his hand up to defend himself, he is going to be more concerned with protecting himself than in hearing what you have to say. If someone throws a punch unwarranted, lie down in the ring. No one wants to fight alone. Right or wrong, silence, not obstinacy, will often end the problem, especially if in public. At any time when you feel you are hurling punches and putting your husband on the defense, stop talking until you can think of a way to communicate without attacking.

g) Learn how to present your feelings so that it is easier for someone to take. A spoonful of sugar helps the medicine go down, and a little statement affirming something positive may help a difficult suggestion be easier to swallow. You may say something like, "You are usually so considerate of my feelings. However, last night when you spoke ill of my family, it was very difficult for me not to take it personally. I was thrown off guard and offended when you were disloyal to them."

h) Give him a chance to respond. If he doesn't understand, let it go. Give him time to think about it. Give him a chance to change; it may not be instantaneous. If I am frustrated, I may even say something like, "How would you feel if I said something negative about your family?" Surprisingly, your husband may not feel the same way if you did the same thing to him, which is what causes some hurt feelings and communication problems. After communicating my feelings in a non-threatening way to let him know how I feel, I give him time to think about it without pressing him. Often, we have to agree to disagree on an issue. It is better than unloading our frustrations on each other.

My husband takes things easier if I exaggerate the point and use a little humor. One thing I tell my husband is that I am so precious he should walk around cupping his hands and holding me delicately to his heart. When he isn't treating me right, I tell him, "You should be carrying me like this… [demonstrating]; instead you are doing this [stomping me under his foot]…" He inevitably ends up cracking up and feeling a little sorrier at least.

i)   Guard against repaying evil for evil. 1 Peter 3:9 (KJV) gives us the way to get a blessing in a hostile situation: "Not rendering evil for evil, or railing for railing: but contrariwise blessing, knowing that ye are thereunto called, that ye should inherit a blessing." It is natural human reaction when attacked to retaliate with a counter-attack. Attacking only makes the other person try to come back in self-defense and a situation goes from bad to worse. Learning to respond intelligently to any attack helps us avoid repaying one evil with another. Remember: it is easier to shut up than sweep up.

j)   Be humble; we all make mistakes. What if someone says something negative about you and it is true. Tell the Lord and the people involved that you did the wrong thing, and you do not want to do it again. They will respect you for it. If we really believe, "Surely there is not a righteous man upon earth who does good and never sins,"[99] and, "All have sinned and come short of the glory of God,"[100] why is it so hard for us to admit we've made a mistake? Our wrongs simply prove that we are members of the human race. The Bible says "… you can't tame a tongue – it's never been done…"[101] If you have pictured yourself to be above sin, then re-consider and make a scriptural re-evaluation about who you are.

8.   A Good Communicator Fuels Solutions, Not Problems.

We can get so caught up in a problem that before we know it, the problem is all we can think about. If we give the problem fuel by over-thinking and dissecting every aspect of it and by rehearsing it over and over in our mind, the problem seems to get bigger and bigger.

Stop thinking about the problem and start thinking about possible solutions. Dr. Susan Nolen-Hoeksema, a professor at Yale University, extensively researched rumination and its effects. In referencing her work, Tartakovsky found that "Ruminating is like a record that's stuck and keeps repeating the same lyrics. ...When people ruminate while they are in depressed mood, they remember more negative things that happened to them in the past, they interpret situations in their current lives more negatively, and they are more hopeless about the future. Rumination also becomes the fast track to feeling helpless. Specifically, it paralyzes your problem-solving skills. You become so preoccupied with the problem that you're unable to push past the cycle of negative thoughts."[102]

I have heard, "Don't curse, don't nurse, don't rehearse, instead disburse and then God can reverse." Don't waste necessary energy mulling over things that can't change; use that energy to creatively find solutions.

9. A Good Communicator Knows What to Do When Solutions are Delayed.

Once you have asked your husband, you have done about all you can do to change his behavior. Trust God either to help your husband change, or to give you the necessary grace to live without a solution. 2 Corinthians 12:9-10 (KJV) says, "My grace is sufficient for thee: for my strength is made perfect in weakness. Most gladly therefore will I rather glory in my infirmities, that the power of Christ may rest upon me. Therefore I take pleasure in infirmities, in reproaches, in necessities, in persecutions, in distresses for Christ's sake: for when I am weak, then am I strong."

Communication "Busters"

There are three "communication busters" that must be eliminated in order for you to have effective communication:

<u>Explosion</u>.

If you get hostile when confronted by your husband, what you communicate to him is that he cannot come close to your weaknesses or you will explode. Anger on one person's part usually precipitates an angry response by the other. It puts your husband in an awkward position because he fears your temper tantrums. If solutions aren't found to problems and problems are ignored long enough, soon it becomes easier to walk away from the relationship rather than solve years of built up difficulties. Try to state objections kindly and trust that your words are the right ones to effectuate a change.

<u>Tears</u>.

If you cry any time your husband tries to talk to you about change, your sobbing will make him feel awkward. Many men don't know how to handle tears, which shuts down problem solving communication, including possible solutions. If your husband feels you are going to cry if he talks to you, he may avoid the conversation entirely or try to give you limited information to prevent your tears. Any barrier to unrestricted communication is not going to help you solve problems together.

<u>Silence</u>.

Many women resort to silence because their only alternative would be to get mad. In this instance, silence is not golden. Not only does it bring any possible solutions to an immediate halt, but also silence gives the message that you totally shut out any input from your spouse.

Psalm 32 is a wonderful Psalm that relates how wonderful it is when a transgression is forgiven. "[H]appy, fortunate, to be envied,"[103] is the one forgiven: "[c]ount yourself lucky – God holds nothing against you and you're holding nothing back from him."[104] When King David was silent and hadn't yet worked through this forgiveness, he was in great physical pain. Only when he acknowledged his wrong and made things right was he able to receive mercy, rejoice, and be glad.[105] You don't have to discuss problems immediately when you are upset; you can wait for an appropriate time to cool off. Silence will not accomplish solutions; it merely extends the time between problem and solution.

The word "metamorphosis" refers to the transformation from an immature form to an adult form in two or more distinct stages.[106] When applying these new principles to your communication, be patient and realize it may take time to complete the metamorphosis.

Chapter 11

Identity Crisis: Roles in Marriage

When I was dating my husband, I was amazed at the things we had in common. We seemed to be a perfect match. However, soon after we were married, differences seemed to arise from nowhere. He was frugal; I was extravagant. My husband likes to think things over to weigh out all the options; I tend to make snap decisions. Soon it became difficult to even find any common ground.

God knows that men and women are more different from each other than we realize at first. I believe He carefully thought through how to best teach us how to live unselfishly during the short lives we have on earth. Remember, He knew we would either have to be unselfish immediately or we would have miserable marriages.

Studying your spouse and how the differences in your background, personality, and gender affects your approach to life and communication can help you understand and perceive your spouse's actions (and non-actions).

In *Sacred Influences,* Gary Thomas says, "To influence a man, you have to learn to talk his language. Many marital problems arise not because of an issue between [people] but because of a breakdown in understanding, between a male and a female. ...I hope to give you an insider's view of the male mind so that you'll learn how to better understand and communicate with your husband.

"...[N]eurological studies show that men may take up to seven hours longer than women to process complex emotional data. Seven hours!...

"Consider the implications... If you have a disagreement just after breakfast, and you take about 15 minutes to get a grip on why you feel so angry, your husband may not get to that place until dinnertime!"[107]

Michael Gurian has been studying how the differences between the brains of women and men affect their marriage relationships through the changing stages that exist during the life of a relationship. "How we handle those stages can make or break a marriage... Understanding the behavioral differences involved can be the key to making love last a lifetime.

"Ultimately men realize that women are right: A relationship is most likely doomed if there isn't enough togetherness. But men are right, too: It is most likely in serious trouble if there is not enough independence. When we are too far away from each other, that amazing love we knew at the beginning will die. Yet when we are so close that one person will not allow the other to be himself or herself, the marriage can't survive. Understanding the strengths of male and female chemistry is the key to success."[108]

Michael Gurian gives the key to a successful marriage as: "Couples live together, raise children, love and are loved, but not because they've become the same as each other—in fact, because they've learned to be happily different."[108]

Be careful you don't take away your spouse's individuality and put your marriage at risk. If you want a more thorough discussion on the differences between male and female thinking patterns, pick up Michael Gurian's book, *What Could He Be Thinking? How a Man's Mind Really Works.* For understanding roles in marriage, learn to appreciate your husband for the man he is, be *happily different,* and respect his individuality. Your husband has a different perspective and different choices. Would you *really* just want him to be another *you?*

What is a good marriage all about? There is a divine order of marriage, as given to Adam and Eve, and it has not changed. A man's needs have not changed, and our marriages can only be successful if we follow the unchanging principles God laid down. His laws are eternal and do not change with the times or circumstances.

Men and women are wired differently, and have different roles within marriage:

Man's Role	Woman's Role
Leader	Helper
Protector	Respecter
Servant	Homemaker

The masculine and feminine roles, as defined above, are not merely a result of custom or tradition, but are of divine origin.

Leader/Helper

It was God who gave man the responsibility to "rule his own household well, keeping his children under control, with true dignity, commanding their respect in every way and keeping them respectful."[109] Paul compared man's leadership of his wife to Christ's leadership of the Church. Ephesians 5:23-24 says, "For the husband is head of the wife, even as Christ is the head of the church…

Therefore, as the church is subject unto Christ, so let the wives be to their own husbands in everything." "In a marriage relationship, there is authority from Christ to husband, and from husband to wife. The authority of Christ is the authority of God."[110] "Wives, place yourselves under your husbands' authority. This is appropriate behavior for the Lord's people."[111]

Before acknowledging leadership roles in various relationships, Ephesians 5:21 (GW), reminds us what kind of heart leaders must have in exercising their roles: "Place yourselves under each other's authority out of respect for Christ." In other words, before a man is in a position to lead the way God intends for him to lead, he must know what it means to be under authority. In order for him to be the "head of the wife, even as Christ is the head of the Church,"[112] he needs to know how Christ leads His Church.

In addition to being God's directive for men to lead in the marriage relationship, it makes *sense* that someone needs to take the lead in the relationship. Even business advisers speak against 50/50 partnerships because a smooth running business needs one partner who has a deciding vote if there is a deadlock. Jesus spoke about what it means to be in charge: "You know that the rulers of the Gentiles lord it over them, and their great men hold them in subjection [tyrannizing over them]. Not so shall it be among you; but whoever wishes to be great among you must be your servant, And whoever desires to be first among you must be your slave— Just as the Son of Man came not to be waited on but to serve, and to give His life as a ransom for many [the price paid to set them free]."[113]

Although the directive for men to lead their families has come under attack because of the redefinition of the family and the undermining of men's roles in the media, leadership was meant to be a freedom and to benefit our familial relationships. The marriage tug-of-war between husband and wife ends when a wife choses to acknowledge her husband as leader. A man rises above the status quo when his wife recognizes him as leader in the home. A woman that came to our Building Better Relationships classes told us that she could have saved thousands of dollars and hours of time spent in marriage counseling if she had just been told to honor her husband as leader in her home.

"Wives submit to your husbands. It used to be those words were heard in nearly every Christian wedding. Today they are hardly ever spoken and in fact are intentionally avoided. Certainly part of the reason for the change has much to do with a renewed sense of equality that women are striving towards. But it also has a great deal to do with the fact that over the years these words have been used as a hammer to get women to do whatever a man says, no matter what. The fact is, these words are avoided today by men and women in large part because most people have no clue what Paul was really saying. So here is your chance to finally get a correct understanding of this very provocative piece of Scripture."[114]

To get a correct understanding of this Scripture, we must hear the challenge. As women, we have the right to choose the dynamics of our marriage relationship and the power to choose to consider our husband as the leader. We also have the freedom to put ourselves under his leadership without the fear of being threatened or abused.

To truly choose *obedience* to your husband as an authority means you choose "compliance with an order, request, or law or submission to another." I love the word, obedience. Inside that work, right smack in the middle, I see the word *die*. Many times we have to *die* to *our* ways to *choose* to obey our husbands.

When Gabrielle Reece explained that she got her marriage back on track by living out an "old fashioned dynamic and abiding by more traditional gender roles," she "created a firestorm in the process:

"Reece elaborated for *Today's* host, Natalie Morales:

> "I think the idea of living with a partner is 'How can I make their life better?' So if I'm the woman and he's the man, then yes, that's the dynamic. I'm willing and I choose to serve my family and my husband, because it creates a dynamic where he is then in fact acting more like a man and masculine, and treating me the way I want to be treated. Which is—I'd like to be cherished, and I'd like someone to look after me in that role."

But, perhaps anticipating the coming controversy, she added: "I think because women have the ability to set the tone, that the ultimate strength and showing real power... is creating that environment. I think it's a sign of strength."[115]

Unfortunately, because we have distorted women's rights to mean that women need to become more like men, women have mistakenly believed that in order to have their rights they need to surrender their gender.

"Certainly the last thing on the minds of pop psychologists and the liberated 21st century human being is that in order to really be fulfilled we should actually submit to others. Yet that is exactly what the Bible teaches, over and over and over again. The wisdom of God is completely counter-intuitive. Jesus said that if you want to gain your life, you must lose it. He said that if you want to be the greatest among people, then you must become the servant of all. The Bible says that if we want to truly live, then we must die to ourselves. In Ephesians chapter 5 Paul says that if we want to be truly fulfilled, then we need to empty ourselves and submit to one another out of reverence for Christ.

"Somehow in our vocabulary, to submit means to give up and be the ultimate loser. It means that someone else is dominant and rules over you and you have no control of your life. Most recently being submissive is defined in terms of 'having no voice.' It is the image of a person who, cowering in such fear and humiliation, can't even speak to defend themselves. What a sad and pitiful definition of a wonderfully powerful and empowering biblical concept.

"Mutual submission is not about one person winning and everyone else losing. It is not about having no voice or no power or no control. The reason it is none of these things is because submission as a biblical concept is fulfilled when everyone submits to everyone else because we love Jesus. Submission is never a one-way street. Paul tells wives why and how to submit to their husbands. But he also tells husbands why and how to submit to their wives, and children to parents and even parents to children.

"You see, what Jesus wants to see happen is that we never have to worry about guarding or building up our self-esteem. We should never have to worry about ourselves because others are loving and serving us, even submitting to us with the result that we have every confidence that we are valued and loved. When we in turn submit to others and esteem them, not only are they built up, but we are too. We are built up because in submitting ourselves to others and deferring to them out of love for Christ, we end up being like Jesus. Whenever we live and love like Jesus there is an empowering as well as a blessing that comes our way.

"But let me give you an even deeper reason to submit to others. It is not simply in order to be a part of God's plan to feel better about yourself and have your esteem built up. The real reason to submit to others is given in the text. We do it out of reverence for Christ. So what does that mean? Jesus made a big deal out of saying that whenever we serve the poor, visit the prisoner, comfort the sick, and so on, we do these things for Jesus and in fact do them to Jesus. When you feed a hungry person, you are feeding Jesus. When you clothe a naked person, you are clothing Jesus, when you house a homeless person, you are housing Jesus. Likewise, when you submit to a brother or sister in Christ, you are submitting to Jesus. You submit to Jesus as he lives in them. So out of reverence for Jesus in them, you need to consider them before yourself. You need to honor them instead of yourself.

"When we submit in that way, it is not about us putting ourselves down. It is really about lifting them up. When a husband submits to his wife it is in order to help her become the most wonderful person in Christ that she can be. He lifts her up. And in the amazing way that God works, that husband ends up being lifted in the process. How? Well he is one with his wife so if she is lifted up, so is he. As Paul says, 'if one of us is honored, we are all honored.' When a parent submits their own desires for the sake of a child and the child is lifted up in love and esteem, then the parent is too, because they are a part of one another. In the Body of Christ, we are all part of one another and when we lift one another up by submitting to one another, in a miraculous way, we are all lifted up."[116]

Woman was created to be a *helper* to man. "Then the LORD God said, 'It is not good for the man to be alone. I will make a helper who is right for him.'"[117] The Hebrew word used for helper is the same word that is used many times to describe the help that God gives to His people. It is by no means an inferior word or state of being. It means to "succor, to help, aid, bring aid to, give/render assistance, lend a (helping) hand to; and assist and support in times of hardship and distress."[118]

Look for ways you can make the space to allow your husband to excel and experience life to the fullest. Don't be a hindrance; urge him to be the best he can be. Give him space to shine. There was always a sign hanging in my mom and dad's house: "Love wasn't put in your heart there to stay, Love isn't love 'til you give it away."

In marriage, there are a lot of decisions to be made. The idea whereby a husband and wife make all their decisions by mutual agreement may sound good, but it is often impractical and unworkable. Some decisions can be reached by mutual agreement, but many others cannot. A husband and wife may never agree on some things. When a decision must be made, *someone* must take the lead. Why do you think it should be *you* over your husband?

You may not think your husband wants to be the leader. You may have taken over so completely that he has stepped aside. You may have made him feel so inept he doesn't want to face your scrutiny. One woman said that after she had decided to acknowledge her husband as the leader in her family, he became a great leader. He told his wife he never felt she trusted him as leader, partly because she always asked someone else to pray at family gatherings instead of him.

Your husband may not be able to make decisions easily. He may be too cautious, or overly concerned about the obstacles in the way. When you consider that twelve spies went to look at the land God promised to give them and only two came back with a good report in Numbers 13, you realize that the *majority* of those men felt like grasshoppers in the sight of the men that possessed the land. They felt unable to possess the land God told them to possess. Many men likewise may be frozen and unable to make decisions because of the obstacles in the way of important decisions that need to be made. When my husband needed make an appointment to see a specialist, all he could see were the obstacles. I encouraged him by helping him make the appointment, driving him there, arranging for a driver to pick him up from there to bring him to the airport, and generally just helped him see that he could conquer the obstacles that seem so huge. I needed to help him by assuring him that I could stand behind him and make sacrifices to enable him to get the appointment scheduled. At another time, my husband was required to drive over two hours each way to work. He did not want to uproot our family to move, but needed to know I was behind him and was willing to support his decision by not complaining when he had to leave early and get home late every night for over a year. Your husband needs to know you are there to help him make the decision by supporting the sacrifices that need to be made *after* the decision is made.

Your husband may feel you are more qualified to lead than he is, but that doesn't change God's order for the family. If he is uncomfortable leading, ask his opinion, and seek his participation in decisions he wants you to make.

What are a few leadership projects your husband can oversee as the leader in your home?

1. Family mission statement.

Each family has been created for a special purpose. Because my husband taught mission statement development at his place of employment, he brought this practice to our family. We created a mission statement to acknowledge what we wanted to do as a family to contribute to the world we live in. Each year the mission statement changed a little depending on the ages of our children. When the children were young, our statement included: "Be nice to people even if they aren't nice to you." Encouraging our family to take responsibility to contribute to the world helps children grow into a secure identity and purpose early in life. Even if you don't have children, or if your children are very small, you should have family meetings at least yearly to review what your family wants to stand for in the world. We minimized the mission statements, laminated them, and gave each family member a copy. When my husband led these meetings, because the children and he became so united in purpose, a heart bond was created between them too.

2. Family Rules.

My Dad was a huge fan of rules. Our family had meetings and rules for everything. When we participated in relay races, picnics, board and card games, and ice-skating and running contests, my Dad announced the rules. He loved rules because we then knew what to expect and where the boundaries were. When we decide rules for the family, we all know what is allowed and what isn't allowed.

Establish rules for daily living, and rules for arguments. Respecting the rules helps us find the boundaries that make true freedom possible.

3. Decision making.

When I first got married, I thought I should help my husband find a job that had better hours than the job he held. At that time, my husband already had a high profile position with the respect of customers and employees that worked for him around the world. After he began to interview locally, I realized that he wouldn't be as challenged nor in as high demand as he was at his present job. Although he was willing to take a local job, he would have to not only take a more limited job position, but he would not be challenged at all. I quickly realized that since my husband was the one working at the job, that he should find a job *he* felt comfortable with.

Other decisions were more complicated. Once my husband felt we should change churches. I didn't understand why he felt so strongly. I didn't want to leave my friends, but I gave him the overriding vote. Later I found out that the timing was perfect for our family because of reasons that neither one of us could have really known.

I believe that the Lord gives my husband special insight and wisdom to lead because that is the order the Lord established for families. I know that my husband isn't perfect, and there have been times when he chose poorly and times when he asked my opinion and we both chose poorly; some of these decisions cost us both financially and personally. I don't expect my husband to be perfect; I only choose to follow him as the leader of our family. Because of my trust in him, I believe he takes decision making very seriously and considers me in the process.

If my husband makes a decision that I disagree with, that will adversely affect me, cause me duress, or go against what I believe in significantly, I pray about how to express myself. Although most matters aren't of this magnitude, when our decisions are about something that affects me in a significant way, I cannot just go along with it without providing my input and reasons for concern. When I pray, the Lord shows me my error, changes the desires of my heart, or shows me that it is something I should talk to my husband about. I like the example of Queen Esther in the Old Testament (elaborated on in Chapter 5).

First, Esther fasted and prayed. (Esther 4:16)

- Second, Esther chose a convenient time to talk about the problem. (After a good meal is an excellent time for communication.) (Esther 15:4 and 15:8)
- Third, Esther gave the results to the Lord. (Esther 4:16)

For example, when I had five small children my husband's employers asked if we would be willing to move to Korea for two to four years. At that time my husband would still have traveled regularly, even if we moved to Korea. When I realized how much time I would be alone with my children in a foreign country, and when I considered the friends my children would have to leave and the disruption to our lives for such a short term, I felt uncomfortable with the move. After expressing these negative sides about the prospective move to my husband, and after considering both the pros and the cons to the move, we decided to pass up on the job opportunity. Although it would have been a pro on the side of my husband's job experience, the cons that the rest of the family would have had to experience weren't worth the one positive part of the move.

At a different time, when my husband wanted to build a home, we purchased a lot. After I met with the builder, I knew I would never be able to follow through with it; so we sold the lot and pursued a different course of action. If your husband knows that you are normally willing follow his lead, he will usually be more understanding when you express strong opposition against a major decision that you feel will negatively impact a large part of your life.

What are some ways you can help your husband excel in his role as leader?

1.   Be a follower.

In order for your husband to lead, someone has to follow his lead. *Let* him lead. Know he will make mistakes. Express your appreciation that he will do the necessary research to reach the best possible outcome. Appreciate him taking the burden of the decision off your shoulders, and tell him so. I often tell my husband how happy I am that he takes worries off me because he handles situations so well. Sometimes, he will say something like, "I'm handling this situation, but if you are going to worry about it, I am not even going to tell you any details about this any more."

2. Don't criticize or undermine his decisions.

Once your husband makes a decision, stand behind him, even if the results aren't what you expected. One time my husband asked if we should trade some stock in. I made a suggestion, but he decided to wait. The decision resulted in us losing a significant amount of money, but I never said anything. About ten years after that happened, my husband and I were leading a class and he mentioned how important it was that when a husband makes a mistake that the wife doesn't rub it in his face. I never thought he realized it at the time, but it was still noteworthy over ten years later that I didn't criticize him or tell him that if he had done it my way, it would've turned out better. In hearing him say that, I realized how easily I could have missed the chance to do something that would be noted for virtue a decade later.

3. Choose "us" as a couple.

In the movie *Family Man,* Kate and Jack discuss whether they will move their family from the suburbs to the center city. Kate was against the move. When she saw he was set on moving, she said, "You know, I think about the decision you made... maybe I was being naive, but I believed that we would grow old together in this house. That we'd spend holidays here and have our grandchildren come visit us here. I had this image of us, all grey and wrinkly, and me working in the garden and you re-painting the deck. But things change. If you need this, Jack, if you really need this, I will take these kids from a life they love and I'll take myself from the only home we've ever shared together and I'll move wherever you need to go. I'll do that because I love you. I love you, and that's more important to me than our address. I choose us."[119]

Choosing "us" means a wife supports her husband's lead and encourages him to make decisions. She doesn't fear whether he will make a mistake or not. The success of the relationship does not lie in the perfection of each decision, but in growing together through the good decisions and the bad ones. I have a friend who supported her husband through two failed attempts at opening his own business. Because of her support, he tried a third business, which was a successful one. His wife was an important key to his success. Because of her support, he survived his mistakes and kept trying.

4. Respect your husband's position.

When you submit to your husband's authority without undermining him, complaining, or otherwise acting like he should be the one submitting to you, you get the added benefit of your children seeing the principle of authority at work. They will learn valuable lessons about submitting to authority when they don't agree. Many women don't understand why teenagers constantly come against authority—teachers, coaches, and bosses—and seem unable to follow any one. Your children will learn the principle *by example.*

God stated the man is to be the leader of the home. To go against this principle is to go against God's directives for harmonious living. We can trust His ways to show us "all things that are requisite and suited to life and godliness," to bring us to spiritual maturity, to grow our faith, to increase our fruitfulness, and to bring us real success in life.[120]

5. Stand together as one.

Even if you don't agree, it is wise to show the children a united stand with your final decisions. When children are growing up, they can interpret what you say differently than what you mean. My husband and I agreed together on what our children could do, and we didn't change our position until we both talked and changed it together. This brought a great deal of consistency in our home. It also brought forth a great deal of conversation and thinking through how to best rule the roost with teenagers in the house. If one of our teenagers asked us if they could spend the night at a friend's or extend the curfew, since these rules had already been established, both of us knew to automatically say "no." We would be sure to talk to each other before we changed a set family policy, whether it applied to our children or ourselves. If it was something that hadn't been talked about or decided, we asked our teens if they had talked to the other parent. It was noteworthy that many times teens approach both parents believing their option is the answer that best suited their situation. For example, our teens would ask their dad if they could go to a party, although he was unaware of facts about the party that I knew about, such as where it was, whether the parents were going to be home, and who was going. Knowing I was privy to more information about school and friend activities, my husband would make sure it was okay with me before he gave his approval.

6.   Voice your opinion.

I usually have an opinion. I laughingly tell my husband he is not married to a vase that is just an ornament without any input. My opinion may consider a perspective that my husband hasn't thought of and vice versa. A wise decision considers all facets of the situation. When you share your opinion, listen to be sure it is not biased or self-serving to your own needs. Make sure you have something worthy to contribute also. Try to be positive and uplifting, and work on finding solutions rather than magnifying problems. Don't limit the scope of your opinions by lack of character or wisdom. Keep up on what is going on in the world. Even when I don't have time to read the entire newspaper, I read the headlines of the *Wall Street Journal* and scan the editorials in it just to broaden my perspective. If you are always working on bettering yourself, you will have something valuable to offer your husband or others when asked for advice. If you live an isolated, self consumed life, your husband will not put his trust in you and seek your advice and if you are one-dimensional, you will not have anything worthwhile to offer.

7. Watch the *way* you voice your opinion.

Your opinion is *your* opinion. Not the mandate, not the benchmark, not a demand. Your insights and opinions are important but may not be the best or right choice. Your kind, helpful, calm tone will give your opinions value.

Listen carefully and thoroughly without interrupting and ask questions. If you have any insights, share them as information others can use to make better decisions. This wisdom is important when your children grow up and leave your home as well—particularly in areas where they are making choices that aren't necessarily ones you want to take control over, but which you feel aren't the best for them. You want to be able to help lead them into wise solutions by giving them information you know or see. For example, when my son and his wife found out they were expecting a child, they had a missionary trip scheduled to Haiti. I shared the risks of traveling to a third world country while pregnant: you are not able to have some of the recommended vaccinations, there are high incidents of fever and parasite infestation, the roads are extremely bumpy when traveling, hospital care is not as reliable should you need medical attention, and food- and water-borne illnesses are classified as high risk. Although I was able to contribute information to them to help them decide how to proceed, I knew that the final decision was up to them. With your husband, your children, or really any one you are helping through a situation, you don't want them just to *do* the right thing but to *know* the right thing to do.

Express your insights and perspective with kindnesses, "The way I see it…" or, "Another way to look at this is…" or, "Have you considered…" or, "The possible results would be…." Try not to control by saying, "The only way to do it is...." Avoid acting like a know it all.

When one of our children in high school began hanging around someone with a less than stellar reputation (to put it mildly) I was not happy. I heard myself constantly giving warnings about character and bad influences, and generally nagging. One day our child grew tired of my judgmental attitude and asked, "Why can't you believe that my friend has re-dedicated his life to God? Why is it I'm willing to give him a chance, but you aren't willing to give him a chance?" I promised my teen that I wouldn't judge as long as he would carefully observe if the friend had truly changed his life habits. I agreed never to bring it up again. My son made his own decision about that relationship and in a few weeks, their friendship dwindled.

If I behave as if I am the only authority on everything that pertains to someone else's life, then that person will end up resenting my smug attitude. In addition, I truly don't desire to be responsible for making every one else's decisions. I trained my children at early ages how to consider all the ramifications, seek wisdom, and be observant and aware of the outcomes of their choices so they could make wise decisions. When they asked me if something was going against God's will, I helped them separate themselves, not listen to outside voices, consider what the Word of God said, and then lift their hearts and voices to the Lord in prayer and ask *Him* if that decision would please Him. As they grew up they learned to separate themselves from outside influences to really hear the voice of God and know the heart of God about the decisions they made.

8. Watch your attitude.

There are many homes where women work outside the home, or men work so many hours they can't attend to things at home, so it necessary to share responsibilities. With the sharing of roles, it is important that women do not use their position or job as a way to undermine or lord it over their husbands. Equally important is the sharing of all roles: the husband and wife will both need to kick in to keep up with jobs at the house—cooking, cleaning, shopping, tending to children, yard work, taking care of cars, and repairing what goes wrong in the house. The *sharing* of roles shouldn't turn out to be a *destruction* of roles, however. Maintaining a respectful and good attitude towards each other in the face of increased demands is imperative if you desire to have a happy home life. I was privy to one young man coming home to find the house a disaster area because his wife had been tending to yard work all day. She worked diligently to surprise him, but he came home and unleashed his frustration on her because the messy house eclipsed his appreciation of the yard work that was done. The situation was quickly escalating into the proverbial mountain out of a molehill until she wisely stopped defending herself and accusing him (which wasn't helping the situation anyway), and calmly told him how she felt after working all day only to have her efforts disregarded because she couldn't get to everything. Had she or her husband held onto a wrong attitude, the night could have easily been ruined, cold water could have been thrown on future efforts to surprise him, and distance from each other could have been created from the unwise choice of adjectives being used. Because she chose to have the right attitude, he was able to see her point and apologize, help her pick up the house, and the rest of the night they enjoyed each other's company.

The two major societal revolutions pertaining to roles in marriage are the Industrial Revolution and World War II. Some of the changes have produced less than desirable results. How many families consider the man as the head of the household, realizing this is a scriptural term? In how many homes today would women admit to being the *helpmate,* even though this term too is scriptural? Does the fact that many women work outside the home, whether for "needs" or "greeds," make God's directives null and void?

Statistics show otherwise. The reason God created order is because He knows what is best suited, that our days on earth be like days of heaven (Deuteronomy 11:21 KJV). Those who live contrary to the design and plan of God, including women who refuse to follow and men who refuse to love their wives like Christ loves the church, cannot expect to live full of joy and peace.

"One of our blessings as wives is that God has ordained that our husband be the leader in our marriage. With groups of ladies screaming today for their rights and many ladies obviously acting as heads of their homes, a Christian woman may wonder if somewhere between Creation and today God has changed His mind. What Scripture supports a woman feeling she must take over the leadership of the home. Because she is more capable, more intelligent, or more spiritual than her husband? Yes, there are men today who actually prefer not to assume the headship role for a variety of reasons: (1) he doesn't want all the hassle; (2) he doesn't want to make a commitment of time to the Lord for direction, nor a commitment to his family; (3) if he can come and go as he pleases, he will have more time for his fun and games; (4) his mother was the head of his childhood home, and he grew up without a male example of real headship; and/ or (5) he doesn't know how to be the leader; and more importantly and above all – he is a sinner and lazy and it takes work to lead so if someone else is willing to do it, he will sinfully step aside and allow it. It is God's ordained wisdom in our homes that the husband be the leader.

"Our men need encouragement to lead. They don't need competition from us with the connotation of, 'I can do it better.' Matthew Henry said, 'A woman was not made out of his head to top him, or out of his feet to be trampled upon by him; but out of his side, to be equal to him; under his arm to be protected; and near his heart to be loved.' How many ways can we say, 'I love you' without the words? Let us become the women God created us to be and let God work on our husband. Marriage is not so much finding the right man as it is being the right woman."[121]

When your husband takes leadership responsibilities in your home, there will be less arguments and contentions over decision-making. When your husband is given his rightful authority, he will stop *fighting for it*. He will be encouraged to have stronger character in considering the impact decisions will have on you and any children in the home. As he makes more and more decisions, he will become more confident, assured, and responsible. Power struggles will be gone from your home, and it will become more peaceful. You will operate more as a team than opponents.

The way we stand behind our husbands can make or break them. It is my goal to help my husband to be the best he can be, while working on being the best I can be. When I get lost in that work, I tend to see the best, feel the best, and encourage him to do the same. When I start looking at his faults, I feed the faultfinding, negative part of me. Remember, what you feed grows; what you starve dies. What a relief when you cast off the job of judge, jury, critic, faultfinder, and nitpicker. Instead, feed good thoughts, good actions, and good sentiments about others, especially your husband.

My mom said, "Two heads make a monster." And we all know women who look and act like monsters. Basically, in the realm of God-ordained jurisdictions, there are two types of power. First, there is the power of headship, as in the head of state, the head of a family, the head of a church, or the head of a company. Second, there is the power of influence in those who serve the ones in leadership—the second in command and the chief advisors. The record of history and the reality of our observations provide ample confirmation that the greater of these two powers is the power of influence.[122]

Our influence should not be undervalued. Power of influence can be used for both good and bad. Joseph, Daniel, Esther, and Nehemiah all used their power of influence to change nations. Eve used her power of influence to encourage Adam to disobey God. Sarah influenced Abraham to have a baby with her servant, which began the Jewish-Arab conflict that still continues. In order for the power of influence to be used effectively, there needs to be a strong harmony and trust between the one in leadership and the chief assistant.[122]

Yes, our husbands will make mistakes, and hopefully if we are patient, loving, and kind, and don't throw the mistakes back in their face, they will learn from those mistakes. You would make mistakes too! You can't just support his leadership when he does just as you would do. It takes meekness to be a good supporter—not weakness. Meekness means power under control. Just because you could make the final decision, just because you could say something unkind, just because you have the information to cut someone down, does not mean you should.

The meek will inherit the earth (Matthew 5:5). In the biblical sense, a meek person has channeled his strengths into serving God and does not seek his own way. Nothing will prove whether you are meek or not like when things don't go the way you think they should.

When I was a legal assistant, I had signature privileges on my boss's checkbook. I wrote checks in his stead for the things he needed. I did not abuse the privilege. We should represent our husbands that way. When we make decisions, we should consider our husband's opinions and directives. Since my husband traveled, I had to run my house in his absence, but I was careful to consider what he would have me do. If we were trying to pay off our house or save for something costly, or when we were sacrificing to put our children through private school, I knew we agreed to stop purchasing anything optional. If I had a reason to want to purchase something, I discussed it with him, knowing that "no" was an answer. In the long run, because of his discipline and our sacrifices, we were able to do much more with our finances than I would've been able to do without his leadership and perspective. I am seeing the effects of this wisdom in my adult children's lives. They work together and exercise discipline in financial choices as they pay off student loans and mortgages.

Protector/Respecter

In a society where men and women work side by side, women have become less aware of dangers, of why they shouldn't attempt work beyond their physical capacity, and even of things they need protection from. When a woman becomes independent, capable and efficient, those initials spell ICE woman. We can come off like we can handle everything ourselves without any help. As if we don't *need* our husbands around.

My Dad didn't even want to come over my house unless he could *do* something for me. When he had surgery on his hip, he became extremely discouraged and depressed because he felt useless. We went through great lengths after his surgery to show our appreciation and convince him that we love him for who he is, not just for what he can do for us. "That's why we are called human beings and not human *doings,*" we told him. When our husbands, or any one for that matter, feel that their lives are not at all beneficial or appreciated by us, it makes them feel frustrated that they cannot offer us anything. We all need to be appreciated, and you cannot make someone feel appreciated unless you allow him or her to be or do something for you to be grateful for.

Women go to extremes to find self-fulfillment, but we often deny our husbands the fulfillment they would feel if they were allowed to protect us and our families in some ways. There are two ways to be closer to someone: (1) do or be something for them; or (2) *let* them do or be something for you. I have found that if I take away the ability of my husband to be able to do or be something for me, we aren't as close.

The Bible says, "Your heart will be where your treasure is."[123] That word, "treasure" means *deposit*. Where you deposit time and energy, your heart will be bound there. Consider how people love their hamsters. Because they invest time and effort into their hamsters, they can even love a hamster! How much more if you invest time and effort into your husband, you will have an increasing love for him. Conversely, if you want him to have an increased love for you, you must allow him to invest time and effort into you.

One woman told me that she didn't understand how far she and her husband had drifted apart. She told me that she never required him to accompany her to places he said he would rather not go, and she never asked him to help her. Sadly, his love for her diminished almost to extinction just as his investments into their relationship had. Another couple was on the brink of divorce; the wife told me she had "fallen out of love" with her husband. She took this principle to heart and decided to make one last investment to save her marriage. She wrote a list of things she could do to invest into her husband. She even posted the list on the refrigerator to remind herself. They are still happily married now, twenty-some years later, and enjoying grandchildren together. It is of utmost importance that you allow your husband to do and be things for you, not necessarily because you *need* him to, but because you know *he* needs to give!

When Dr. Phil describes the role of the man in the family, he indicates that the role of a protector means protecting his wife's self-esteem and self-worth as well as the children's. It can also mean protecting your way of life and guarding against any threats to the things that you and your family value.[124]

If you haven't let your husband help you lately, here are some ways to start:

1. Ask for help with heavy groceries, things that you can't reach, or moving furniture or heavy boxes. Again, playfully say something like, "Those muscles weren't just given to you to look good: can you help me lift these heavy packages?" I say that to my sons too, and love when they smile.

2. When you have a problem that you can't fix. I'll ask my husband to make a call if I'm having a difficult time negotiating a price on new tires or other items that he would be more likely to know whether the price is fair or not. Gary is pleased to make a tough telephone call or deal with mechanics or builders who may think I am easier to push around.

3. If you are having a problem, ask him for advice. When I realized I had left my phone on the trunk of the car when I went to drop a meal off to a sick friend, I was very upset about losing my phone. My husband came home from a business trip the next day, got on his bicycle and followed the road that I took with my car, observing the trajectory the phone took when I rounded a curve on the road. He found the phone almost a mile away, face down in the dirt on the side of the road.

4. When you are overwhelmed, ask him if he would mind helping you out. When we were in Florida and my four-month old granddaughter was put into the hospital, I couldn't think of anything except getting home. My husband stepped in and made some telephone calls, and within minutes we were heading to the airport for the next flight with all arrangements made. I have tried to switch flights before and was unable to do so without incurring exorbitant fees.

5. I ask him to pray with me if I am trusting in the Lord for an answer to prayer, going through something, or speaking at

an event. I know that our unity and agreement in prayer is powerful.

You and I must *choose* to lean on our husbands. The dichotomy of knowing you can handle situations and challenges on your own and choosing to lean on your husband is settled with one question. Even if you *can* handle trials and tasks alone, would you choose to? If you continually disallow your husband to provide some of your needs or be leaned on, soon you will find he has become unaware of your needs, and you *will* be on your own. Even if I could handle a situation, he will often solve a dilemma with qualities that I don't possess. And the bonus is that he loves to be needed.

To invite chivalry into my marriage relationship, I must *allow* my husband to care for and protect me. In the process, I respect his time, efforts, and calendar, as I would want him to respect mine. I am grateful for the things he does for me. Ephesians 5:33 (GW) tells us, "...wives should respect their husbands." I love how the Amplified Bible expands the word respect: "[that she notices him, regards, him, honors him, prefers him, venerates, and esteems him; and that she defers to him, praises him, and loves and admires him exceedingly]." Put these action verbs on a note card and post them on a mirror as a checklist and reminder of how to respect your husband.

Servant/Homemaker

Your husband is called to provide for his family. 1 Timothy 5:8 (AMP) states, "If anyone fails to provide for his relatives, and especially for those of his own family, he has disowned the faith [by failing to accompany it with fruits] and is worse than an unbeliever [who performs his obligation in these matters]." Ephesians 5.25 (THE MESSAGE) puts it this way, "Husbands, go all out in your love for your wives, exactly as Christ did for the church—a love marked by giving, not getting." The way Christ loved the Church, your husband is to show love toward you. Jesus didn't come to be served but to serve.[125]

Give your husband opportunities to serve. Encourage him, tell him he is important to you, and admire his personality or skills or nature. Don't take on the "I can do it myself" attitude. Let him invest in you and his heart will be with you too. Without whining, tell him what troubles you, what you worry about, what pressures you face, your hopes, your dreams. If you do, your husband will be able to understand encourage and support you more than you realize. Ask him to help you make ways to help some of your aspirations come true.

Our role as homemaker shouldn't be taken lightly. "It takes hands to build a house, but only hearts can build a home."[126] We have been told we can "have it all," but increasingly we are finding that something has to give when we take on too much.

To make your house a *home* is more than just funding it with cash. I love to picture various houses without the impact of the woman who lives there. I am sure the house would present itself quite differently! When we were looking for a cabin up north, I could tell which cabins had a women's touch and which cabins men owned. The men's cabins were basic and functional, with a variety of animal heads and even taxidermy squirrels and other small animals randomly placed. Most had fishing poles, hunting guns, and other sporting paraphernalia out. After seeing such obvious differences, I asked for my husband's support in not allowing any cabin we purchased to look like a hunting and fishing expo that would scare our grandchildren.

Being a homemaker is much more than furnishing and decorating a home and keeping it up. Being a homemaker encompasses everything that turns your house into a home. Feeding your family healthy, foods. Learning to live simply. Giving your family a place to keep their belongings organized. Having a system for household duties. Keeping your house clean and organized. Keeping your perspective. A clean and organized house is important, but don't obsess over housework. My mom had a sign in our kitchen: "My home is clean enough to be healthy and dirty enough to be happy." A warm friendly environment in a home that welcomes others is so much more important than perfect decorating or the latest fad in furniture. A home full of children who are being trained and loved, not merely watched, is a haven. Provide a place where children know their stories are listened to, their triumphs are rejoiced with, there is someone to hold them when they're sick, someone to take care of them, and someone who is interested and involved in their school events and activities.

It is generally in a woman's nature to make her home a place for the family to relax and enjoy. Paul encouraged us to be homemakers, "So that they will wisely train the young women to be sane and sober of mind (temperate, disciplined) and to love their husbands and their children, To be self-controlled, chaste, homemakers, good-natured (kindhearted), adapting and subordinating themselves to their husbands, that the word of God may not be exposed to reproach (blasphemed or discredited)." (Titus 2:4-5 AMP) However, some women do not naturally take to cooking or decorating. If that is you, pay someone to help you as you increase your knowledge and skills in homemaking. Some men are wonderful cooks and love to putter around the kitchen. Develop your talents and your gifts, and alongside your husband's gifts and talents make your marriage strong.

Anne-Marie Slaughter is a professor of politics and international affairs at Princeton University, and the mother of two teenage boys. She served as the director of policy planning at the State Department from 2009 to 2011. In a July/August 2012 article *Why Women Still Can't Have It All,* she states, "…Yet I also want a world in which, in Lisa Jackson's words, 'to be a strong woman, you don't have to give up on the things that define you as a woman.' That means respecting, enabling, and indeed celebrating the full range of women's choices. 'Empowering yourself,' Jackson said in her speech at Princeton, 'doesn't have to mean rejecting motherhood, or eliminating the nurturing or feminine aspects of who you are…' We will properly focus on how we can help all Americans have healthy, happy, productive lives, valuing the people they love as much as the success they seek."[127]

As women, we have choices. We choose to pursue our definition of success. Each of us needs to define up front what we want our lives to stand for. It helps to visualize our relationships and families and what our priorities in life are to be. Decide your definition of success at the beginning: what do you want to say at your 50th wedding anniversary; what does being a successful parent look like? Only when we define these goals early, will we be able to make the tough choices that will help us to live out our priorities. Only when we purpose what we want to stand for early, will we be able to purposefully and intentionally deal with the bombardment of choices that we will face.

What have you done to make your house a home? Learn a few feminine arts and skills. Learn to cook a little better. Get organized. Get help. Learn to be thrifty. Read books on parenting. Invest and devote time to the welfare and happiness of your family.

Maybe you need to work at a paying job or you have professional skills or a career that puts you into a work environment outside your home. "Bentley University's Center for Women & Business conducted a survey of 1,000 college educated men and women born since 1980 to provide a more in depth picture of the career aspirations of Millennials and the values driving those aspirations… A majority of respondents say that having a successful marriage (63%) and being a good parent (57%) are among the most important things in their lives when they think of the goals they value. Most respondents (62%) define 'good parenting' as spending as much time with your children as possible. If companies want to tap the loyalty and the career aspirations of this generation for leadership development, they should create a work environment that respects personal values, especially related to family."[128] When a woman works outside of the home, especially when she places her top priorities on her home and family, often she must hire someone to help with the chores and learn to delegate work to others. Your love of home and family will shine through if you place a great importance on finding those who can help you live out your priorities as faithfully as possible.

Use what you have available. When Moses, in Exodus chapter 3, was issued a directive from God to lead the Israelites into the Promised Land, he questioned his ability to do such a huge job. After he set out all the things he was concerned about, God simply asked him, "What's that in your hand?"[129]

What is in your hand to accomplish all you need to do? Maybe you can't serve a made-from-scratch dinner every night, but you can utilize some of the quality fruit markets or whole food places in your neighborhood to help you with healthy dinner starters and add a few things to make a dinner that is good for your family. Maybe you can't sew or make curtains for your home, but you can pick up inexpensive flowers from any local grocery store and put them in a vase on the counter to add a warm touch to your home.

We make excuses why we can't do what we want for our families. I am inspired by women who plan ahead enough to prepare crock-pot meals, or practice menu planning, or cook ahead and freeze things. If we use some creative energy, we may find we may be able to come a little closer to our ideals if we would just take advantage of opportunities available instead of wasting so much energy complaining or giving up.

Chapter 12

Set Your Pace

Newton's first law of motion applies to my life constantly: "An object at rest stays at rest and an object in motion stays in motion with the same speed and in the same direction unless acted upon…"

When I am in a routine and keep the pace, it is actually easier than all the preparation and efforts necessary to get a break. When I was anxious to get away from my responsibilities and take a mini-vacation or night off, I had to work even harder to catch up. The break actually turned into an increased load on me.

It is also unfavorable to wait for my husband to give me a break. When either of a couple is looking for a way out or seeking fairness in taking a break, both individuals are destined to find that balance on a seesaw is virtually impossible. When I was looking for a way to make my own life easier, I failed to notice the needs of my husband, I found that my life would never be so easy that I could focus on giving my husband a break instead of me, and I started to resent times when it seemed he had a break and I didn't. This 50-50 proposition never works. Marriage needs to be 100-100. You need to regard your spouse's needs as more important than yours (Philippians 2:3[130]). You will find true joy and provision in giving 100%. These Scripture verses encouraged me in this regard:

If your first concern is to look after yourself, you'll never find yourself. But if you forget about yourself and look to me, you'll find both yourself and me." (Matthew 10:39 THE MESSAGE)

"Self-help is no help at all. Self-sacrifice is the way, my way, to finding yourself, your true self." (Matthew 16:25 THE MESSAGE)

"Listen carefully: Unless a grain of wheat is buried in the ground, dead to the world, it is never any more than a grain of wheat. But if it is buried, it sprouts and reproduces itself many times over. In the same way, anyone who holds on to life just as it is destroys that life. But if you let it go, reckless in your love, you'll have it forever, real and eternal." (John 12:24-25 THE MESSAGE)

"Give, and you will receive. A large quantity, pressed together, shaken down, and running over will be put into your pocket. The standards you use for others will be applied to you." (Luke 6:38 GW)

"[Be] ...mindful of the words of the Lord Jesus, how He Himself said, It is more blessed (makes one happier and more to be envied) to give than to receive." (Acts 20:35 AMP)

I learned that I needed to be more reasonable and realistic in my expectations of what a break really signified at each stage in my life. Directing as much resourcefulness and efforts as I could toward training my five children to get along and even have a quiet time, training them to behave and stay busy while they went with me on errands, and really working at keeping up with things, I found that the increased peace, harmony, and order in my home didn't require me to have as many breaks as I needed when I wasn't working as hard. As long as everything was close to being in order, I found that a short latte break to catch up briefly with a friend on the phone was more effective than having a longer break that resulted in disorder and chaos.

Your husband is to be intimately acquainted with you, as commanded in 1 Peter 3:7 (GW) "…live with your wives with understanding…" In order to do that, you must allow him in by telling him your deepest feelings, fears, and joys—the part of you he can't easily see.

My circumstances have required me to be self-sufficient because my husband travels quite a bit, so I have had to get the cars fixed, get minor and major repairs done in the house, and even had to move from one house to another while my husband was working. *Having* to do without my husband is different than *wanting* to do without him. I had to manage to get quite a routine going when he was away and I was either homeschooling or had five children in private school all involved in various activities.

Sometimes, in the rush of things, it became easier to not have to consider another person's welfare when I already had to consider so many other things. When my husband came home, I almost became irritated, because now, instead of just running out the door to get to one of the children's sports games, I had to be sure there was dinner for my husband, and that he was informed of how to catch up with us. I didn't want my husband to feel that he was interrupting my routine unfavorably. I then made a "ruling decision," that my husband's home is his safe place, the place he can come and take his hat off at the end of the day and not have to worry about answering to others. In that "ruling decision," I wanted my husband to know he was always welcomed and appreciated when he was home. I then had to make sure that my attitudes, actions, and lifestyle went along with that ruling decision. By planning ahead, I was able to show him my excitement that he made it home to be with us, have something ready for him to eat, and have an address and time where games and other events were if he were able to join us.

It is important to have an idea of the "ruling decisions" that govern all other decisions. For example, I wanted my children to grow up in a happy home. That ruling decision dictated how much I could take on each day to still keep that decision solid. That decision mandated that we be involved in charity work at all times, because you cannot be joyful when your world is centered on selfish pursuits. I made a ruling decision that I wanted my children to be kind and thoughtful. Because of that ruling decision, I incorporated many activities, picked out entertainment, disciplined, instructed babysitters and family, and purposefully managed life to support that ruling decision.

Let me ask you, what exactly is your personal ruling decision regarding your husband's role in your family? Do you give him his rightful place so he can function as the leader, protector, and servant? What is his place? Do you ask his opinion? Do you make him feel appreciated? Admired? Does he know you don't want to live without him?

I know many women who have had to live without their husbands unexpectedly. A dear friend of mine, who has seven children and who was so in love with her husband, received a call from him one night when he was on his way home from a sports game. "See you in a few minutes," he said. Instead of seeing him show up at her doorstep, a sheriff came to say her husband was in a car crash and didn't make it.

Did she live without him? Yes. Did she *want to* live without him? No. Yes, you can live without your husband if you have to, but do you really want to? Does he know how important he is to you? You have to <u>let</u> him be important to you. Because he is. More than you often realize.

It is a mystery how you become one with your spouse when you marry. I think as you grow together and really make it your business to know your spouse and love him despite your differences, you actually begin to understand how he feels even before he tells you.

So many times I will think something and Gary will do exactly what I was thinking.

Although the marriage is the event that makes you one, it really seems more like a process that needs to be worked out day after day. It becomes a choice. Here are a few ways to work on becoming one:

- Care about what your husband cares about.
- Feel your husband's emotions; even if he holds things inside, try to understand what emotions he is feeling and feel those emotions with him.
- Try to anticipate his needs and meet them.
- Somehow touch base with each other during the day, even if just for a minute.

How are you "one" day by day? Think of ways each day to show your oneness in a tangible way. Be consistently ONE-derful. My husband counts on me in the following ways:

- I always am excited to hear from him, and I let him know!
- I feel his emotions with him; I rejoice with him if he's rejoicing and I'm sad if he is sad.
- I give him the benefit of a doubt when necessary.
- I try to turn his mood around if he is feeling low.
- I try to make him laugh if he's sad.
- I can be trusted with his secrets.
- I look for the best in him, and disregard the worst.
- I make time for whatever is important to him.
- I don't cater to my emotions but cater to facts.

What can your spouse count on from you? Are you consistent, or does your spouse have to wonder what kind of mood you'll be in? Work on your list of what your husband can count on.

Karen Budzinski

When I ran the marathon, I was about to hit the wall at the eighteenth mile of the 26.2 mile race. Runners know that moment: with 18 miles behind you and 8.2 miles before you, it is a time when you feel you have given your all and there is nothing left to give—the wall.

There are several *walls* in life: in fact researchers Holmes and Rahe have listed life events in a stress scale, giving numbers according to the stress levels each life event causes. With over 41 events on the list,[131] we seem destined to trudge through life hitting impassable roadblocks all along the way.

God has a different plan for our lives. His plans are for "peace and not evil, to give you an expected end." (Jeremiah 29:11 KJV) He desires to do "superabundantly, far over and above all that we [dare] ask or think [infinitely beyond our highest prayers, desires, thoughts, hopes, or dreams." (Ephesians 3:20 AMP) God wants my days to be "...as the days of heaven upon the earth." (Deuteronomy 11:21)

The key to getting the most out of the present—this life God gives us—is to live with God's power instead of our own. With His "super" coupled with our "natural," He gives us the power and ability to live beyond our means and abilities. He takes us to higher heights. Terrible twos turn into terrific twos. Teenagers begin to contribute, equipping their parents to enjoy the fruit of their labors. Depression becomes reflection; and instead of the seven-year itch we look for God's plan and purpose in our marriages through each changing season of it. Instead of the empty nest syndrome, parents get excited as they see their children sent out like arrows in the hands of a mighty warrior, hitting the target square on.

How can we live this kind of life? By living life the way God planned it to be.

My grandparents and parents taught me that all you really have is what you give away. What have you tangibly given today to demonstrate to your spouse how much you love him? What have you given of your time, your talents, your efforts, to the one who means the very most to you? Every day we need to really show our spouse just how much we love and appreciate him... not just by what we say, but mostly in what we do.

Tag along with your husband, do an errand for him, surprise him with his favorite food or movie, serve him dinner with a smile, snuggle with him when you'd rather be getting something else done, write a special note, choose his favorite restaurant, have a great conversation about his job and his dreams. Lavishly and extravagantly give away your self and your love to him.

In order to correctly pace yourself, you need to address your unique situation as well. There are unique yet analogous challenges both for women who stay at home and for women who work outside the home.

Women Who Stay at Home

1. Be sure your choice supports rather than undermines the success of your marriage relationship.

According to a Forbes survey, 84% of working women told *ForbesWomen* and *TheBump* that staying home to raise children is a financial luxury they aspire to.[132] If you are able to stay at home, be grateful and utilize the opportunities. Your choice to stay home requires sacrifice, but choose to focus on the positive aspects of your role and you will find your life more enjoyable.

2. Don't feel justified in putting pressure on your husband to take over when he gets home.

A woman who stays at home isn't able to take a break from the demands on her day. She may feel overwhelmed with the job of keeping and maintaining the house while tending and caring for children. She may feel it is unfair for her husband to relax when he comes home from work, while her job never ends. She may feel justified in requiring her husband to split duties or even take over duties so she can take a break too. She may need a break, but he likely needs one as well. Talk to your husband and work out a schedule that gives you a break yet doesn't put undue pressure on him. Leave some things undone so that you and your husband can enjoy time together in the evenings.

3. Remember to keep the end in mind.

One day those children will leave the home to make their own lives—and that day comes sooner than you think it will. Build your marriage relationship and your friendship so that those empty nest years will be the best years of your marriage.

Women Who Work Outside the Home

When women work to supplement family income, utilize their education, contribute to society, or because they enjoy it, their responsibilities at home don't go away. Instead, working women are required to constantly balance demands from both work and home. It takes extra efforts, planning and fortitude to build relationships with your husband or children when so many voices clamor for your attention. It takes tolerance to let some things go in the house, socially, and otherwise that are impossible to attend to because of your busy schedule. One thing I realized when I sent my children to school was that although I was choosing a school that supported my belief system, I was still ultimately responsible for the training of my children. Although I was working outside the home, I was still ultimately responsible to be a wife and mother, and as such put those roles as my top priority. My husband does the same: although his work schedule leaves him very little room for choice, and even though we have to work our birthday celebrations and some holidays around his schedule, he ensures he is present for major life events and he stays connected.

I feel often that women must juggle roles, but when you juggle you have to realize that you must release some balls to grab others. Juggling doesn't work when you try to hold on to all the balls at the same time, or try to get someone else to grab some of the balls you are trying to juggle. When you need to work outside the home, you need to be *extra careful* you don't suffer the negative statistics of it.

When I homeschooled my children, I did a lot of research on the pros and cons of homeschooling. I didn't put my head in the sand and choose to be ignorant that, although there were a myriad of advantages, there were also disadvantages too. Instead, I studied, made tweaks and corrections, and worked hard to ensure that my children wouldn't suffer the negative aspects of homeschooling. For example, my children were still involved in a lot of teamwork activities at church, in city sports, and in the community. We held open house events where others could see their hard work. We kept to a strict schedule so they didn't think they could just do their work with their own timing. We had a dress code so I wasn't raising them to believe they could do their schoolwork in their pajamas. Each year they minimally accomplished what the syllabus indicated they would learn in school at their grade level.

When you are working outside the home, work extra hard at home to be the wife and mother you want to be. Make sure you are working outside your home to make it better and not to destroy your values. Some helps to prioritize your family's success if you work outside the home:

1. Be sure your choice supports rather than undermines the success of your marriage relationship.

The Forbes survey also shows, "…more than one in three [working women] resent their partner for not earning enough to make that dream [staying home to raise children] a reality.[132] [A]pproximately half of working moms agree their overall happiness would increase if they didn't work. More than a third (34%) of working moms admit that their work performance was slacking a bit and they wished they were home with baby after returning to work. In fact, 47% agree that their overall happiness would increase if they weren't working."[133]

Don't begrudge or blame your spouse for your schedule. Remember that you and your spouse are a team. Playing the blame game will not make the situation better and will only hurt your relationship. If you and your husband work together and communicate, you may be able to find a solution that will get you both to a place where you are able to handle your role more joyfully.

Cut down your hours as much as possible when situations at home are stressful. Be on guard that your work outside the home doesn't make you discontent or desirous for more material goods. When you're working outside the home, you may be surrounded by others who have more stylish clothes, take nicer vacations, or have newer cars, homes, jewelry, or any number of other material possessions. Discern between your wants and your needs so you don't find yourself working more than you want to. It may be wise to forego getting newer things until there is a better season for you to work more.

2. Don't feel justified in putting pressure on your husband to take over when he gets home.

A woman who works feels that since she and her husband both work, they should split all the other jobs 50-50 too. It is more important that you concentrate on the 100-100 formula instead of keeping track of how much the other person can or should do for you.

Adjust your expectations. If you are away from your home all day, it is unreasonable to expect that you can have a three-course dinner on the table and have the house perfectly clean. Adjust your expectations to meet your schedule. If you are having a demanding time at work, don't put extra demands on yourself at home. I made a decision that I would rather serve Cheerios™ with a smile for dinner than a three-course meal with a complaining ugly attitude.

Constantly review your priorities and make sure you are living out your priorities. Is it more important to make an elaborate dinner or to be at your daughter's soccer game? Is it more important to dump your responsibilities on your husband and nag him to help, or to let some things go or hire a helping hand and enjoy the little time you have together?

Remember that your husband worked all day too. Rather than trying to outdo each other in demanding things for yourself, try to outdo each other in helping the other person have a break. Do everything possible so you can enjoy your evenings together and keep your home as your safe place rather than generating more pressures at home than either of you have at work.

Control the pressures that are on you at home, and stop pressuring your husband when he is home. A man is entitled to time for himself, for recreation, study, and regrouping. He should be able to be involved in church service or civic service. My husband, at one of the busiest times in my life raising small children, decided to become a precinct delegate in the midst of his work travel schedule. I supported him. I did not want to take away his ability to make the world a better place. I support him when he takes away from the scarce time we have as a family to mentor young men too. It is not right for a man to spend his entire time and energy to simply give things to his family.

Make your home purposefully be a safe place for your husband and for yourself—the place you can hang your hat, be yourself, get refreshed, and rest up for the demands outside those closed doors. Be sure that demands do not come from you and your expectations for your husband once he gets home. It will take away time that you and your husband could have given each other, your home, and your children. It takes a lot of time to teach children the values of life, how to live, standards to follow, and how to build strong family ties.

In my husband's case, his job is so demanding that he has no choice but to devote almost all his waking hours to it. I know the same is true for doctors, dentists, emergency vehicle workers, volunteers, and any one else that needs to address emergencies around the clock. My husband's drive to provide for our family took him up the corporate ladder so that now, in his position, it is impossible for him not to constantly work or he will lose his position. Although I worked many times to get us through different seasons, my husband has carried the primary responsibility for providing for our household. The sense of competition and the stress of competing create a terrible strain on men. It is the stress of competing in a race versus just going out for a run. Many times the competition is not only for preferment and advancement; it is often for his job itself. Every man knows that if he falters or lets up his drive, he can and will be easily replaced.

No level of employment is really free of this endless pressure. Quotas are in place and scrutiny constant. There is no field of endeavor that a man may enter where he can count on complete economic safety;

competition, year-in, year-out performance is his life's lot. He cannot turn aside from his work with a clear conscience. Some men feel guilty or demeaned when his wife is more successful at work than he is. It takes a pretty amazing woman to not make her husband feel inferior when she is more successful at work than he is. I do know of several very successful marriages where a woman was able to keep her husband knowing he is the man of the house when she was vastly more successful in business than he, but it is a definite tribute to the attitude and character of the women. I know other successful women that have constantly belittled and downgraded their husbands because their husbands' jobs didn't seem as successful or they made significantly less money, and the results were not exemplary.

In order for a woman to be truly successful, she should be able to recognize the purpose and value of her husband regardless of the differences in position or salary. After my daughter was firmly established in her career as a dentist, she and her husband were excited that he was able to quit his secular job to work in full-time ministry. She works alongside him, in charge of the medical missions team, and he is helping her with the business side of her practice. They work together, and she is as big a part of his success for the Kingdom of God as he is in her success as a dentist.

3. Keep the end in mind.

Just as the stay-at-home wife needs to do, don't get so bogged down with the moment that you lose sight of your friendship and marriage relationship. Your relationship with your spouse is much more important than worrying and stressing about things to be done.

Make sure your husband knows you still need him. In the long run, it can damage your relationship if your husband is made to feel that since you are making your own money that you no longer need him. It is important to every human being to be needed as well as wanted.

The dynamics of rank or competition have no place in a marriage and success depends on your attitude. If you lord it over him, brag about making more than him, or minimize his position in life, you can be sure that your marriage is going to bear the wounds you have inflicted. If, on the other hand, you acknowledge and honor his leadership, have a good attitude, your marriage can be rich and rewarding.

Cherish the Moment

My Mom said, "...too many people let the precious moments of life slip by unappreciated."

I have noticed the dangers of waiting to live. People seem to be waiting for some event before they can appreciate their lives. "When I graduate..." or "When I start my new job..." or When I start making money..." or "After I have the baby..." or "When I get a house..." etc. Instead of waiting for that event to happen, enjoy life. Enjoy it today; enjoy this moment. Today is not a dress rehearsal.

Before I had children, I had heard parents wish that their baby slept through the night, then that their baby would start walking, then talking, then get to school, then graduate, then get through college, and then find the right mate. Then they wished their child were home again! They unfortunately wished their child to the next stage only to wish they could go back. I never understood this type of thinking, so I decided a long time ago that I would never do it. I try to cherish each stage I'm in.

In marriage, there are unique challenges you can find yourself wishing would go away. When you first get married, there are the challenging times of being busy, trying to have children, paying off school or house debts, demanding work schedules with burgeoning careers. Challenges of raising children, then teens, increased financial requirements of these things, house and career moves, keep escalating. Then come the challenges of aging together, together with physical and emotional trials that accompany retirement and old age.

Most seasons of life can be difficult and challenging. It is easy to wish yourself to the next season. Avoid wishing to fast forward your life or wish yourself into the next season, because you can be in danger of wishing your entire life away. With each season come unique challenges and frustrations as well as unique joys and things to celebrate. Learn to slow your life down by looking for the good in every hill and every valley because your life will go by quickly enough.

It is the same with big events that should be happy times. We can allow ourselves to be so distracted and so overwhelmed that we fail to enjoy the happiest times of our lives. I fought against this in my life. I made sure that if I was moving to a different house or having a baby, or planning a big party, shower, or wedding, I would make it an awesome experience from beginning to end. This has to be decided because it will not automatically happen. You have to fight to enjoy these wonderful, yet demanding, times. When you find things heating up in the rush and emotion of such large things, you have to take steps to be sure you do not let anything or anyone rob you of your joy. Much of the process is accomplished by just making the decision to enjoy the whole process on purpose.

Look for the reason that this day is the time of your life; and live today reflecting that awareness. You can't drive forward successfully while looking in the rear view mirror. That is why the rear view mirror is so small in your car. Also, "Give your entire attention to what God is doing right now, and don't get worked up about what may or may not happen tomorrow. God will help you deal with whatever hard things come up when the time comes."[134] Live your life the best you can today, and make it such a beautiful day that it will be worth remembering.

Ungratefulness will rob you of the blessings of each day. If you are not grateful for what you have, you will always be concentrating on what you don't have. If you are grateful for what you have, it will be enough. You will be able to rejoice with others even when they have more or better than you, because you are so grateful for what has been given to you.

Find reasons to appreciate your husband. It never fails to amaze me how I have been blessed with a man who committed to walk through life with me—all the ups, downs and in-betweens. He has known me from way back when. He knows the reason behind my joys and tears and looks deeply enough to see my heart. Over the years, I have seen the best in him and I have not expected perfection from him. He has done the same for me. We have both invested into our relationship with constant efforts. We have lived by the Word of God. We love each other without trying to change each other. I allow him space to grow and I don't rely on him for my sole source of joy.

Look at yourself and find reasons to appreciate who you are. Do yourself a favor and give up perfection. Instead, simply strive for excellence. Don't be so hard on yourself. Appreciate who you are, and focus on your strong points. Don't get hung up on little imperfections so that you can't enjoy who you are and live out 100% the life God created you to live. May you live all the moments of your life![135] Fully present, fully alive![136] Give yourself some room!

Don't hold other people responsible for your happiness: it will sap your life of its joy. Let it go, give it up, lay it down, forget about it. Set people free. The ministry of reconciliation has been committed to each one of us. "Live life so completely that when death comes to you like a thief in the night, there will be nothing left for him to steal!"[137]

In John 16:33 (AMP), Jesus said, "I have told you these things, so that in Me you may have [perfect] peace and confidence. In the world you have tribulation and trials and distress and frustration; but be of good cheer [take courage; be confident, certain, undaunted]! For I have overcome the world. [I have deprived it of power to harm you and have conquered it for you.]" Although our lives aren't guaranteed to be without storms, we can have peace in the midst of them. Life is a parable, and we see the demonstration of this in the eye of the hurricanes and tornados. The winds may be rotating and disaster all around, but there is a place in the center of the storm where everything is relatively calm. Biblical peace is not tied to your circumstances in life nor removed by trials or tribulation. Isaiah 26.3 (AMP), "You will guard him and keep him in perfect and constant peace whose mind [both its inclination and its character] is stayed on You, because he commits himself to You, leans on You, and hopes confidently in You."

Changing the Trend

The following is from an insightful article from Suzanne Venker, author of *The War on Men*, shared in its entirety by permission:

> "The battle of the sexes is alive and well. According to Pew Research Center, the share of women ages eighteen to thirty-four that say having a successful marriage is one of the most important things in their lives rose nine percentage points since 1997... For men, the opposite occurred...

> "Believe it or not, modern women want to get married. Trouble is, men don't.

"The so-called dearth of good men (read: marriageable men) has been a hot subject in the media as of late. Much of the coverage has been in response to the fact that for the first time in history, women have become the majority of the U.S. workforce. They're also getting most of the college degrees. The problem? This new phenomenon has changed the dance between men and women.

"As the author of three books on the American family and its intersection with pop culture, I've spent thirteen years examining social agendas as they pertain to sex, parenting, and gender roles. During this time, I've spoken with hundreds, if not thousands, of men and women. And in doing so, I've accidentally stumbled upon a subculture of men who've told me, in no uncertain terms, that they're never getting married. When I ask them why, the answer is always the same. Women aren't women anymore.

"To say gender relations have changed dramatically is an understatement. Ever since the sexual revolution, there has been a profound overhaul in the way men and women interact. Men haven't changed much – they had no revolution that demanded it – but women have changed dramatically.

"In a nutshell, women are angry. They're also defensive, though often unknowingly. That's because they've been raised to think of men as the enemy. Armed with this new attitude, women pushed men off their pedestal (women had their own pedestal, but feminists convinced them otherwise) and climbed up to take what they were taught to believe was rightfully theirs.

"Now the men have nowhere to go.

"It is precisely this dynamic – women good/men bad – that has destroyed the relationship between the sexes. Yet somehow, men are still to blame when love goes awry. Heck, men have been to blame since feminists first took to the streets in the 1970s.

"But what if the dearth of good men, and ongoing battle of the sexes, is – hold on to your seats – women's fault?

"You'll never hear that in the media. All the articles and books (and television programs, for that matter) put women front and center, while men and children sit in the back seat. But after decades of browbeating the American male, men are tired. Tired of being told there's something fundamentally wrong with them. Tired of being told that if women aren't happy, it's men's fault.

"Contrary to what feminists... say, the so-called rise of women has not threatened men. It has [made them mad]. It has also undermined their ability to become self-sufficient in the hopes of someday supporting a family. Men want to love women, not compete with them. They want to provide for and protect their families – it's in their DNA. But modern women won't let them.

"It's all so unfortunate – for women, not men. Feminism serves men very well: they can have sex at hello and even live with their girlfriends with no responsibilities whatsoever.

"It's the women who lose. Not only are they saddled with the consequences of sex, by dismissing male nature they're forever seeking a balanced life. The fact is, women need men's linear career goals – they need men to pick up the slack at the office – in order to live the balanced life they seek.

"So if men today are slackers, and if they're retreating from marriage en masse, women should look in the mirror and ask themselves what role they've played to bring about this transformation.

"Fortunately, there is good news: women have the power to turn everything around. All they have to do is surrender to their nature – their femininity – and let men surrender to theirs.

"If they do, marriageable men will come out of the woodwork."[138]

Whether or not you blend some of the more traditional roles in marriage, it is paramount that you allow your husband to operate in the roles of leader, protector, and servant and that you operate in the role of helper, respecter, and homemaker. When you follow God's order for your home, there will be more peace and harmony there. Make your husband feel needed in his family; verbalize praises that encourage his contributions to your home and family. Let him know you like when he's around. Many times I'll tell my husband, "I love you being home! You are making it a lot harder to do without you next week!" He loves to come home; it is his safe place where he is honored and a place where he feels special. That's what home should be!

Chapter 13

Problems Ahead

Self Destructive Habits, and
Effective Problem Solving

Self Destructive Habits

1.   Perfectionism or Healthy Pursuit of Excellence

Unfortunately, we get confused while pursuing excellence and end up with the problem of perfectionism. Inevitably, this tendency is carried over into our relationships and the expectations we put on our husband's shoulders. How do you know the difference between excellence and perfectionism? The following lists will help us see how dangerous it can be if we allow perfectionism instead of pursuing excellence when it comes to your relationships.

> **Perfectionists** reach for impossible goals.
> **Pursuers of Excellence** enjoy meeting high standards that are within reach.
>
> **Perfectionists** value themselves by what they do.
> **Pursuers of Excellence** value themselves by who they are.

Perfectionists get depressed and give up.
Pursuers of Excellence may experience disappointment, but keep going.

Perfectionists are devastated by failure.
Pursuers of Excellence learn from failure.

Perfectionists remember mistakes and dwell on them.
Pursuers of Excellence correct mistakes then learn from them.

Perfectionists can only live with being number one.
Pursuers of Excellence are happy with being number two if they know they have tried their hardest.

Perfectionists hate criticism.
Pursuers of Excellence welcome criticism.

Perfectionists have to win to keep high self-esteem.
Pursuers of Excellence finish second and will still have a good self-image.[139]

Perfection is being right; Excellence is being willing to be wrong.
Perfection is fear; Excellence is taking a risk.
Perfection is anger and frustration; Excellence is powerful.
Perfection is control; Excellence is spontaneous.
Perfection is judgment; Excellence is accepting.
Perfection is taking; Excellence is giving.
Perfection is doubt; Excellence is confidence.
Perfection is pressure; Excellence is natural.
Perfection is the destination. Excellence is the journey.
—Anonymous

Life is full of imperfect things and imperfect people. Although I love doing a little bit of everything, I am the proverbial "jack of all trades and master of none." What I've learned over the years is that learning to accept each other's faults and choosing to celebrate each other's differences are two of the most important keys to creating a healthy, growing, and lasting relationship.

That's my prayer for you today. That you will learn to take the good, the bad, and the ugly parts of your life and lay them at the feet of God. Because in the end, He's the only One who will be able to give you a relationship where a few imperfections and lapses don't become a deal-breaker. In fact, understanding is the base of any relationship, be it a husband-wife or parent-child or friendship!

> "Don't put the key to your happiness in someone else's pocket – keep it in your own." (Anonymous)

2. Smolder or Communicate

Many beautiful women believe that it is better to hold irritations and annoyances that bother them inside rather than to take the time and effort and to work through solutions by communicating them to their husbands. Pushing the dirt under the rug doesn't get rid of it though; it just piles up under there until you start tripping over the huge bump or finally deal with it.

You are not doing yourself or your husband a favor by hiding your feelings from him. Not communicating how you feel can result in resentments and bitterness. Learn some basic precepts about meaningful communication to learn to come up with solutions rather than smoldering inside.

Why Am I Afraid to Tell You Who I Am? Refers to five different levels of communication:

- The fifth level is cliché conversation, such as …How's the family?
- The fourth is reporting facts about others, simply words and conversations…designed to keep us aloof and removed from people.
- The third is ideas and judgments, where we begin to approach an area of real communication.
- The second level is feelings and emotions, where, as husband and wife, we begin to share the feelings that are underneath the ideas and judgments expressed.
- The first level is complete emotional and personal truthfulness in communication.

For us to survive in marriage, first level communication is a must. When we develop an openness and honesty within our relationship we say, "I can tell you how I really feel without you judging that feeling." This level of communication is very difficult because we fear being rejected.[140]

I often refer to the Scripture that says God made His acts known to the children of Israel, but His ways to Moses (Psalms 103:7). Interestingly enough, the children of Israel told Moses they didn't want to approach the mountain where God was speaking. They saw the mountain shaking and smoking and they were concerned that they would die if God spoke directly to them, so they told Moses, "Just tell us what God says and we'll do it." Moses wanted a relationship with God enough to approach the mount, and as in every relationship, he knew something in him would probably have to "die," but the relationship was worth it. That's why Moses intimately knew God's ways—why God did the things He did. But Israel only knew God from the outskirts and only knew what He did and didn't understand why.

As I share my heart with Gary, I try to communicate the whys of my actions—my analytical reasoning, the "inside scoop." Then my husband is on board with me. For example, I shared with my husband the reasons for not coming against authorities in our children's lives. If we encouraged them to come against the authorities in their lives, whether their teachers, coaches, or police, we were also showing our children that when they don't agree with us, they should come against us regardless of our authority. When a teacher said my son was talking out of turn, I went to school with him as he apologized and worked through a solution with the teacher. When the coach put my son on the bench, I encouraged my son to speak with his coach to find out why and then work on the issues that had him on the bench. By explaining these types of insights, the "whys," to my husband he understood and made sure he was with me. So together we stood with our children's coaches, teachers, or bosses and showed our children the value of authority. My catch phrase to remind myself of this principle with my husband, children and others is, "Don't just show your *ways,* tell your *whys.*"

By talking in first level conversations, we shared our dreams for our future. Before we even had children, we talked of our dreams for them. Our involvement in our children's lives today wasn't planted in our hearts recently; we rehearsed what we wanted to do in those early conversations. If you don't reveal what your heart is how can someone know it? If you don't hear your husband's deepest desires, how can you know what is important to him?

Because we talked at that level-one depth and because we got on the same page about how we wanted to put money towards our children's higher education beyond traditional college or their first house, we lived like we were destitute and packed money away so those dreams became a reality. Had we not talked about it early enough, it would have been impossible to do it. Talk to your spouse about the "what ifs" and what you admire that others do and what you don't want to do that you see others do. When a husband and wife have these conversations, they begin to walk toward the same goals.

Communication is a difficult concept to master. Most of us stay at a superficial level. The difficult part about communication is that you can have it down pat at one point in your life, yet let it lapse at another point. Good communication isn't a one-time decision; rather, it is an ongoing work and process. If I don't make an attempt to deal with the important issues in a strong, intimate communicative basis, then my husband is not going to enter into a risk-like situation and share himself openly with me either.

If you decide to pursue open communication together, be aware of the potential difficulties at first. If either of you haven't felt secure enough to tell the other person your true feelings, the feelings that have been bottled up for so long may seem overwhelming at first. Be patient with each other. Make free and truthful communication your goal. Avoid being defensive or justifying a point of view or fighting about perceived hurts and wrongs. Give each other a lot of understanding. Take the time to work through every perceived wrong or pain.

Communication will help you grow together; without communication you will grow apart. Be intentional. Look, find, figure out, make the time to converse and connect with each other in meaningful ways.

> "Dialog is to love what blood is to the body. When the flow of blood stops, the body dies. When dialogue stops, love dies and resentment and hate are born. But dialogue can restore a dead relationship. Indeed, this is the miracle of dialogue: it can bring a relationship into being, and it can bring into being once again a relationship that has died. There is only one qualification to these claims for dialogue: it must be

mutual and proceed from both sides, and the parties to it must persist relentlessly."[141]

3.   Understand or Demand

When your husband comes home each day, do you greet him with a warm smile or a list of problems? Do you let the children rush in and climb all over him or make complaints? After everyone greets their father, do you encourage him to go into his room where he can take off his shoes, change his clothes, and have a little peace and quiet (which I sometimes call piece of quiet) before expecting him to jump in to home life? This is a good wife's way of protecting her husband and allowing him some transition time. What is your way of welcoming your husband home? What is your way of giving him time to transition from demands and frustrations at work and overcrowded highways to home life?

If your husband is not able to take you out to dinner or to other social events, do you try to understand? Do you try to see things through his eyes as well as through your own? When I was leading a discipleship class with the pastor of our church, I realized that my husband could not control his schedule enough to be home and available so that I could be there on time. After being embarrassed and late several times, I arranged for a babysitter to cover for him. The same problem happened when we were invited to dinner. I learned that I could plan on my husband being home on "as the plane flies" time, which wasn't a fixed time on a clock. I realized it was easier to let people know we couldn't be there than to be extremely late or not show up at all because planes were delayed for hours or cancelled. Although we had to give up social events, I realized that my husband was just as frustrated, and exhausted, trying to make it to things and not being able to control events to get him places on time. I could have hammered at my husband and nagged him and tried to change the situations, and he couldn't have changed the airlines or the traffic, and I would have lost the good relationship I have with him.

The principle is that I forgo my own needs in preference to my husband's greater need to unwind. I don't want to be demanding, adding to his burdens. Wives of builders, carpenters, and painters have to do the same thing—forgo the jobs they would like done at home to prefer their husband's greater need to unwind. Sometimes what you desire which would make your home life more enjoyable are out of reach financially. As much as these items, repairs, or renovations would mean to you, your husband's health and happiness should mean more.

A wise wife should understand her husband's motives. If I don't agree with my husband's plans or decisions, I am able to express myself honestly, but usually I am more understanding when I can see and understand his motives. My husband's intentions are usually better than his delivery because he is unable to direct his own schedule because of work constraints. So I often say, "Gary, you get an A for intentions." This bit of humor helps us both step back and be sure we understand each other.

Children tend to adopt the attitude of their mother. If you feed your children negativity about your husband, they will see their father through that filter. If you emphasize his positive traits, they will sift their thoughts of him through those words. Discuss with your husband privately about mistakes, failures, or shortcomings, but speak only positive comments with your kids and others. It takes great discipline, but the reward is great.

If your husband spends a lot of time away from home, it might be easy to get upset with him. Your understanding will curb your demands. For example, my brother-in-law is an excellent golfer, and he takes a lot of clients golfing. My sister has been very wise in her demands about his time and has praised him for taking time to play golf with his sons and other family members. If your husband has the comfort and assurance he needs to function at full capacity, and if he is always met with understanding, you can be sure he will be home as often as possible.

Men need down time. My son once said, "Mom, I think when I'm sleeping." The demands, expectations, and frustrations in your husband's life are great. Don't add to the pressure; make time for rest, recreation, and down time.

4. Bomb Diffuser or Bomb Detonator

Anger can be a good thing—it is a powerful emotion that, when targeted like a laser beam, can be a conduit for positive changes. However, explosive anger can cause much damage to a relationship, like a bomb exploding.

> "Anyone can become angry—that is easy; but to be angry with the right person, and to the right degree, and at the right time, and for the right purpose, and in the right way—that is not easy."--Aristotle[142]

When you have feelings of anger simmering, or if you see signs of it in your spouse, it is wise to understand and use some of the techniques that a bomb diffuser has to utilize. Have you ever watched a movie or seen a person diffusing a bomb? It takes skill and patience. Keep these few steps in mind when you need to diffuse potentially explosive and destructive elements in your relationship.

<u>Realize what you are dealing with.</u> Take a good look at the situation, analyze the problem, picture the desired outcome, and look at the obstacles in between.

<u>Take apart the detonator</u>. As in a bomb, look for the override mechanism that will stop the explosion from happening. What can you say or what body language will stop the timer?

<u>Get rid of the bomb's explosive elements.</u> Carefully and gently get to the root of the problem that could explode and get it out of the way. You may say, "Is the real issue the expense?" or "I really didn't mean to sound so angry."

<u>Stop toxic levels of radiation from being released.</u> The uranium inside of bombs combines with other elements to become fatal. If they are kept apart there is no danger. What combinations of words or issues are lethal in your relationship? Does your insistence on a girls' night out where singles frequent cause your husband to feel jealous? Does his desire to play cards with the guys threaten you? Does his golf or love of football inconvenience you? When angry, don't bring up these toxic areas and don't rehearse all the old hurts or disappointments. Keep the argument focused on the current problem not all the issues that you have ever faced. If you link, you sink. Stick to the subject at hand and don't link past events or situations to it.

The Bible reminds us, "When angry, do not sin…"(Ephesians 4:26, AMP). When I want to control my anger, I like to use the same reminder I used when I taught my children to cross the street: stop, look, and listen.

<u>Stop</u>

The adrenaline that rushes through your system can cause destruction if you allow it. Take a deep breath, and purposefully stop. Do not react immediately. I have found several helpful tools to slow down my anger.

1. I remove myself from the situation that was making me angry. Physically go into another room, into a nearby large closet, or simply walk away. If I'm on the phone, I say, "I need to call you back" and hang up as quickly and politely as possible. Time and space allow me to cool down and act calmly without adrenaline making me over-react.
2. I remember these key words: "It is better to shut up than sweep up."
3. I ask God to help me: "Lay It Down, Let It Go, Give It Up, or Forget About It."
4. I read Psalm 39 (AMP), which has some amazing advice for difficult situations:

<u>Know when to "shut up" and when to "speak up."</u>
"I said, I will take heed and guard my ways, that I may sin not with my tongue; I will muzzle my mouth as with a bridle while the wicked are before me. I was dumb with silence, I held my peace without profit and had no comfort away from good, while my distress was renewed." (Psalm 39:1-2 AMP)

I have often muzzled my mouth for the sake of the relationship.

<u>Look</u>

<u>Muse (or "Look!")</u>
"My heart was hot within me. While I was musing, the fire burned; then I spoke with my tongue: Lord, make me to know my end and [to appreciate] the measure of my days—what it is; let me know and realize how frail I am [how transient is my stay here]. Behold, You have made my days as [short as] handbreadths, and my lifetime is as nothing in Your sight. Truly every man at his best is merely a breath! Selah [pause, and think calmly of that]! Surely every man walks to and fro—like a shadow in a pantomime; surely for futility and

emptiness he is in turmoil; each one heaps up riches, not knowing who will gather them." (Psalm 39:3-6 AMP)

These verses remind me to take a look at myself and how frail I am, and how much perspective I need. I need to calmly think of how transient little disagreements are and to realize that at my best I am just a breath!

Verses 7–13 continue this train of thought by helping me to place my expectation and hope in the Lord, who has delivered me from all my transgressions. He helps me muzzle my mouth. When I acknowledge and realize my own vulnerability to do the wrong thing, I am better equipped to open my mouth with the law of kindness and forgive as I have been forgiven. Only through received grace can I give grace. Deciding to muzzle my mouth and change my perspective isn't easy. These decisions require me to put away my pride.

"Who says that you are any better than other people? What do you have that wasn't given to you? If you were given what you have, why are you bragging as if it weren't a gift?" (1 Corinthians 4:7 GW)

"And now, Lord, what do I wait for and expect? My hope and expectation are in You. Deliver me from all my transgressions; make me not the scorn and reproach of the [self-confident] fool! I am dumb, I open not my mouth, for it is You Who has done it. Remove Your stroke away from me; I am consumed by the conflict and the blow of Your hand. When with rebukes You correct and chasten man for sin, You waste his beauty like a moth and what is dear to him consumes away; surely every man is a mere breath. Selah [pause, and think calmly of that]! Hear my prayer, O Lord, and give ear to my cry; hold not Your peace at my tears! For I am Your passing guest, a temporary resident, as all my fathers were. O look away from me and spare me, that I may recover cheerfulness and encouraging strength and know gladness before I go and am no more!" (Psalm 39:7-13)

Karen Budzinski

268

I went through Lamaze classes for childbirth and since then I have discovered those techniques are valuable for hostile and aggressive situations in relationships. When your body is tensing up, take a cleansing breath, candle blow air through your lips, shake your body to make sure you are not tensing up everywhere, walk around (or away), get a drink of water, count, focus on something else to divert your attention, and one of the *most* important methods: be quiet! Especially if you know nothing good is going to come out of your mouth.

Listen

Listen and trust the Lord to act on your behalf.
Listen to the Word of God and apply it to your situation. If we reach an impasse because we can't agree, I release the matter to the Lord.

"Entrust your ways to the Lord. Trust in Him, and He will act on your behalf." (Psalm 37:5 GW)

"Hear my cry, O God; attend unto my prayer. From the end of the earth will I cry unto thee. When my heart is overwhelmed: lead me to the rock that is higher than I." (Psalm 61:1-2 KJV)

"Cast thy burden upon the Lord, and He shall sustain thee: He shall never suffer the righteous to be moved." (Psalm 55.22 KJV).

The Bible commands us to overcome evil with good (Romans 12:21), and to trust the Lord to handle our adversaries.

Although King Saul sought to kill David, and David had the opportunity to kill King Saul (1 Samuel 24:4-7), David refused to harm the king because David honored him as God's anointed. David had the promise of the throne, and had a good case for self-defense, but he still chose to wait for the Lord. King David is my hero because he truly was a man after God's heart. He went after God's heart always. He fell and got up and kept going forward. He trusted God to fulfill His promises and change those in authority over him and didn't take action against those in authority. I want to be more like him. No matter how bad the situation, ^{we} can trust that God is more powerful, and His plans cannot be sabotaged.

Resolve

After I have stopped, looked, and listened, then I can open my mouth with the proper perspective and wisdom. This is the key to problem solving instead of problem escalation. "A gentle answer turns away rage, but a harsh word stirs up anger." (Proverbs 15:1 GW) If you purpose not to open your mouth until you have established these steps, you will be successful in conquering the destructive aspects of anger.

Effective Problem Solving

I heard that when racecars are built, they are built to crash. The designers build in fortification so the driver will sustain the least possible injury. Special seat tilts and special frame engineering and materials are tested in high impact tests so that the car provides protection for the driver.

In marriage relationships, the crash will come. Wives can fortify and protect the relationship for those conflicts.

"I have told you these things, so that in Me you may have [perfect] peace and confidence. In the world you have tribulation and trials and distress and frustration; but be of good cheer [take courage; be confident, certain, undaunted]! For I have overcome the world. [I have deprived it of power to harm you and have conquered it for you.]" (John 16:33 AMP)

What do we do when our world comes crashing in on us? An unexpected doctor's report, financial woes, job loss, auto accidents? Have we prepared for the crash? Can we withstand the crash with the least injury to our relationship? Here are some tips to help you fortify your marriage:

1. When life is running smoothly, use your time wisely to build closeness and understanding. Make special memories, handle little annoyances well, and consider how your communication styles need buffing up. If we are not in a battle, we should be preparing for the next battle. Keep short accounts, appreciate each other, and learn better communication skills.

2. Put extra absorbent materials into your relationship. Pour extra love, understanding, gentleness, kindness, and every other fruit of God's Spirit into your relationship so that when things crash there is a buffer of insulation all around!

3. Have some fire extinguishers ready and know how to ward off little fires before things escalate. Develop some key phrases, such as "Hey, remember, we are on the same team."

4. Become an expert at forgiveness. The book *What is Forgiveness,* describes what it means to forgive. "Psychologists generally define forgiveness as a conscious, deliberate decision to release feelings of resentment or vengeance toward a person or group who has harmed you, regardless of whether they actually deserve your forgiveness… Experts who study or teach forgiveness make clear that when you forgive, you do not gloss over or deny the seriousness of an offense against you. Forgiveness does not mean forgetting, nor does it mean condoning or excusing offenses. Though forgiveness can help repair a damaged relationship, it doesn't obligate you to reconcile with the person who harmed you, or release them from legal accountability. Instead, forgiveness brings the forgiver peace of mind and frees him or her from corrosive anger… In that way, it empowers you to recognize the pain

you suffered without letting that pain define you, enabling you to heal and move on with your life."[143]

Forgiveness is a choice; it is a decision. Remember, emotion follows action; don't wait until you feel like it. How many times should you forgive someone? As often as it pops up in your mind. Peter asked Jesus, "Lord, how many times may my brother sin against me and I forgive him and let it go? [As many as] up to seven times? Jesus answered him, I tell you, not up to seven times, but seventy times seven!"[144] In Matthew 6:12 (AMP), we are instructed to pray, "…[F]orgive us our debts, as we also have forgiven (left, remitted, and let go of the debts, and have given up resentment against) our debtors."

My mom defines unforgiveness as, "drinking poison and expecting the other person to die." Besides this obvious benefit of forgiving, there are good reasons to forgive listed in Scripture. Find at least one of them that compel you. Forgiveness gives you a heart like God. Forgive as Christ has forgiven you. If you receive forgiveness for all your sins, it is wrong to fail to forgive someone of so much less. You will be forgiven in the same way that you forgive others.[145]

Forgiving doesn't always mean forgetting. It may take time. When you are reminded of the offense, cast the thoughts out and replace them with other thoughts or Scripture.[146]

In some instances, forgiveness does not necessarily mean that everything has been worked out. When my sister and I had too many misunderstandings and heated discussions to unravel, we decided to do what any good knitter would do when the yarn becomes too tangled to work with. We agreed to cut off the tangled mess, tie a knot to a new ball of yarn, and begin our relationship again. Although the knots couldn't be worked out, we left them behind to move forward in our relationship.

A dear friend felt she was encumbered by unforgiveness. She needed to release these feelings to the Lord, so she decided to do it in a visual way. She purchased helium balloons and with a sharpie wrote her issues on the balloons. Then she went to a park, prayed over the balloons, and then let the balloons go, watching as they disappeared.

Forgiveness opens your life up to move in the direction God calls you to move. "It is hard to steer a parked car. A vehicle that is barely moving is easier to turn than one that is sitting still. When we attempt to obey what we hear God calling us to do, our lives become more open to the guidance of the Holy Spirit…. If you are not experiencing blessings, maybe you are like a parked car. If you continue to beg God for clarity, maybe you are ignoring an earlier answer he has already given. Start moving in the direction he called you and see if your life is not more easily steered!"[147]

5. Keep growing spiritually. When you get closer to the Lord, the fruit of His Spirit will be more and more evident in your own life. "…[T]he fruit of the [Holy] Spirit [the work which His presence within accomplishes] is love, joy (gladness), peace, patience (an even temper, forbearance), kindness, goodness (benevolence), faithfulness, Gentleness (meekness, humility), self-control (self-restraint, continence). Against such things there is no law [that can bring a charge]."[148] Knowing who you are in Christ will empower you to be the best you that you can be.

6. Develop a way to work through smaller problems without ugliness. Sometimes when my husband is overloaded and starts to get short with me or frustrated with me, I tap him on his shoulder, look at him in the eye kindly, and say, "Remember when you used to be really <u>nice</u> to me?" Sometimes injecting an element of humor or lightheartedness into a situation diffuses the tension, "Hmm… and I was just thinking about what I should get you for your birthday."

We need to find ways to defray tough situations. Kindly respond when you can, without overanalyzing everything or making mountains out of every molehill. Sometimes when Gary asks me if I'd like to do something I don't want to do, rather than launch into a lengthy explanation, I may just say, "No, thanks!" One of my daughters and her husband have a tagline, when confronted with a mistake they've made, to simply say, "I'm sorry, I wasn't thinking." This keeps a small mistake small instead of escalating the situation into something bigger than it needs to be.

7.   Develop some Rules of War. Successful married couples argue, but they take a gentle approach to start the conversation, and they know how to exit an argument if it begins to escalate, and quickly repair the damage.[149] Why are there no laws for relationship wars? Even in international warfare, there are rules of engagement. Establish some argument guidelines before the argument gets heated. Here are some suggestions.

Declaration of war. Promise to let each other know when you are upset.

Acceptance of surrender. Develop a signal that allows a truce.

Treatment of prisoners. Use kind, gentle, loving words. Never hit below the belt.

Prohibition of certain weapons that could cause suffering unnecessarily. Establish what statements are off limits. What taboo subjects (such as mother-in-law, past bad business decisions) are not allowed in arguments?

Avoid "Friendly Fire." Although it is a misleading term, "friendly fire" is the unfortunate circumstance when someone is shot down by a person who is on his or her side. I have seen this happen when women are with family or friends and think it is okay to poke fun at or belittle their spouse to seem funny.

8. Avoid being wounded or wounding others. Wounded animals act unpredictably, and wounded people aren't much different. Pain because of past experiences is a real emotion. Wounded people might over react or react inappropriately— if you add to the pain. If you have unresolved wounds, seek treatment. If you have been hurt, abused, taken advantage of, unappreciated, cheated on, seek the Lord's help along with professional help. When you are healed, choose to move on. Put the past behind you. Be sure you keep moving forward.

9. Handle problems quickly. Whenever the degree of closeness, love, and companionship of your relationship with your husband begins to decline, even slightly, face the problem now. Little frustrations and problems, when not addressed, can chip away at your relationship without being noticed. Take the time to make things right.

10. Realize that what you can't see will hurt you. One of my favorite features of our truck is that the side mirrors show cars hidden in the blind spots. If I couldn't see the cars driving in my blind spots, major accidents could occur. I wish it were that easy to see the blind spots in my relationships—those hidden problems that cause me to sideswipe or bump into the one I love. If you have the same issue with multiple people, take a good look at yourself: you could have some blind spots that need to be brought into clear vision to avoid further problems.

Realize that others have blind spots too. Don't take your husband's moods or attitudes so personally. If someone tried to come through the door in a wheelchair, you would try to help. But if someone has problems relating to others you aren't willing to overlook their relationship handicap. Be sure you don't make someone else's problem become your own by acting as though it is directed at you. For example, when I used to do a home-based business, my daughter helped me conduct a class where a woman had a horrible attitude towards me. I cheerfully helped her and encouraged her and overlooked her obvious attitude problem. After the class, my daughter asked me, "How were you so nice to that woman. She was so mean to you; she didn't like you." I told my daughter, "She doesn't even know me, so I can't take her problem personally. She probably has that problem relating to people in general and it's not really directed at me." Sometimes others may not even be aware of their crabby attitude so I try to consider it a handicap that they aren't even aware of and it makes it easier for me to "open the door" for them.

11. Define some of your unique contributions. You have unique characteristics that make you one of a kind. What does your husband know about you and expect of you? Does he know how you will react? Does he depend on you to act and react in a certain way?

When my son–in–law Brandon comes home, Christa (my daughter) makes a huge deal over his entrance. She runs to him and throws her arms around him. If she didn't respond in this way, it would not only be sad for Brandon, it would be sad for any one privileged to see her response to him. I hope when they are celebrating their 50th Wedding Anniversary she is still responding to him in the same way.

12. Consider how you and your husband respond to each other. Did you lose some enthusiasm along the way? Are you close?

Your husband will react to the positive or negative changes you implement in your marriage. Make steady progress and tell him how you are trying to change. Be prepared for testing to begin, so you won't react inappropriately.

Women are under a lot of pressure. Each day brings different demands and frustrations. Often we can't keep up with all that is expected of us. Time and energy have limits. I've been told I appear to have so much energy. Truth is I often feel like someone treading water in the middle of the ocean.

When I feel frustrated, I reevaluate my day's activities honestly and objectively. Do I need to cut work hours? Do I need to be more realistic about time I am spending away from my home? I cannot expect to accomplish anything around the house if I am not home. Do I need to put the telephone away so I can attend to the backlog? I may be blaming other people or circumstances when it is my own inefficiency at fault. Sometimes simply getting to bed earlier and waking up earlier helps me to be more effective and efficient.

I know when my fuel tank is low. I also know my routine: over-commit, over-do, over-extend, over-schedule, and then I want out of everything! I can tell when the end is coming. I am not charitable towards others. I am unkind and impatient with others' shortcomings. I start expecting others to take on some of the loads I have taken on myself. I am frustrated and easily irritated even on the road, in a restaurant, or with strangers. When this happens, I cross everything off my schedule, don't answer the phone, stay inside and disconnect. Then the whole cycle starts over.

I have tried unsuccessfully to eliminate this cycle from my life, but I have learned I need down time after major commitments or I will experience burnout. When I begin to get impatient, I try to lighten my load. I make commitments for limited times. For example, when I was homeschooling, I committed to one year and then reassessed before deciding for the next year. I didn't commit to a 12-year homeschooling program.

If you are feeling pressure and are frustrated by routine chores and normal problems, perhaps some of these tips that helped me can help you:

- I hire an inexpensive Mother's Helper—a girl too young to babysit alone but old enough to amuse and keep my children from being underfoot so I can get a few things done in the same or the next room.

- I constantly review my calendar and checkbook to be sure my time and money is going to my priorities. For example, I broke away from being in a carpool because I loved being the first person my children connected with after school, and I wanted to be the one they talked to about their day. I refused to give up those moments no matter how convenient a carpool seemed.

- I break larger projects into smaller tasks. If I have to do a lot of filing of papers or clean the basement or attack Mount Never-Rest (my laundry room), I repeat this phrase, "Never underestimate the value of a minute." If I only have a couple of minutes, I do a small task toward my overall goal. By the time I'm ready to tackle the whole project, much of it is done already.

- I set a timer when I take phone calls. With small children, long conversations are not an option. Set your answering machine and your timer; tell your friends you'll call them later. I bought a hands-free telephone headset. When everyone is in bed and I'm finishing a task such as scrubbing my kitchen floor, I call people back. Makes my chore more fun, and I talk to friends too.

- I am careful not to commit to many activities; my "yes" to the many requests for my time and energy is actually saying "no" to the needs of my family. That simple revelation equips me to say "no" to requests that rob my family of time. When I say "no," I know I am saying "yes" to my family's needs.

Because women are nurturing and compassionate, we want to help others, but our children, our husbands, and our homes are our priority.

- I stay connected purposefully. I put names in a jar of those I really want to stay connected to, and when I have a few minutes, I call or email one of those people.

- I try to make wise choices. Sometimes, in an effort to "get out" or have a "break" it causes more havoc and disruption and problems than if I just give up getting out for a season. It just doesn't pay to try to get out more often when it causes suffering to make up for lost time! For example, as much as I love my tennis league, when I am going through seasons where I know investing in a practice every week and driving to far away games will cause more problems than good, I opt out of the league and try to play with friends locally instead. When I feel there is a season in my life that offers me more time, I go back on a league.

- Every morning I make a list of twenty things I need to get done and put the most important ones first. Anything not accomplished goes on the next day's list.

- I constantly tweak my schedule. I purposefully choose to enjoy my life, and sometimes enjoyment means scratching items off the calendar or postponing activities to another season. Readjust your schedule; be fully present and fully alive.

- I purpose to be 100% where my body is at all times. This sounds funny, but so many times I have attended a work event with my husband, but my mind would be at home with my children. I've wished I was somewhere other than where I was much too often. I finally decided to be present mentally as well as physically. It is one of the most awesome decisions I've ever made. This commitment also helps me say no when I realize I don't really desire to commit to an event or invitation 100%.

Try conscientiously lifting the loads and demands rather than creating more. Instead of trying to get away, try making your home more of a peaceful haven you don't need to get away from. Take control of your schedule. Take a break from social media to concentrate on the real people in your life. Pressures can be temporarily relieved when your home is in order and your children are well behaved. You will receive the fruit or harvest from your hard work, and your work will be a testament to others.[150]

Don't try to over discuss the thoughts in your head. Some thoughts need to be cast out. Develop a bigger perspective than your inner thoughts. Your thoughts can be skewed because of personal issues. In 1 Kings 19, when Elijah was running away from Jezebel, he was so depressed he prayed he might die. What Elijah *really* needed was to sleep, eat, and drink something. Many times when we are out of sorts and our thoughts are off track, take a good look at your schedule, what you have been eating and drinking, and determine if you just need to rest and eat properly to get your emotions back in balance.

Addressing Addictive Destructive Behaviors

Sometimes problems in your home or relationships aren't your fault. Even though it is your responsibility to check yourself first as you searching for the reasons for the problems. Some difficulties are beyond your control.

If you can, see a professional counselor. Friendly advice from your acquaintances or well-meaning-but-wrong advice from others may not be the best for you. Even some pastors or religious leaders may give you wrong advice. Ask God for discernment. You may be told to try harder, to avoid making him so mad, and to soldier on. You may be reminded that God hates divorce. Or be told it is your fault. Never stay in a situation that is dangerous to you or your children.

If you are being physically or emotionally abused, you need professional help. Wives can fall into the co-dependent habit allowing her husband to continue in unhealthy patterns. If your husband indulges in alcohol or drugs or hurls insults at you or tries to keep you like a prisoner in your home or if he refuses to pay the bills or pay for groceries or constantly criticizes and belittles you, he is an abuser. If he thinks he can treat you badly because you allow him to, you have developed co-dependent habits and need a professional to help you.

It is important that if you or your children are at risk, you must get to a safe place. Separation allows for a time of prayer and fasting and counseling to get your marriage back together if you are safe. If you are not at risk, you need to find out if there is a way to break the pattern so you can look forward to a different kind of future together.

If the policeman were to drive by you screaming at the top of their lungs and waving their fists at you, would you *really* not drive as fast? If he made a sad face or shook his head at you, would you really care? Your screaming, "waving your fist," or your sad face may not be a strong enough motivation for your husband to want to go through the trouble of changing an abusive habit.

Don't internalize or cover up for serious issues. When a husband verbally or emotionally or physically abuses his wife, she should not tolerate him abusing her. Remember, it is not your fault, and, no matter how scary it is, there are many great organizations to help in these types of abusive situations, and you should seek professional help as soon as possible. When things at home require you to cover up or lie, result in you being constantly belittled or feeling intimated, your marriage is in a hostile position. You have to know that by trying to just "soldier on" in the face of things that are overtly hurting you or doing without things you truly need, you are not doing your marriage any favors by not addressing these types of serious issues.

"Domestic abuse, also known as spousal abuse, occurs when one person in an intimate relationship or marriage tries to dominate and control the other person. Domestic abuse that includes physical violence is called domestic violence."[151] Emotional abuse is not only equally damaging, but sometimes even more so because the scars cannot be seen. "An emotionally destructive marriage is one where one's personhood, dignity, and freedom of choice is regularly denied, criticized, or crushed. This can be done through words, behaviors, economics, attitudes and misusing the Scriptures."[152]

"God wants us to live abundantly in His blessings. He will not entrap us, or force us to stay in our own traps to uphold an institution. The institutions of our loving God are never more important than the people within them."[153]

"There are myriads of reasons why marriage relationships break down. God hates it when a heavy, inflexible grid of legalism is imposed on people and they are broken and turn away from Him as a result. Marriages are intended to be life long and every attempt should be made to reconcile and recapture the first love that founded the relationship. But in this imperfect world, God's provision of divorce is sometimes vital, and can be lifesaving."[154]

"Jesus answered them, 'I assure you, most solemnly I tell you, Whoever commits and practices sin is the slave of sin.'" (John 8:34 AMP)

"…You know well enough from your own experience that there are some acts of so-called freedom that destroy freedom. Offer yourselves to sin, for instance, and it's your last free act. But offer yourselves to the ways of God and the freedom never quits. All your lives you've let sin tell you what to do. But thank God you've started listening to a new master, one whose commands set you free to live openly in his freedom!" (Romans 6:16–18 THE MESSAGE)

Don't be afraid to seek professional help if you are in over your head. It is better to get help early with the problem than to wait 15 years to get help. A third party may be able to help work out problems in a way that will bring more harmony to your relationship. It is not a weakness to seek help; rather it is strength. Remember what we have observed about the best of the best in the sports and art world—the best are still taking lessons, are still being coached, and are taking advice of third parties.

Chapter 14

Joy in the Journey

Financial Strength

Since money problems are often the number one problem in marriage and believed by some experts as the number one cause of divorce, we need to take a look at becoming financially strong to keep our relationships stronger.

"We Owe We Owe, It's Off to Work We Go!" I am so grateful that my husband and I both hate being in debt. This belief doesn't mean that we never were in debt, only that we believed the Scriptural admonitions that "the borrower is servant to the lender,"[155] we were to "owe no man any thing but to love one another,"[156] and that God desires us to be content with little,[157] letting our moderation be known to all.[158]

We moved seven times, each time paying our house off, and then moving to a larger house when we were financially able. When we borrowed money for each house, we made sure our monthly payments didn't strap us. As soon as we signed mortgage papers, we lived simply. We even hung little signs in our closet with $500, $100, $50, $10, and $5. The signs equaled the amount we owed the bank. As we prepaid our principal, we pulled the signs off the wall until the debt was paid.

Compare this strategy to the financial attitudes of too many people. Some are not interested in paying off loans right away; others take trips and spend money even though they owe hundreds and sometimes thousands of dollars in loans. I have spoken to people who are deluded into believing that they are so far into debt they might as well just keep spending money, because they'll never pay off their loans anyway.

God's best for you is to live modestly and free of debt. If you are in debt, stop spending money unless the item is a necessity; sell what you can, work an extra job if possible. Until your debts are paid off. Then you are free.

"Let your character or moral disposition be free from love of money [including greed, avarice, lust, and craving for earthly possessions] and be satisfied with your present [circumstances and with what you have]; for He [God] Himself has said, I will not in any way fail you nor give you up nor leave you without support. [I will] not, [I will] not, [I will] not in any degree leave you helpless nor forsake nor let [you] down (relax My hold on you)! [Assuredly not!]" (Hebrews 13:5 AMP)

Financial freedom has rewards:

1. It is satisfying to desire something, work to save enough money, and then purchase it. When we first got married, we made lists of items we wanted to purchase. We saved until we were able to afford those items, reevaluated our need, desire, and priority of purchasing the item, and then purchased the item. This process was challenging, rewarding, and free of mandatory choices. It helped me realize that I wanted to teach my children these principles and help them gain the same benefit that comes from wanting something, working towards getting it, and then having the reward of

actually getting the item. Many times, in the process, my desire changed for the item and I actually realized I would rather not purchase it. This process also made me realize that the item was a real representation of weeks, months, or even years of my life or my husband's life as we worked hard to get it.

2. It is rewarding to get a paycheck and be able to decide what to do with the money instead of paying off old financial obligations.

3. It is gratifying to pay the actual price devoid of interest and credit fees.

4. It is enjoyable to go on a trip or purchase an item with cash instead of credit.

5. It is pleasing to know you own what you purchase and that the bank or financial institution has no claim on your possessions. When I was younger and before I realized the importance of living debt free, I wanted a sports car. I borrowed money to buy one. I had a great job as a legal assistant and thought I made a lot of money. However, the $350 car payments per month were cumbersome on top of my housing and living expenses. It strapped me for cash, and I was paying high interest rates but not a lot on the principal of the car. Then my car was totaled when it was parked on the street, and I was forced to keep paying on the car because I owed more for it than it was worth.

6. It is empowering to know you have the power to do without things and actually live below or at least within your means. One of history's true men of God, Watchman Nee, desired to live without covetousness. He made it a practice to actually purchase six of whatever he wanted and give five away and keep one. He wanted to be sure he was living well below his means.

"…godliness with contentment is great gain. For we brought nothing into this world, and it is certain we can carry nothing out. And having food and raiment let us be therewith content. But they that will be rich fall into temptation and a snare, and into many foolish and hurtful lusts, which drown men in destruction and perdition. For the love of money is the root of all evil: which while some coveted after, they have erred from the faith, and pierced themselves through with many sorrows. But thou, O [wo]man of God, flee these things, and follow after righteousness, godliness, faith, love, patience, meekness." (1 Timothy 6:8-11 KJV, emphasis added.)

7. It is liberating to enjoy good things without having the upkeep and maintenance of owning them. For example, as a photographer, I felt I should get a large format printer since many photographers owned one. I thought I would print photo packages at my home. I purchased a professional model and then a true large-format model. Because I wasn't working with them every day, the ink dried out, and I never was able to get the color calibrated between my various computers and devices. Owning that printer was frustrating, time consuming, and expensive. It seemed to always be in the repair shop. I spent too much time trying to figure out why the printers weren't printing correctly. Yes, I did manage to print a few photo packages, but the money I spent went well beyond the money I saved. I could have ordered Costco™ prints or prints from photography service sites and not had the hassle, financial costs, or hours of wasted time.

I have learned, especially with now having another home up north, that the more things you *have* the more things you have to *service*. I purged what I did *not* want to service any more. Getting rid of a lot of technical products eased the frustration I was experiencing in dealing with those complicated items.

When my children were little, we enjoyed visiting a friend with a pool, or we went to the public pool for open swim times. I brought snacks, picnic lunches, and drinks for my family. When the day was over, I felt such relief to pack up and go home without worrying about pool maintenance and upkeep. Later, when we purchased a home with a built-in pool, I discovered first-hand what I had been saved from in those early years. The pool required me to monitor the chemicals, and service and maintain a dehumidification system to ensure the humidity didn't adversely affect our home. I ran the shark to clean the pool, covered the pool, and skimmed it. On top of that, the liner was costly to repair and the pool heater had to be maintained. Eventually we decided not to pour thousands of additional dollars into the pool. We closed the pool and had it taken out; it was a huge relief.

If you desire or require some expensive equipment, be sure you not only have the money to purchase these costly and time-demanding items, but also the money to maintain them.

Do you want a deck? Consider the cost of the deck, but also consider that every two years you need to have the deck re-stained and retreated. Do you want a hot tub? Consider the cost of the chemicals to maintain it, the bromine, saline, or chlorine tablets, the alkaline, and ph adjustment chemicals to keep the hot tub in good working order each year. Also consider the time investment to maintain it. If it is still within your financial and time expenditure means, then you have made a balanced decision.

Debt Eliminates Choices

1. Debt puts your future in bondage. When you assume debt, you assume that you will be able to maintain your job at your current salary. You are basing your debt to income ratio on your current situation. Accordingly, you are assuming

that you will not be involved in any accidents, have any sickness, or experience any unexpected burden on your finances, such as an unexpected water heater problem or roof replacement. You assume that nothing could happen which would require you to take unexpected time off of work. You assume that your job will continue without interruptions due to downsizing or salary cuts.

2. Debt is a breeding ground for discontentment. You are not content with the things you can afford, so you can't wait to get things you cannot afford. Because you don't own the things you buy, you get bored and disinterested and unsatisfied because you end up focusing on the next thing you need or want.

Learn to be happy with much as well as with little, and your joy will not be tied to the things you own. Luke 12:15 (AMP) reminds us, "And He said to them, Guard yourselves and keep free from all covetousness (the immoderate desire for wealth, the greedy longing to have more); for a man's life does not consist in and is not derived from possessing overflowing abundance or that which is over and above his needs."

Philippians 4:11-13 (THE MESSAGE) says, "Actually, I don't have a sense of needing anything personally. I've learned by now to be quite content whatever my circumstances. I'm just as happy with little as with much, with much as with little. I've found the recipe for being happy whether full or hungry, hands full or hands empty. Whatever I have, wherever I am, I can make it through anything in the One who makes me who I am."

3. Debt takes away your choices. No longer can you decide what to do with the money you make, because it is all to be doled out for bills and to creditors. You are paying for rapid depreciation. No longer can you decide to take a less stressful

job if it pays less or take a sales job based on commission. You can't decide to take time off or to stay at home with your baby and take time off of work. You can't be a generous giver to others because you have overspent on yourself.

Top Financial Challenges in Marriage

There are several reasons why financial issues top the charts when it comes to marital disharmony. The problem is not how much money you make, because there are many couples that don't make a lot of money yet still are able to manage their money and make ends meet. My dad had six children, seventeen grandchildren, plus great-grandchildren. My mom didn't work. They not only balanced the budget, had us in private school, and lived below their means, they were known as extravagant givers, went on many vacations, saved towards retirement, and had money in the bank. Compare this to ultra rich celebrities who have filed for bankruptcy. Notice some of the top financial problems and the character trait that enables you to address those problems.

1. Budgeting Takes Discipline.

Make a plan to live the life you want to live: not only now but for your future. The choices you make financially for your future will dictate your spending habits for the present. For example, before Gary and I had children, we talked about our hopes and dreams and plans to be a part of our children's lives when they came along. We knew we wanted to enroll them in a Christian school and to help them go to college. We knew that vacations, however simple, even camping, were a priority for us. We knew that we wanted to help them with their weddings and give them a down payment to be used for higher education after college or for their first home. We could not put our heads in the sand and deny that our home would need regular maintenance and repairs, too. We've had to replace furnaces, hot water heaters, roofs, and have squirrels and other pests eliminated. We had car accidents and repaired cars. We faced surgeries and emergencies for our children and ourselves. All these needs demanded large amounts of money. We lived in a 950 square foot home until we were able to scrimp and save to get to the next level. We lived on next to nothing. I bought used clothing for my children and myself. I rarely purchased new clothes. We budgeted and stayed within our budget so when (not if) these demands hit, we were ready and prepared for the storms.

Living with the goals in mind requires discipline. In order to achieve our goals for our children, we lived well beneath our means. We stayed out of debt. I believe that most people don't realize just how much they cannot afford because they fail to consider putting enough money aside for their future plans and emergencies that are sure to arise. I also believe that foolish and extravagant spending eliminates the ability to choose your future priorities. Until we had money set aside for what we wanted to do for our children, our biggest vacations were in borrowed cabins. We lived on a fraction of what we made in order to have money to use toward our priorities. If I can not afford to buy something today and need to charge it, *what* would make me think I can afford to have money for expenses *plus* pay for the item tomorrow? In other words, if I can't afford it today, it is probable I won't be able to afford it tomorrow either. Holding off on purchases until we had the money for them made sure we could afford the items when we bought them.

If you can stay out of debt and live in a house you can afford to pay off quickly, you will eliminate thousands and even hundreds of thousands of money in interest. By eliminating mortgage or car loan or other payments, and then stashing the money you would have paid for those loans plus the interest, you will amass large amounts of money. But it will take saying no to a lot of things, including eating out, having the latest fashions, and drinking Starbucks coffee regularly. (According to the Stop Buying Expensive Coffee and Save Money Calculator,[159] drinking a Starbucks instead of office coffee during the workweek costs you well over $10,000 over a 10-year work period.) You cannot have instant gratification or feed materialism, but if you commit to eliminate debt, you will be able to live out your priorities more effectively and without stress.

We used an envelope system that allocates funds for certain categories. Although I was very hostile towards the envelopes at first (it seemed that the envelopes shouted "no" to me), I soon realized a newfound freedom because I knew exactly how much money to spend on gifts, babysitters, gas or other cost categories. I learned to be extremely frugal and spend less on gas if I needed to spend more on something else. It was a great system that taught me some good life lessons and choices. I learned to be very creative in planning meals, planning around what was on sale. I didn't waste a penny and was able to stash a little away here and there for my mad money. Because of these disciplines, I became less needy for things that didn't matter, and I was able to enjoy what I purchased.

2. Compulsive Purchases.

I never purchased something that wasn't on a list. I raised my children that way too. If we were shopping and they saw something they thought they had to have, they weren't allowed to purchase unless they had told me beforehand. Avoid compulsive purchases, which often only satisfy you for a minute. You know you are compulsively buying if some of the items you felt you needed to buy are sitting unused in your home. There is now a disorder named CBD (Compulsive Buying Disorder), and instead of Alcoholic Anonymous, compulsive spenders have Debtors Anonymous. Now there are even television shows about hoarding. Know that you will never remain debt free if you get an emotional rush or meet physiological needs by shopping with money you have or money you don't have.

Be practical. Realizing that you need to be out of debt more than you need another pair of shoes or any other item is the first step in avoiding compulsive purchases or over buying. Getting in touch with your practical side (it's in there somewhere!) is the second step. If you want to be debt free, you may not want to pay $1,000 for a Louis Vuitton purse unless you calculate the impact on your financial picture. If your finances allow such a purchase and the cost doesn't hinder your financial goals, fine. However remember that this expensive bag will wear out or go out of style, and consider if you could be just as happy with a look-alike bag. Perhaps the money you save can be applied towards debt, be spent on another need, or you might consider giving the money to a charity or worthy mission project.

There is no stress to me as horrible as financial stress, and, when necessary, I have happily lived without extras to avoid that kind of pressure. I was as happy in my 12x60 trailer as I am in my four-bedroom home. I have made my happiness portable, knowing full well I can be happy vacationing in a tent as well as a five-star hotel. Be practical and know where it just doesn't pay to spend money.

3. Debt to Income Ratio

Making a lot of money does not ensure financial freedom. Those who make less money can enjoy financial freedom too.

Debt to income ratio is a comparison. Total the amount of your monthly payments to service your debt. Include credit card payments, loan payments, housing expenses, including property taxes and insurance, and any homeowner fees, garbage collection fees, etc. Divide your monthly debt repayments by your gross income per month (although for a more realistic comparison, use your net income).

Then multiply that number by 100 to get your debt to income percentage. For example, if you pay $200 on credit cards, $300 on a car payment, and $1,400 per month in other housing and miscellaneous expenses, your total commitment is $2,000 per month to debt. If you make $60,000 per year, your gross income is $60,000 divided by 12 months or $5,000 per month. To figure your debt to income ratio, divide the $2,000 by the $5,000, which is .4 or 40%. Sadly, the average debt to income ratio is 125% in America. You need to start seeking help if your ratio is over 35%.

Two of the principles that helped me live within my means are (1) it is possible whatever my means are at any given time; and (2) I have no right spending money until it is mine to spend. My husband and I took it to the next level because we wanted to avoid paying interest. Although bankers and financial advisors told us that house debt and even other debt was good debt, we tried to live by the Scripture "… the borrower is a slave to the lender." (Proverbs 22:7 GW) As long as the bank owned my house or I owed money for other items, I felt it wasn't really mine. As long as I owed the bank money, I did not feel I had any "extra" money to spend—because it was the bank's money until the loan was paid off. Because of that attitude, I lived well below my means, which resulted in habits I still incorporate into my life now, even though my husband and I are debt free.

Living from payday to payday doesn't leave enough money for a desperate need, such as a medical treatment or coverage that insurance doesn't cover. Sadly, when we squander money on things we don't need, we may not have enough money for something we really can't live without. If you are wise, you will limit your optional spending to focus on your compulsory spending. Refuse to let your money be spent to make you self confident; instead spend your money to make you self sufficient. Displays of wealth and possessions that you can't afford are deceptive and will push you to the edge of a cliff. Learn self-sufficiency so you don't have to expect someone else to bail you out when emergencies arise. Learn to entertain yourself without leaving home. Learn simple joys of picnicking in the park or swimming at the local municipal pool. When I travel with my husband for his work, I am amazed to see just how much money people will spend to fly halfway around the world to go to a park, walk through the woods, sit at a beach, and go to restaurants and stores, many of which are available where we live. Save money for travel but also enjoy the attractions closer to home. Make your home so amazing and stress free that you don't have to pay large loads of money to get away from it. When people tell me they have to get away from everything, especially when they don't have children, I wonder what they are trying to get away from. I work hard to make my home a place of peace and joy, and I enjoy my life at home, so that when I choose to go somewhere, it is because I want to go there and not to escape from my normal life.

4. Leisure Shopping.

Shopping for fun, so called recreational shopping or shopping therapy, needs to be avoided if you are going to stay out of debt. Unless I have money to spend and have considered what I will buy, I avoid shopping. Shopping emphasizes how much you *don't* have. It feeds your greed and your desire for more. Buying gadgets, clothes, or home décor that you don't need and do not have money for will keep you from buying necessities such as groceries or from paying your electric bill. If you continually live beyond your means, get professional help. Stop going to the malls for recreation or hobby, but fill your days with more meaningful hobbies, such as charity work, family days, sports, gardening, cooking, and crafts.

Plan and prioritize the way you spend your money. When we first got married, I realized I couldn't have all the little things and the bigger things too. I learned to save towards something bigger. At other times, I realized I couldn't have bigger items, so I started to appreciate the smaller things I was able to have. Make priorities. My husband and I decided we would never complain or skimp on anything that had eternal value. We had to do without a car for a while. I worked into the early morning hours doing side work for an attorney. I babysat during the day and started a small home sales company. I even made soap and washed out Ziploc bags, but we were able to enroll our children into Christian school, which was a big priority. When it is time to give gifts such as Christmas or birthdays, learn to be creative, but don't give gifts you cannot afford. Learn to say, "I can't afford it" or "I'm sorry I can't go; this isn't a priority for me right now."

5. Insecure in Who You Are and What You Make.

If you are counting on your possessions to make you feel good about yourself, you are already in trouble. If you feel you have to sport name brand purses, shoes, and clothes that movie stars are wearing, beware. Remember they purchase those items out of their excess money, while you may have to forego necessities to purchase them. That difference is huge. If you think you are missing out because you don't have the latest and greatest luxury items or home conveniences, you are in danger because envy turns into desire, then greed.

If you feel that it is important to keep up with your friends' lifestyles, or if you believe you would be happier if you had more, you may be allowing pride to make your financial decisions. I have a friend who is blind and he told me that he is "ahead of the game" because he doesn't base his opinion of others on what they look like, what they wear, or what they drive. Before you make that next purchase, ask yourself, "If no one could see this item except me, would I still want it?"

6. Set Limits and Boundaries.

Begin to watch for the details by tracking where your money is spent. Find an app or program online to help you. One of my friends uses Quick Books to track expenditures so she and her husband can manage money better and stretch it farther. Others use tools such as YNAB (You Need a Budget)[160] or Mvelopes[161] (an online version of the Envelope Plan my husband and I used for years). You will never be able to get your arms around your financial picture without knowing just how much is coming in and where it is going out. As you pay your bills, also pay yourself by starting a savings plan. We have always had an emergency fund, which we refused to touch unless a real emergency arose. If we had to deplete it, we didn't spend money on any extras until we had the fund in place again. We calculate an approximate amount to spend on vacation, and each month, we put 1/12th of that amount aside so when vacation time comes, we have the money. If you have debt, plan a way to pay it down as quickly as possible. Living debt free makes the future brighter and allows choices, not captivity. Debts impinge your future together so make a plan to be debt free so you'll have alternatives. Set boundaries on the amount of money that each of you can spend without consulting the other. If one of you tends to spend and one of you likes to save, set limits and establish priorities together. Establish some discretionary income for each of you, even if it is only $20 per week. You need to know that you don't have to ask your spouse or have him ask you to be able to make a small purchase.

In setting limits and boundaries, don't punish others for your misplaced priorities. If you spend a lot of money on travel and the newest fashions, but are unable to give your niece a small birthday gift or unwilling to pay when you are out with others, take a look at your spending habits; you may find your priorities are out of sync. I believe in the biblical laws of sowing and reaping. The Lord has supernaturally shown my grandparents, my parents, my husband

and me, and now my adult offspring the supernatural laws of giving and receiving. Proverbs 11:24 (THE MESSAGE), "The world of the generous gets larger and larger; the world of the stingy gets smaller and smaller."

Your checkbook reveals what you feel about stewardship and what you believe about biblical principles.

"Give and you will receive. A large quantity, pressed together, shaken down, and running over will be put into your pocket. The standards you use for others will be applied to you." (Luke 6:38 GW)

"[Remember] this: he who sows sparingly and grudgingly will also reap sparingly and grudgingly, and he who sows generously [that blessings may come to someone] will also reap generously and with blessings." (2 Corinthians 9:6 AMP)

"Let each one [give] as he has made up his own mind and purposed in his heart, not reluctantly or sorrowfully or under compulsion, for God loves (He takes pleasure in, prizes above other things, and is unwilling to abandon or to do without) a cheerful (joyous, 'prompt to do it') giver [whose heart is in his giving]. And God is able to make all grace (every favor and earthly blessing) come to you in abundance, so that you may always and under all circumstances and whatever the need be self-sufficient [possessing enough to require no aid or support and furnished in abundance for every good work and charitable donation]. As it is written, He [the benevolent person] scatters abroad; He gives to the poor; His deeds of justice and goodness and kindness and benevolence will go on and endure forever! And [God] Who provides seed for the sower and bread for eating will also provide and multiply your [resources for] sowing and increase the fruits of your righteousness [which manifests itself in active goodness, kindness, and charity]. Thus you will be enriched in all things and in every way, so that you can be generous, and [your generosity as it is] administered by us will bring forth thanksgiving to God." (2 Corinthians 9:7–11 AMP)

"Tell those rich in this world's wealth to quit being so full of themselves and so obsessed with money, which is here today and gone tomorrow. Tell them to go after God, who piles on all the riches we could ever manage— to do good, to be rich in helping others, to be extravagantly generous. If they do that, they'll build a treasury that will last, gaining life that is truly life." (1 Timothy 6:17-19 THE MESSAGE)

Reduce expenses. Put aside gym memberships. Trim the luxuries. I refused to purchase an individual pod coffee maker until very recently. It is much cheaper to make coffee in your coffee pot rather than pay for individual containers. A fax machine, photo printer, hot tub, and even many lawn and household tools are not necessities and can be used or rented usually within a mile from your home. Reducing expenses sets you free from maintenance and operational expenses and time. Before you make a purchase costing more than $300, wait a few days; you may discover you can do without it. You may end up with a lot more time and money, but even more important, a lot less stress and more peace.

Karen Budzinski

The Way You Make Me Feel

I love this poem about Friendship:

> Oh, the comfort –
> The inexpressible comfort of feeling safe with a person,
> Having neither to weigh thoughts,
> Nor measure words – but pouring them
> All right out – just as they are –
> Chaff and grain together –
> Certain that a faithful hand will
> Take and sift them –
> Keep what is worth keeping –
> And with the breath of kindness
> Blow the rest away.[162]

How do others, specifically your spouse, feel with you? Are you a safe place? Does your spouse feel accepted just as he is or do you have him "jumping through hoops" to be what you want him to be? Do you allow others to express themselves to you until you understand their viewpoint, or do you go on "de-fense" and partition yourself from them? Do you seek to understand rather than undermine? Do you allow your husband to rephrase things that you may have interpreted differently than what he was trying to say? Make him feel safe and enjoy the "inexpressible comfort" defined in the poem above.

If others see you together, is your spouse proud to introduce you? Make sure he doesn't want to say, "Hello, this is my wife, and can't you just tell by the look on her face how miserable she is?"

Wives sometimes repel their husbands rather than attract them. If he feels worthless around you, chances are he isn't going to crave more time with you—nor want to go out of his way to please you. If your husband feels like a million dollars around you, he will want to be

300

around you more and he will want to please you. Maya Angelou said, "I've learned that people will forget what you said, people will forget what you did, but people will never forget how you made them feel."[163] I have counseled couples that are amazing individuals, yet neither is able to make their spouse feel special. Setting a too-high standard for your spouse will leave you isolated and alone. Live your life with charisma and you will inspire devotion, favor, loyalty, and enthusiasm in others by your presence. How do you espouse charisma?

- You're interested in others, not just interesting.
- You make others feel important. You already know everything about yourself, so why not take the time to learn about others when you have a chance?
- You listen more than talk. You are interested in others' lives, their children, and their accomplishments. You want to hear about their challenges.
- You are an energy giver and not an energy taker.
- You have good manners.
- You stay focused intently on what someone is saying without looking around for someone better to talk to or checking your phone or computer even for a glance.
- You let someone else shine, without trying to one-up them with a better story.
- You are careful in your choice of words.
- You don't gossip or laugh at others, so people know you won't gossip or laugh at them.
- You are more concerned about how others feel than how you feel, and will go to great lengths to demonstrate that concern in words and deeds.

What do others remember about you? Do they feel loved? Have you appreciated others, or have you taken people for granted and had even a little attitude of entitlement? When someone goes out of their way for you, do you understand and acknowledge it? Are you grateful? If something is important to those you love, do you make sure it is important to you, if only for that fact alone?

Joy in the Journey

"Focus on the journey, not the destination. Joy is found not in finishing an activity but in doing it."[164]

It is so much fun to be around someone who is excited and enthusiastic about life. We need to take more time to smell the roses strewn along the path of our every day lives.

Enthusiasm is contagious and magnetic. I love the word enthusiastic; it comes from a Greek word meaning divine inspiration, to be inspired or possessed by a god. From 'en' (in) and 'theos' (god).[165] The way I see it, when you are enthusiastic, you show that you are in Christ. When I see my enthusiasm for life waning or I am becoming disillusioned with life or people, I know I need to get closer with the Lord. I don't want to become the opposite of enthusiastic: dull, impotent, apathetic, uninterested, weary, or weak.[166]

My mom taught me to love little things all around me, so joy follows me everywhere I go. You need to carefully train your eye to look for a random flower in a crevice in the desert. You need to stop the car to appreciate the first flowers of spring, the glorious buds on a flowering tree, an incredible sunset, or a few deer by the side of the road.

In the fall I often took my children to Dodge Park to see the incredible fall leaves; we loved taking big handfuls of color and throwing the leaves into the air and all over ourselves. We often stopped to count flying geese overhead or watch leaves playing "tag" in the wind. We paused at a favorite maple tree every day in the fall to delight in the new colors; we gathered our favorite leaves off the ground and made wax paper crafts. Stopping to see how ants build their homes or watching a leaf bug in action or admiring beautiful wildflowers growing in unexpected places teaches your family to delight in little things.

Being enthusiastic means that you are exuberant and appreciative when others please you. When we first got married and I started cooking for Gary, he was so appreciative that he always exclaimed, "This is the best ever!" about my food. I was very excited to keep trying new recipes to impress him. It made giving to him fun instead of routine.

When your husband buys a gift or does something special for you, what kind of response does he get? Women who know how to communicate their gratitude are usually the women who receive the sweetest gifts. If you act as if your husband owes you and you are ungrateful, your husband may find little joy in giving gifts to you.

I tried to teach my children the art of being a grateful recipient when they were given a gift. I instructed them to say three or four sentences about why they liked the gift, what they would do with it, or how they had wanted or needed something like that. As they got older, they thought other people were not grateful because they didn't know how to express their gratitude. Gratefulness makes giving and receiving joyful.

Keep your zest for life, pep in your step, a lighthearted sense of humor, a twinkle in your eye, and enthusiasm for the future. This type of woman is refreshing to be around. One dear friend of mine, who was getting older, told me that whenever people marveled at her age, she told them, "It's just a number." Living young-at-heart made her attractive.

Let the peace of God rule; let anger, malice and wrath be put away, and be kind and kindhearted forgiving others. Feel cute, and if you don't, ask yourself, why not? Push yourself. Don't allow yourself to grunt when going up and down stairs or getting up and down from a chair. Be pleasant. Be interesting. Stop complaining.

Be sure you don't become comfortable dressing dowdy. Go through your wardrobe and throw out some old tired clothes; stay as fashionable as you can within your budget. Keep yourself healthy and in good shape. Be sure to incorporate nutrition and exercise into your daily routine; you will be able to maintain a much more youthful, vibrant lifestyle, resulting in vitality and good health.

If you are overweight and have accumulated extra pounds, keep working on it. Don't give up. As you get older, extra weight will tax your body and result in sicknesses and diseases that will make your life difficult and painful. Start now.

Here are a few reminders to live with joy:

1. Find invisible, buried treasures inside of you. What is in you that you need to bring out? I believe most women have much more tolerance, patience, and fortitude than they even realize until they pull it out from deep inside them.

2. Don't allow negatives to take up space. Get rid of "can't" and "couldn't" for a positively wonderful relationship.
3. Evaluate your decisions in the present and how they affect the future. Then, change the present immediately if it will adversely affect your future.
4. Ask: what can I do to make the situation better? Then do it immediately and don't waste precious time.

5. Achieve big goals through small steps. There are little duties you can do and steps you can take that will ultimately achieve much larger goals.

6. Develop the ability to hate the right things. Hate the things that should be hated:
    *   time wasters—arguing, overindulging in social media
    *   prayer effectiveness robbers—unforgiveness
    *   laziness—any attitude or habit that prevents you from doing what needs to be done or promotes lack of empathy

7. Do not strive to be noticed or to get all the credit. After all is said and done, who cares who had to give in to make it right?

8. Do not make decisions based on fear of how others will react. Do the right things, over and over again.

9. Give back more than you are given, especially in relationships.

10. No hang-ups allowed. I'd like to hang a sign around my neck: No Hang-ups. Do not let bad attitudes such as unforgiveness, bitterness, or anger hang you up and stop you from the innocence and freedom you can have without them. Have you been hurt in a previous relationship? The person you're with now didn't do that to you—move on. You have two choices: to nurse it or reverse it. Relive or nurse your hurts and you'll be miserable.

Day in and day out it is tough to maintain joy in the journey. It has to be a dedicated, consistent effort—an on-purpose and no-excuses lifestyle. As the daily grind becomes tedious or monotonous, we become selfish and exhausting. Daily chores threaten our joy. Our days become a blur of emptying garbage; getting rid of anything growing inside our refrigerators; spit up, throw up, and dirty diapers; cleaning toilets; doing laundry; flossing and brushing teeth; cleaning tubs and changing bedding; washing floors and wiping counters; shopping and cooking; paperwork and mounds of bills to pay; not to mention working at a place where you are only as good as your last performance, feeling you could be replaced at any time. Add to these daily anxieties the need to fix broken things in your home and a host of other unpleasant jobs to be done again the very next day. Your spouse faces similar demands and disagreeable task too.

Responsibilities overwhelm and we wonder, "Is **this** what my life is all about?" Going through a million motions and never feeling appreciated? No wonder we feel weary and depressed. So we take a break to watch television and as soon as we begin to watch we see marriage depicted in a negative light, romanticized affairs, and violence and language we don't care to see.

Our culture has promoted the message that if you find the ideal person, then you can have a happy marriage. However, no person will ever be ideal, and if the end goal in marriage is happiness then happiness based on externals will be unreachable or unsustainable. The happiness of learning how to love someone and what love really looks like is the happiness that marriage is really about.

What tempts couples to give up on marriage?

1. Feeling Important and Noticed.

Everyone wants to be appreciated and admired. Everyone wants to feel like his or her opinion matters and that someone cares enough to listen. We want to feel attractive and that someone wants to be around us. We want to feel special to someone and know that someone cares about us. When we don't receive appreciation in marriage, we might look for it elsewhere.

2. Romance.

Women love to share sunsets, hold hands, have the door opened for us, have someone look into our eyes with deep love. Women feed into this desire for romance by reading romance novels or watching chick flicks where romance reaches heights often unknown to the real world. Each of us has an idea about romance and if our husband can't figure it out, we feel deprived.

3. Sex and Intimacy.

Unfortunately, married status is not a boundary for our sex-starved world. Sex has become a casual sport not a commitment. Husbands who feel unappreciated at home will soak up any positivity about them like a parched sponge soaking up water in a thirsty land. Women who are alone thrive on compliments and affirmation. Demanding schedules leave physical and emotional sexual needs unmet and spouses become vulnerable to outside influences that draw them away from faithfulness.

4. Just Plain Fun.

Sometimes the daily monotony leaves very little time for laughter, fun, and enjoyment. There are days we wish we could forget our obligations and get away to go play a round of golf or tennis. When breaks aren't possible, we would welcome an opportunity to throw our head back and have a good laugh.

I have walked next to many couples as they have flirted with departures from their obligations in order to find these desires outside their marriage. It never ceases to amaze me how oblivious people are to the first brief departures from their routine. They seem to make little mentions and little steps in going outside their normal routine, but run back to tag "safe" in between their little blips

These departures are first voiced in statements such as: "I'm done giving," "I need more time out with the guys (girls)," "I am taking a vacation without my spouse," "What's wrong with going out and getting a few drinks with my friends?" All of a sudden, one of the partners may look for an obvious source of enjoyment that does not include his or her family. Any questions are met defensively and with justification for their new focus.

What happens to the person who decides to leave his or her life of responsibility to succumb to these temptations? Does he or she really live happily ever after; is the grass really greener on the other side? Inevitably, he or she enters another life of responsibility or takes on a stepfamily. Now the responsibilities of the new life blended with the prior life become even greater. Life can seem greener on the other side of the fence, but it still has to be mowed. Leaving one relationship for another not only requires you to mow the new lawn, but you'll have the other lawn to tend to as well.

He or she may have been noticed and appreciated and even romanced by someone new and exciting, and the affair may have been exciting and fun, but eventually they have to go back to work; empty garbage; get rid of anything growing inside their refrigerators; deal with spit up, throw up, and dirty diapers; clean toilets; do laundry; floss and brush teeth; clean tubs and change bedding; wash floors and wipe counters; shop and cook; fill out paperwork and pay mounds of bills.

The wonderful fling has boomeranged back with a thud. On top of it all, the demands from the first relationship place stresses on the new one. Your new spouse doesn't have the same parental influence or interest in the children and possibly doesn't understand your split devotion. Your new spouse would rather you didn't communicate with the other parent of your children—making life terse and unpleasant when such communications are necessary. Your ex may find someone else and ultimately add another personality to the confusion in your life, your new spouse's life, and the lives of your children. Now you probably have more bills to pay and alimony and child support bills to worry about. Now schedules need to be juggled and your children live between parents. You may have lost a lot of money, good friends, and family members in the split. Your new spouse may not have considered all the physical and financial ties you still have with your past. If you thought it was difficult with the first relationship, adding all these additional components has not made things easier. In fact, the difficulties have increased as the responsibilities have doubled and tripled.

What is the answer for the couple that decides the life of responsibility is too much to bear? What do they do when they want to feel important and noticed, desire to be romanced, crave sex and intimacy, and want more plain fun? Going from one relationship to another leaves many dazed, bruised, and wounded people in the wake, especially children who need to figure out what marriage is supposed to be about.

The most important answer is to meet the needs of your spouse inside of your marriage:

1.   Feeling Important and Noticed.

Why can't the desire to be admired, appreciated, and noticed by the opposite sex be fulfilled at home? I teach "inside-out living" which means you should be the best you can be at home with those who are with you every day. Take time to listen to your spouse, let him know he is attractive to you, work at and put some effort into enjoying just being around him. Help him feel special and find tangible ways to demonstrate that you care about him. Be blind to his faults and see only the good in him. "Love begins by taking care of the closest ones - the ones at home."[167]

2. Romance.

Take time to have a candlelit dinner, get someone to watch the children, and go for a walk. Plan a picnic lunch for the two of you. Incorporate romance into your life purposefully. Plan a date night where you refuse to talk about problems but purpose to enjoy each other's company. Write love notes. Surprise each other. Make time for each other, even if your children need to go out of their way to accommodate. It is good for the children to see you and your spouse take time for romance. The best gift you can give your children is a good marriage.

3. Sex and Intimacy.

Does your husband feel like a macho man around you? Admire his masculinity. Compliment him. Hold hands and keep kissing. Make sure you communicate your love with touch. I am not a really touchy person, but my husband is, so I make time for hugs, snuggles, and kisses. Never withhold sex or make sex conditional on your needs being met. Intimacy needs to be a top priority in your life. For your husband, it is both physical and emotional. Don't kill your husband's emotions for you or put undue physical stress on him by refusing to have sex with him. Do not make your spouse vulnerable to outside influences that draw him away from fidelity to you. Not many people go shopping for something they have at home!

4. Enjoy Each Other.

Husbands and wives should go on a date at least once a week if possible, leaving children with suitable caregivers. Some form of sports or recreational activity should be enjoyed together, even if it is just walking. And take time to laugh together—enjoy each other. Go bicycling, roller skating, or canoeing together. Leave issues and problems at home; incorporate positivity and fun into your relationship.[168]

As heavy as your life of commitment and responsibility is, you should be doubly creative to make it fun and enjoyable as much as possible. Appreciate the one who committed to love you all your life, and don't make it an impossibility to do so.

I learned so much when I worked at Gilda's Club,™ a cancer support group. These patients faced death, yet they chose to appreciate every day. One lady told me, "I used to complain about the weather. Now, I am just so happy to be alive. I don't care if it's raining, snowing, sleeting, or hailing. I appreciate every moment I'm given." I have seen brave women in their early twenties holding onto chairs to make their way around to help others, gasping for breath but still giving to others and focusing on others. There is no excuse for us to live with pettiness and selfishness. I often left Gilda's Club™ challenged and have developed very little patience for anyone who is petty, picky, or ungrateful.

True Intimacy

I think the best example of true intimacy is found in the biblical account of Adam and Eve. *And they were both naked, the man and his wife, and were not ashamed* (Genesis 2:25).

Adam and Eve were open, honest, transparent, not concealed, vulnerable, even susceptible to criticism or attack, before each other. Nothing to hide. No sin had entered the earth. They didn't know about lying, cheating, or deception at that point. No wonder they were transparent.

The best way to keep intimacy intact with your spouse is to keep your communication and your heart open, honest, transparent, not concealed, vulnerable, even susceptible to criticism or attack. Don't hide your feelings. Don't lie, cheat, or deceive. Choosing openness will lead to the kind of intimacy that Adam and Eve had.

Learn these few words and practice them regularly:

- I'm sorry
- Please forgive me
- I was wrong

Practice saying these words while you're vacuuming; practice them while driving in your car; speak them out loud and speak them often. Most of all, grow the habit of speaking them regularly to your spouse. Use these words sincerely and specifically.

"Humble yourselves [feeling very insignificant] in the presence of the Lord, and He will exalt you [He will lift you up and make your lives significant]." (James 4:10 AMP)

"Therefore humble yourselves [demote, lower yourselves in your own estimation] under the mighty hand of God, that in due time He may exalt you." (1 Peter 5:6, AMP)

My mom once told me about a beautiful woman who loved her husband so much that she often signed her name: "Art's Trudy."

Put your husband's name and your name together like that. I am "Gary's Karen." How wonderful to be so aware that you belong to someone.

"Love is a mighty power, a great and complete good. Love alone lightens every burden, and makes rough places smooth. It bears every hardship as though it was nothing, and renders all bitterness sweet and acceptable. Nothing is sweeter than love, nothing stronger, nothing higher, nothing wider, nothing more pleasant, nothing fuller or better in heaven or earth; for love is born of God. Love flies, runs and leaps for joy. It is free and unrestrained. Love knows no limits, but ardently transcends all bounds. Love feels no burden, takes no account of toil, attempts things beyond its strength. Love sees nothing as impossible, for it feels able to achieve all things. It is strange and effective, while those who lack love faint and fail. Love is not fickle and sentimental, nor is it intent on vanities. Like a living flame and a burning torch, it surges upward and surely surmounts every obstacle."[169]

Do you love your husband like that? Do you even know what your husband loves? What would he like to do to be fully alive? Are you aware of his dreams, hopes, hobbies, and desires? What can you do to help him reach his goals? When you identify so closely with your husband that you walk in the realization of his dreams, you are truly his. And you both will shine!

Love is wonderfully unique; the more you give, the more you have. "In the arithmetic of love, one plus one equals everything, and two minus one equals nothing."[170]

"You'll be trying to live a science-fiction novel if you ever expect to fully understand your husband. He probably can't even understand himself! Men seem better able to accept this, while wives often feel as though they have to understand their husbands. They can't accept that some things about their men don't make sense and may never make sense. Sometimes, you simply have to accept that this is the way a guy is—and love him accordingly."[171]

When multitudes of little things annoy you about your husband, sometimes the real problem is that you are so easily annoyed. I used to think I needed to change what annoyed me; then I realized that sometimes the problem is simply that I allow myself to be bugged by too many things that are morally neutral or merely inconvenient.

Become a woman of understanding; learn how and when to communicate in such a way that your husband can fully participate. Part of living with someone is learning to accommodate them, and that adaptation to him includes all his nonsensical habits and rituals. Don't let petty annoyances poison your relationships. Live with, and even celebrate, the mystery. "It doesn't make sense, but that's the way he likes it, and that's good enough for me."

A Love That Lasts

You have taken a journey with me to study and use the tools to live out our priorities in our relationships. We left excuses behind to apply ourselves to an extreme relationships workout. We lifted some of the ideals we have settled for in our relationships to new standards. We've thought about and challenged some of our pre-conceived ideas, and hopefully developed and applied some new skills.

With the spirit of a champion, in order to keep improving your relationships, keep working on being the best you can be and challenging yourself to the next level.

"For everyone who comes to Me and listens to My words [in order to heed their teaching] and does them, I will show you what he is like: He is like a man building a house, who dug and went down deep and laid a foundation upon the rock; and when a flood arose, the torrent broke against that house and could not shake or move it, because it had been securely built or founded on a rock." (Luke 6:47–48 AMP)

Epilogue

Thank you for going on this journey with me to build better relationships. If you truly challenged yourself to work hard to bring your relationships to the next level, your relationships should be showing the effects of your efforts.

Remember to continue to work to make your relationships keep getting stronger and better. Stagnating or not working on relationships means that you are growing further apart. It takes consistent commitment and devotion to keep getting closer with our spouse and others.

Commit to growing with each other and reaching the full potential for your relationships. Bring out parts of you that you haven't utilized to be the best you can be, and to help those around you be the best *they* can be as well. Keep working on eliminating negative attitudes and habits you may have fallen into. Evaluate your decisions in the present by what results they will bring in the future. Have the courage and tenacity to change the present immediately if it will adversely affect your future.

Don't waste precious time: if you see a need for change, effectuate the change immediately. Like flicking on a light switch floods the room with light, your immediate "flick of the switch" can change things instantly. Be on guard for time wasters and laziness, and continually weed those things out of your life or keep them in proper perspective.

God can use your marriage to teach you how to love. If you don't run from the challenges that marriage presents, your marriage will make you a more unselfish, stronger, and wiser person.

When you find yourself falling into bad habits, or when you are losing steam in your pursuits, go through the book and workbook again. Every time you do, you will find new things to work at.

I know this journey has equipped you with tools to keep building better relationships. Keep your toolbox handy, and your work ethic strong, and your relationships will reflect your efforts!

End Notes

Chapter 1

[1] Andy Stanley, *Louder Than Words: The Power of Uncompromised Living*, (Multnomah Books, 2004)

[2] Nancy Reagan, Ronald Reagan, *I Love You, Ronnie: The Letters of Ronald Reagan to Nancy Reagan*, (Random House Publishing Group, 2002)

[3] Mother Teresa of Calcutta, as quoted in Ame Mahler Beanland, *Celebrating Motherhood: A Comforting Companion for Every Expecting Mother*, (Conari Press, 2002)

[4] *They Died With Their Boots On*, Raoul Walsh, Errol Flynn, Olivia de Havilland, 1941

[5] Bolton, D. H., Egypt Search forum: *What is a "Good Wife"?* posted 5 Sept. 2002. http://www.egyptsearch.com/forums/Forum2/HTML/000865.html

[6] Anonymous men polled, ranging in age from 25 to 38 years old

[7] Wikipedia, Antony and Cleopatra, http://en.wikipedia.org/wiki/Antony_and_Cleopatra

[8] http://shahjahanlife.tripod.com/biographyofshahjahan/id2.html http://tajmahal.gov.in/taj_story.html

[9] Evans, Becky, Mail Online, posted 19, June 2013. http://www.dailymail.co.uk/news/article-2344329/Devoted-husband-spends-life-savings-build-scale-replica-Taj-Mahal-honour-dead-wife.html

[10] http://www.pbs.org/empires/napoleon/n_josephine/emperor/page1.html

[11] http://mentalfloss.com/article/20872/10-great-love-affairs-history

Chapter 2

[12] Why Are Tree Roots Important?
http://1800cuttree.com/content/why-are-tree-roots-important

[13] 2 Corinthians 5:17

[14] Ephesians 1:6

[15] 2 Timothy 3:16-17

[16] Psalm 45:7

[17] Psalm 16:11 and 1 Chronicles 16:27

[18] Matthew 12:34

[19] Nancy Reagan, Ronald Reagan, *I Love You, Ronnie: The Letters of Ronald Reagan to Nancy Reagan,* (Random House Publishing Group, 2002)

[20] USA Today, May 1, 2005, *Determined Dana*

[21] *Somewhere in Heaven: The Remarkable Love Story of Dana and Christopher Reeve,* July 8, 2008, Hachette Digital, Inc.

[22] **What I Really Want To Say**
Words and Music by Steven Curtis Chapman
(c) 1999 SPARROW SONG and PRIMARY WAVE BRIAN
(CHAPMAN SP ACCT)
SPARROW SONG Admin. at CAPTITOLCMGPUBLISHING.COM
All Rights Reserved Used by Permission
Reprinted by Permission of Hal Leonard Corporation

[23] Winston Churchill

Chapter 3

[24] For example, see the forum entitled Most Important Things Woman Should Know About Men to Keep the Relationship Going, http://shareranks.com/9884,Most-Important-Things-Women-Should-Know-About-Men-to-Keep-the-Relationship-Going#b

[25] *Sacred Influence: What a Man Needs from His Wife to Be the Husband She Wants*, Gary L. Thomas, Zondervan Publishers, 2006

[26] The word [nouthetic] comes from the Greek New Testament. It has, within it, three elements-concern, confrontation, and change. Nouthetic counseling is counseling that involves face to face confrontation by one person to another, out of loving concern for him, in order to bring about the changes God desires in his life. That in a nutshell, is what Nouthetic counseling is all about. Jay Adams, http://www.nouthetic.org/what-is-nouthetic-counseling

Chapter 4

[27] Ralph Waldo Emerson, www.finestquotes.com

[28] *The Holiday.* Dir. Nancy Meyers. Universal Pictures (2006).

[29] http://affaircare.com/articles/love-extinguishers-what-are-they/

[30] Adapted from http://affaircare.com/articles/love-kindlers-what-are-they/

[31] William Shakespeare, www.thoughtcatalogue.com

[32] www.merriam-webster.com

[33] **Who Will Love Me For Me,**
Writers/Publishers: Jennifer Heller, David Heller/
Butter Lid Publishing (ASCAP)
All Rights Reserved
Used by Permission
Reprinted by Permission of Whizbang, Inc.

319

[34] the Love Revolution, Joyce Meyers, FaithWords Publishers, 2009

[35] Steven Stosny, Ph.D., *Freedom to Love*, published September 13, 2010 in *Anger in the Age of Entitlement*, http://www.psychologytoday.com/blog/anger-in-the-age-entitlement/201009/freedom-love

[36] *What About Bob*. Dir. Frank Oz. Touchstone Pictures (1991).

[37] http://www.nanacompany.typepad.com

[38] 1 Corinthians 13.7 (KJV)

[39] Felleman, Hazel, ed *The Best Loved Poems of the American People*. Garden City, NY: Garden City Books, 1936 and Dinah Maria Mulock Craik, *A Life for a Life*. London: Collins' Clear Type Press, 1900. As quoted on www.potw.org

[40] http://www.elegantwoman.org/womanhood.html

[41] *Can Eye-Rolling Ruin a Marriage?* Researchers Study Divorce Risk, Tara Parker-Pope, Wall Street Journal, August 6, 2001,, http://online.wsj.com/news/articles/SB1028578553586958760

Chapter 5

[42] Barbara and Allan Pease. Why Men Don't Listen and Women Can't Read Maps. NY: Broadway Books, 1998, as quoted at http://arlenetaylor.org/index.php/gender-differences-br.html

[43] Google reference tool

[44] John Gottman, Nan Silver, *What Makes Marriage Work?* Psychology Today, March 1, 1994, http://www.psychologytoday.com/articles/200910/what-makes-marriage-work

[45] http://www.etymonline.com/index.php?term=winsome

[46] *Fascinating Womanhood,* Helen Andelin, Bantam Dell, Division of Random House, Inc., March 1975, Pacific Press edition March 1965

[47] *The Emotionally Destructive Marriage,* Leslie Vernick, WaterBrook Press, 2013.

[48] Mary Jean Irion, http://www.goodreads.com/quotes/101242

[49] *Sacred Influence: What a Man Needs from His Wife to Be the Husband She Wants,* Gary L. Thomas, Zondervan Publishers, 2006

[50] Originally referred to in disconnected link: http://www.theartofloveandintimacy.com/2007/05/did-you-marry-right-person-zig-ziglar.html Also referenced at http://toughwords.wordpress.com/2012/04/10/did-you-marry-the-right-person/

Chapter 6

[51] http://www.tesh.com/story/love-and-relationships-category/romantic-comedies-set-up-unrealistic-expectations/cc/13/id/1215

[52] *Strike the Original Match,* Dr. Charles R. Swindoll, Multnomah Books, December 1, 1980.

[53] Roy Croft, http://www.drgamm.com/romanticreading.html

Chapter 7

[54] http://www.freemaninstitute.com/quotes.htm

[55] *Fascinating Womanhood,* Helen Andelin, Bantam Dell, Division of Random House, Inc., March 1975, Pacific Press edition March 1965

[56] *Capture His Heart,* Lysa TerKeurst, Moody Press, 2002

[57] *Sacred Influence: What a Man Needs from His Wife to Be the Husband She Wants,* Gary L. Thomas, Zondervan Publishers, 2006

[58] Maurice Maeterlinck, *Thoughts from Maeterlinck,* Dodd, Mead and Company, May 1903.

[59] John Ortburg, *When the Game Is Over, It All*

Goes Back in the Box, http://www.goodreads.com/
quotes/404867-gratitude-is-the-ability-to-experience-life-as-a-gift

[60] *Emotional Blackmail: When the People in Your Life Use Fear, Obligation and Guilt to Manipulate You,* Susan Forward and Donna Frazier, HarperCollins Publishers, 1997

[61] *How to Act Right When Your Spouse Acts Wrong,* Leslie Vernick, Waterbrook Press, 2003

Chapter 8

[62] The Call of Wisdom: Insight From the Book of Proverbs, Alice and Karen Mason Mathews, RBC Ministries, 1970.

[63] *Sacred Influence: What a Man Needs from His Wife to Be the Husband She Wants,* Gary L. Thomas, Zondervan Publishers, 2006

[64] *Steel Magnolias,* Dir. Herbert Ross, TriStar Pictures and Rastar Films (1989).

[65] Jim Burns, HomeWord, *10 Things Guys Wish Women Knew About Men,* http://www.cbn.com/family/marriage/Burns_MenWishWomenKnew.aspx

[66] *How to Act Right When Your Spouse Acts Wrong,* Leslie Vernick, Waterbrook Press, 2003

[67] *Sacred Influence: What a Man Needs from His Wife to Be the Husband She Wants,* Gary L. Thomas, Zondervan Publishers, 2006

[68] R. M. Salley, *Have You Figured Out Your Value Added Proposition?,* http://www.divinecaroline.com/life-etc/career-money/
have-you-figured-out-your-value-added-proposition

[69] Mary Fairchild, *The Healing Power of Laughter, Warning: Laughter May Be Hazardous to Your Illness,* http://www.christianity.about.com/od/
topicaldevotions/qt/laughtertherapy.htm

[70] Joe Love and JLM & Associates, Inc., *Developing Your Sense Of Humor,* http://joeloveinternational.com/articles/senseofhumor.htm

[71] Brian Regan, *Me Monster,* https://www.youtube.com/watch?v=vymaDgJ7KLg

[72] Mitch Temple, *Strengthening Marital Commitment,* http://www.focusonthefamily.com/marriage/strengthening_your_marriage/commitment/strengthening_marital_commitment.aspx

[73] Andrew Ryan, http://bioshock.wikia.com/wiki/Andrew_Ryan

Chapter 9

[74] Psalm 55:19 (AMP)

[75] 2 Corinthians 3:18 (KJV)

[76] Proverbs 4:18 (AMP)

[77] Isaiah 59:12, Roman 3:23, Romans 6:23, John 3:16, Romans 5:8, John 1:12-13, Matthew 11:28-29, Revelation 3:20, John 8:32 and 8:36, Romans 8:2, 1 Corinthians 5:17, John 16:33, 1 John 4:4, Romans 8:37, Philippians 4:13, Psalm 60:2, Matthew 28:20

[78] Malachi 3:17 and 1 Peter 3:22 (THE MESSAGE), Ephesians 3:20 (AMP)

[79] *The Right Words at the Right Time,* Marlo Thomas, Atria Books, 2002

[80] Proverbs 18:21 (THE MESSAGE)

[81] http://wishmesweetdreams.blogspot.com/2012/04/i-learned-from-mygrandfather-that-when.html

[82] *Divine Secrets of the Ya-Ya Sisterhood.* Dir. Callie Khouri (book by Rebecca Wells). Gaylord Films (2002).

[83] http://quotationsbook.com/quote/8337/

[84] Belinda Elliott, CBN.com Senior Producer, *Marriage Secrets Every Woman Should Know,* quoting Shannon Ethridge, co-author with Greg Ethridge of *Every Woman's Marriage: Igniting the Joy and Passion You Both Desire,* Waterbrook Press, 2006, https://www.cbn.com/family/marriage/elliott_EveryWoman.aspx

[85] James E. Faust, http://www.goodreads.com/quotes/tag/potential

[86] John 13.35 (NLT) "Your love for one another will prove to the world that you are my disciples."

[87] Viktor E. Frankl, http://www.goodreads.com/work/quotes/3389674-ein-psychologe-erlebt-das-konzentrationslager

Chapter 10

[88] David and Vera Mace, We Can Have Better Marriages If We Really Want Them, Abingdon, 1978.

[89] 2 Corinthians 12:9-10 (AMP)

[90] www.pbc.org/system/message_files/12389/4872.pdf

[91] Douglas S. Drummond, *How Sperry Teaches Listening Skills,* http://www.sellingpower.com/content/article/?a=8011/how-sperry-teaches-listening-skills/&page=1

[92] Douglas S. Drummond, *How Sperry Teaches Listening Skills,* http://www.sellingpower.com/content/article/?a=8011/how-sperry-teaches-listening-skills/&page=2

[93] 1 Corinthians 13 (GW)

[94] 1 Corinthians 13:5-8 (GW)

[95] http://www.newswire.ca/en/story/1316915/direct-approach-and-ineffective-communication-lead-to-2012-striking-of-trestle-in-roberts-bank-british-columbia

[96] *Silent Messages: Implicit Communication of Emotions and Attitudes,* Albert

Mehrabi, Wadsworth Publishing Company, July 1972.

[97] Molly Edmonds, *How Anger Works,* http://science.howstuffworks. com/life/inside-the-mind/emotions/anger2.htm

[98] Paul Hastings, Royal Lemington Spa, *Why Stress Makes You Dumb,* http://www.realsmart-hypnosis.com/makes/dumb.html

[99] Ecclesiastes 7.20 (AMP)

[100] Romans 3.23 (KJV)

[101] James 3.8 (THE MESSAGE)

[102] Margarita Tartakovsky, M.S., *Why Ruminating is Unhealthy and How to Stop,* World of Psychology, http://psychcentral.com/blog/ archives/2011/01/20/why-ruminating-is-unhealthy-and-how-to-stop/

[103] Psalm 32:2 (AMP)

[104] Psalm 32:2 (THE MESSAGE)

[105] Psalm 32:3-11

[106] Google reference tool

Chapter 11

[107] Sacred Influence: What a Man Needs from His Wife to Be the Husband She Wants, Gary L. Thomas, Zondervan Publishers, 2006

[108] Michael Gurian, *The Science of a Happy Marriage,* Reader's Digest, August 2004

[109] 1 Timothy 3:4 (AMP)

[110] 1 Corinthians 11:3 (THE MESSAGE)

[111] Colossians 3:18 (GW)

[112] Ephesians 5:23-24 (KJV)

[113] Matthew 20:26-28 (AMP)

[114] Dan Lacich, *Provocative Bible Verses: Wives Submit to Your Husbands,* October 12, 2009, (Quoted by permission.) http://provocativechristian.wordpress.com/2009/10/12/provocative-bible-verses-wives-submit-to-your-husbands/

[115] Erica Ritz, *Former Volleyball Star Gabrielle Reece ignites Controversy With Marriage Advice: Being 'Submissive' Is a Sign of Strength,* April 14, 2013, http://www.theblaze.com/stories/2013/04/14/former-volleyball-star-model-gabrielle-reece-ignites-controversy-with-marriage-advice-being-submissive-is-a-sign-of-strength/

[116] Dan Lacich, *Provocative Bible Verses: Submit to One Another,* April 14, 2009, (Quoted by permission.) http://provocativechristian.wordpress.com/2009/04/14/provocative-bible-verses-submit-to-one-another/

[117] Genesis 2.18 (GW)

[118] Google reference tool

[119] *The Family Man,* Dir. Brett Ratner, Universal Pictures (2000).

[120] 2 Peter 1:3 (AMP), 1 Corinthians 3:1-2, Hebrews 5:12-14, Romans 10:17, Psalms 1:2-3, Matthew 4:3-11, Ephesians 6:17, Hebrews 4:12, Joshua 1:8, James 1:25

[121] Glenda Hotton, Psalm 65, May 7, 2012, http://www.glendahotton.com/?m=2012&paged=4 ((Quoted by permission.)

[122] Mike and Connie Walsh, *Common Deceptions that Destroy Marriage Oneness,* Institute In Basic Life Principles, January 1, 2001.

[123] Matthew 6:21 (GW)

[124] Dr. Phil, *The Role of the Man in the Family,* http://www.drphil.com/articles/article/347

[125] Matthew 20:28 (GW)

[126] Author Unknown, http://www.quotegarden.com/housewarming.html

[127] Anne-Marie Slaughter, *Why Women Still Can't Have it All,* July/August 2012, http://www.theatlantic.com/magazine/archive/2012/07/why-women-still-cant-have-it-all/309020/

[128] Millenials in the Workplace Executive Study, http://www.bentley.edu/centers/center-for-women-and-business/millennials-workplace

[129] Exodus 4:2 (GW)

Chapter 12

[130] Philippians 2.3 (AMP), "Do nothing from factional motives [through contentiousness, strife, selfishness, or for unworthy ends] or prompted by conceit and empty arrogance. Instead, in the true spirit of humility (lowliness of mind) let each regard the others as better than and superior to himself [thinking more highly of one another than you do of yourselves]."

[131] *41 major life stressors,* Susan Erasmus, Health24, December 2013, listing sources as nih.gov; health24.com; Wikipedia.com, http://www.health24.com/Mental-Health/Stress/Stress-management/41-major-life-stressors-20120721

[132] Meghan Casserly, *Is 'Opting Out' The New American Dream For Working Women, September 12, 2012,* http://www.forbes.com/sites/meghancasserly/2012/09/12/is-opting-out-the-new-american-dream-for-working-women/

[133] Meghan Casserly, September 12, 2012, *ForbesWoman And TheBump.Com 'Parenthood And Economy 2012' Survey Results,* http://www.forbes.com/sites/meghancasserly/2012/09/12/forbeswoman-and-thebump-com-parenthood-and-economy-2012-survey-results/

[134] Matthew 6:34 (THE MESSAGE)

[135] Jonathan Swift, http://www.brainyquote.com/quotes/quotes/j/jonathansw101069.html

[136] A phrase coined by Tim Storey, http://storeystyle.com

[137] http://www.searchquotes.com/quotation/Live_life_so_completely_that_when_death_comes_to_you_like_a_thief_in_the_night,_there_will_be_nothin/23455/

[138] Suzanne Venker, *The War on Men,* November 26, 2012, http://www.foxnews.com/opinion/2012/11/24/war-on-men/ (Quoted by permission.)

Chapter 13

[139] Miriam Renée Adderholdt, Ph.D. and Jan Goldberg, Perfectionism: What's Bad About Being Too Good?, January 15, 1992.

[140] John Powell, *Why Am I Afraid to Tell You Who I Am?*,Thomas More Pr; December 1995, as referred to in Communicate for a Better Sex Life, Dr. Kevin Leman, https://www.cbn.com/entertainment/books/TurnUptheHeat_pg2.aspx

[141] Reuel L. Howe, *The Miracle of Dialogue,* 1963. http://edutrue.tripod.com/a-files/eduquotables-2.html

[142] http://www.brainyquote.com/quotes/quotes/a/aristotle132211.html

[143] Greater Good: The Science for a Meaningful Life, *What is Forgiveness,* http://greatergood.berkeley.edu/topic/forgiveness/definition

[144] Matthew 18:21-22 (AMP)

[145] Ephesians 4:32; Colossians 3:13; Matthew 18; Mark 11:25; Luke 6:37; Matthew 6:14-15

[146] 2 Corinthians 10:4-5

[147] John King, *Steering a Parked Life,* March 12, 2007, http://johnkking.wordpress.com/page/10/

[148] Galatians 5:22-23 (AMP)

[149] *Can Eye-Rolling Ruin a Marriage?* Researchers Study Divorce Risk, Tara Parker-Pope, Wall Street Journal, August 6, 2001, http://online.wsj.com/news/articles/SB1028578553586958760

[150] Proverbs 31:31 (AMP)

[151] *Domestic Violence and Abuse,* http://www.helpguide.org/mental/domestic_violence_abuse_types_signs_causes_effects.htm

[152] *The Emotionally Destructive Marriage,* Leslie Vernick, WaterBrook Press, 2013.

[153] *Marriage and Divorce Myth #2 – Is Divorce A Sin?* http://www.rockymountainministries.org/mythbusters/17-mythbusters/57-marriage-and-divorce-myth-2-is-divorce-a-sin-marriage-and-divorce-myth-2-is-divorce-a-sin.html

[154] *Marriage Divorce Myth #1 – Does God Hate Divorce?* http://www.rockymountainministries.org/mythbusters/17-mythbusters/56-marriage-and-divorce-myth-1-does-god-hate-divorce-marriage-and-divorce-myth-1-does-god-hate-divorce.html

Chapter 14

[155] Proverbs 22:7 (KJV)

[156] Romans 13:8 (KJV)

[157] 1 Timothy 6:8 (KJV)

[158] Philippians 4:5 (KJV)

[159] http://www.hughcalc.org/coffee.cgi

[160] http://www.youneedabudget.com/?utm_source=google&utm_medium=cpc&utm_campaign=(roi)+branded&utm_content=ynab&utm_

term=ynab&gclid=CMar2bOsqr4CFXQiMgodbWMANQ#_

[161] http://www.mvelopes.com

[162] Craik, Dinah Maria Mulock. *A Life for a Life*. London: Collins' Clear Type Press, 1900, as quoted at http://www.potw.org/archive/potw273. html

[163] http://www.goodreads.com/ quotes/5934-i-ve-learned-that-people-will-forget-what-you-said-people

[164] http://www.goodreads.com/author/quotes/86189.Greg_Anderson

[165] Online Etymology Dictionary, http://www.etymonline.com/index. php?search=enthusiasm

[166] http://thesaurus.com/browse/enthusiastic

[167] Mother Theresa, http://www.brainyquote.com/quotes/authors/m/ mother_teresa.html#AXq0EQZjmBM7uFYd.99

[168] Adapted from *The Straight Life,* by Dr. James Dobson, now contained in *Dr. Dobson's Handbook of Family Advice,* Harvest House Publishers, Eugene, Oregon. Copyright 1998.

[169] Thomas A. Kempis, http://www.worldinvisible.com/library/ akempis/imitation/chapter%2042.htm

[170] Mignon McLaughlin, http://ilovelifequotes.com/love-and-life quotes/

[171] *Sacred Influence: What a Man Needs from His Wife to Be the Husband She Wants,* Gary L. Thomas, Zondervan Publishers, 2006

CPSIA information can be obtained at www.ICGtesting.com
Printed in the USA
LVOW12*1507090814

398110LV00002B/2/P